Opera on *Video*

Alan Blyth was born in London. He was educated at Rugby School and at Pembroke College, Oxford, where he was on the committee of the University Opera Club. After working for *Encyclopaedia Britannica* as a music editor, he became a freelance music critic with *The Times* and the *Financial Times*, specialising in singers and opera. He was on the music staff of the *Daily Telegraph* from 1976 to 1990, and assistant editor of *Opera* magazine from 1967 to 1984. He is now on the magazine's editorial board. He has reviewed vocal records for *Gramophone* for the past thirty years. He contributes regularly to Radio 3's *Record Review* and to its series 'Interpretations on Record', and to Radio 4's 'Kaleidoscope'. He has edited three volumes of *Opera on Record*, and his other publications include *Opera on CD* (also published by Kyle Cathie), *The Enjoyment of Opera, Remembering Britten*, and *Wagner's Ring: an Introduction*. He has contributed many entries to the *New Grove Dictionary of Opera* and is record consultant to the *Viking Dictionary of Opera*. His interests outside music include wine and gardening.

Opera on Video

THE ESSENTIAL GUIDE

ALAN BLYTH

KYLE CATHIE LTD

First published in Great Britain by
Kyle Cathie Ltd
20 Vauxhall Bridge Road
London SW1V 2SA

Copyright © 1995 by Alan Blyth

ISBN 1 85626 175 1

A CIP catalogue record for this book is available from
the British Library

Typeset by SX Composing Limited, Rayleigh, Essex
Printed in Great Britain by Cox and Wyman Limited, Reading

CONTENTS

CONTENTS

INTRODUCTION

Opera on video is often frowned on by superior persons as an inferior imitation of the original. Unlike them, many opera lovers who don't have easy access to an opera house and/or can't afford the asking price for tickets find the alternative of video a godsend: in any case the medium ought to be accepted for what it is, in most cases a reasonable facsimile of notable occasions in the theatre. It serves another vital purpose, one that gains in importance as the years pass, of providing a historical record, albeit a haphazard one, of opera performance, stretching back to the 1960s and in some cases even earlier.

We are fortunate to be able to catch on video artists such as Callas, Gobbi, Tebaldi, Corelli, Sutherland, Sills and Janet Baker from an earlier generation of singers. Soon surely to become historic documents are all the videos enshrining performances by Domingo, Pavarotti, Te Kanawa, Cossotto, Zancanaro, Cappuccilli to mention only the most frequently filmed singers, not to forget conductors such as Solti, Muti and Abbado. We are now lucky enough to be gaining a tranche of Russian operas performed at the Kirov by the stirring generation of young Russian singers.

I don't think it is patriotism that has made me aware of, and delight in, the high standards prevailing over the past twenty-five years at Covent Garden, English National Opera and Glyndebourne. Even stagings not received enthusiastically at the time emerge as enjoyable readings, e.g. Covent Garden's *Andrea Chénier*, and Glyndebourne's *Il barbiere di Siviglia* to offer just two examples, and Covent Garden's *Otello* is, for instance, preferable to other versions on offer. In terms of preparation and execution the two houses compare favourably with the Metropolitan (tediously traditional and over-dominated by Levine) and La Scala (uneven). Praise is

due, *tout court*, to Brian Large for his sterling and indefatig-
able work as a video director of discernment and high skill.

We might wish that more had been done to preserve the
past (what would we not give for a Callas *Traviata* or *Norma*),
but be thankful that so much is preserved. By the way I
decided to concentrate almost entirely on official issues as the
availability, at least in Britain, of pirated performances is haphazard and the results of very variable quality – although
video addicts will know that many treasures, e.g. Caballé's
Orange Norma, are occasionally to be had from fringe
dealers.

While the great majority of videos are taken from live performances a significant minority are films made expressly for
the medium. The most successful progenitors of this genre
have been the late Jean-Pierre Ponnelle who, when he
avoided a penchant for excessive movement, provided some
delightful performances, Franco Zeffirelli, Götz Friedrich and
Petr Weigl, the imaginative Czech director, whose films of
two very English works, Delius's *A Village Romeo and Juliet*
and Britten's *The Turn of the Screw*, graphically show how
opera can be successfully taken out of the realms of the
theatre and opened out into the countryside without dele-
terious results. It is a pity few have followed in the footsteps
of these three pioneers, but lack of money is probably the
reason for the absence of more of these kinds of film.

As regards systems, VHS still holds virtual sway but its
hegemony may soon be challenged by a video CD system
which may be successful where laserdisc seems to have
failed. Those who have bothered to invest in laserdisc will
vouch for its obvious superiority, in both visual and aural
terms, over tape, but the inability to record on laserdisc, the
expense of the hardware, and the paucity of software (at least
in Britain) has meant that sales have been infinitesimal in relation to those of VHS. The most recent generation of hi-fi
stereo VHS videos, when played on a first-class TV set and
through a good stereo system, can provide excellent results.

In assessing the videos I have tried to keep in balance judgment of the visual and aural aspects, which don't always
match. Inevitably sound quality is variable, picture less so. At
least with performances relayed from an opera house we seldom get the over-prominence of the orchestra, except at the

Met, so aggravating on many CDs. Most video directors, Large and Humphrey Burton in particular, are sensitive musicians who know that musical values must sometimes take pre-eminence as against visual ones, yet they also try to give, as far as possible, as wide a view of a production as is possible given the medium's limitations.

Finally, I would enter a plea for more subtitles and more informative, better laid out booklets.

It remains to thank those at Polygram (in particular Sophie Beck), Warner Classics (Harriet Capaldi), EMI, VAI, Pickwick and Castle Video who have supplied product to make this guide possible. I also acknowledge the advice and/or help of John McHugh at the Coliseum Shop, Max Loppert and Alice Lindsay of *Opera* magazine, Jane Morley and Deirdre Tilley in the preparation of the book.

Alan Blyth
September 1995

NB Where the laserdisc number corresponds to that of the VHS, I have refrained from repeating it, simply using the style 'LD:-1' to indicate its availability in the alternative medium. Where subtitles are provided, that is indicated after the number. The order of versions is no guide to order of preference. The operas are presented in the chronology of composers and composition.

Alan Blyth's 30 Favourite Videos

Monteverdi: *Il ritorno d'Ulisse in patria*: Glyndebourne
Handel: *Xerxes*: ENO
Mozart: *Figaro*: Vienna State Opera
Mozart: *Cosi fan tutte*: Gardiner production
Rossini: *Il barbiere di Siviglia*: Glyndebourne
Rossini: *Guglielmo Tell*: La Scala
Donizetti: *Mary Stuart*: ENO
Verdi: *Ernani*: La Scala
Verdi: *Siffelio*: Covent Garden
Verdi: *La traviata*: La Scala
Verdi: *La traviata*: Glyndebourne
Verdi: *Otello*: Covent Garden
Verdi: *Falstaff*: Covent Garden
Wagner: *Tannhäuser*: Bayreuth (Friedrich staging)
Bizet: *Carmen*: Rosi film
Mussorgsky: *Khovanshchina*: Kirov
Rimsky-Korsakov: *Sadko*: Kirov
Puccini: *Madama Butterfly*: La Scala
Janáček: *Jenufa*: Glyndebourne
R. Strauss: *Salome*: Friedrich film
R. Strauss: *Elektra*: Friedrich film
R. Strauss: *Der Rosenkavalier*: Bavarian State Opera
R. Strauss: *Intermezzo*: Glyndebourne
Debussy: *Pelléas et Mélisande*: Welsh National Opera
Bartok: *Bluebeard's Castle*: Szinetár film
Prokofiev: *L'amour des très oranges*: Lyon Opera
Britten: *Peter Grimes*: ENO
Britten: *Billy Budd*: ENO
Britten: *The Turn of the Screw*: Weigl film
Britten: *A Midsummer Night's Dream*: Glyndebourne

(For details refer to text.)

Claudio Monteverdi (1567–1643)

L'Orfeo
Dietlinde Turban (Euridice), Trudeliese Schmidt (Musica/Speranza), Glenys Linoos (Messenger/Proserpina), Francisco Araiza (First Shepherd), Philippe Huttenlocher (Orfeo), Roland Hermann (Apollo), Werner Gröschel (Pluto), Hans Franzen (Charon). Monteverdi Ensemble of the Zurich Opera House/Nikolaus Harnoncourt. A film by Jean-Pierre Ponnelle. Decca VHS 071 103–3; LD:−1.

Monteverdi, the first opera composer of consequence, is known to have written seven works for the stage, but only three survive complete. *L'Orfeo*, the first, dated from 1607, when it was given at the court of Mantua. Unlike the other two, its instrumental forces are specified. Languishing in the archives for several centuries, it was at last resuscitated in 1904 by Vincent D'Indy. Since then it has been performed in many editions, most frequently of late in that by Harnoncourt, who has made a close study of the original sources of all Monteverdi's operas. In collaboration with Ponnelle, Harnoncourt staged the three works at Zurich during the 1970s. Over the years the ideas of both the progenitors were developed, and as this *Orfeo* shows the results could be at once historically correct and highly entertaining.

In his film, Ponnelle obviates the static nature of the piece, in which nothing much happens dramatically, by the ingenuity of his production. Within his own decor, he set it as a court entertainment with some of the chorus as spectators commenting on the action. The predominant sense of pastoral bliss in the opening scenes of courtship and marriage of Orfeo and Euridice is rudely broken by the appearance of the black-clad figure of Linoos's lamenting Messenger telling of Euridice's death through a snake bite. Orfeo's descent to the Underworld, particularly his encounter with the shadowy figure of Charon, is elaborately and pointedly shown; so is his reunion with his beloved.

Orfeo is usually given to a tenor but its tessitura lies well within the range of a high baritone such as Huttenlocher, who conveys all the varying emotions of his lengthy part, but his tone tends to be woolly, wanting the clarity of timbre the part really calls for. All the supporting roles are reasonably well taken, and it is interesting to hear the young Araiza, who went on to greater things, so appealing in the young Shepherd's important solos.

Harnoncourt coordinates his forces with all his customary gifts for intense expression, and Ponnelle draws committed performances from every member of his cast. Picture and sound are excellent.

Il ritorno d'Ulisse in patria
Janet Baker (Penelope), Anne Howells (Minerva), Ian Caley (Telemachus), Richard Lewis (Eumeaus), Benjamin Luxon (Ulisse). Glyndebourne Festival Chor, London Philharmonic Orch/Raymond Leppard. Dir: Peter Hall; video dir: David Heather. Pickwick VHS SL 2005. Subtitles.

Ulisse is probably the greatest of Monteverdi's three surviving operas partly because of the nature of its story, which tells of Penelope's steadfastness and fidelity during Ulysses's long absence of twenty years fighting abroad, in face of the importuning of her unwelcome and grasping suitors. She eventually wins her reward for her loyalty when her husband/hero at last returns. Monteverdi clothes the tale in music of surpassing eloquence, notably in Penelope's long monologue at the opening of the work and in the scenes depicting Ulysses's return home in disguise to scatter the unwelcome suitors for his wife's hand.

Glyndebourne's 1973 staging, in Leppard's over-ornate but enjoyable edition (the rich string sound is definitely not authentic), was one of Peter Hall's several imaginative re-creations of the baroque tradition at the theatre. His staging is spectacular with its flying gods, heaving seas and amazingly swift changes of scene, all set in John Bury's ingenious unit-set with a tiled floor based on a Pintorrichio painting. This superb but never overwhelming background is a fit frame for one of Janet Baker's most compelling interpretations. She conveys all the loneliness, bewilderment and steadfast love for her husband by means of her dignified acting, piercing eyes and, of course, impassioned, finely shaded singing. Nobody who has heard her repeated 'torna' in the opening scene could ever forget its moving inflections. For her alone, this video is essential viewing and listening.

Luxon is an upright, heroic Ulysses who nicely marries sympathy with determination, and his singing is warm and sensitive. By his side is the goddess Minerva guiding him to his desired goal. Veteran Richard Lewis is touching as the old shepherd Eumaeus who also helps the hero make his way home. Robert Lloyd is a sonorous Neptune, Virginia Popova makes much of little as Penelope's faithful old nurse Ericlea, but unfortunately the demands of TV timing (from where this video originated) caused not only the loss of her final scene but also that of the gluttonous Iro, magnificently portrayed by Alexander Oliver. There is another excision in the gods' final meeting.

Neither picture nor sound (mono) is up to modern standards. Nevertheless this is a performance not to be overlooked.

L'incoronazione di Poppea

1. Rachel Yakar (Poppea), Trudeliese Schmidt (Ottavia), Paul Esswood (Ottone), Alexander Oliver (Arnalta), Eric Tappy (Nero), Matti Salminen (Seneca). Monteverdi Ensemble of Zurich Opera House/Nikolaus Harnoncourt. Dir: Jean-Pierre Ponnelle. Decca VHS 071 406—3; LD:—1.

2. Maria Ewing (Poppea), Cynthia Clarey (Ottavia), Anne-Marie Owens (Arnalta), Dennis Bailey (Nero),

Dale Duesing (Ottone), Robert Lloyd (Seneca). Glyndebourne Festival Chor and Orch/Raymond Leppard. Dir:
Peter Hall. Castle VHS CVI 2040. Subtitles.

The plot of Monteverdi's last opera, familiar from the Roman
historian Tacitus, runs counter to the conventions of literary
morality (as Peter Hall tells us in his introduction to the Glyndebourne version) in allowing the adulterous love of the
emperor Nero for the spoilt, scheming Poppea to triumph,
leaving his wife Ottavia distraught in exile and his friend-
philosopher Seneca committing suicide for opposing his
master's will.

Two copies of the score survive, both containing emenda-
tions. Conductors have to make their own choices regarding
instrumentation and voice parts. For Glyndebourne (1984)
Leppard opts for a luscious sound with an unsuitably large
number of strings. Harnoncourt at the Zurich Opera (1979),
who plays more of the score than Leppard, is sparer in his
scoring while allowing a varied palette of sound. For Nero,
originally a soprano-castrato role, both conductors pick a
tenor. For Ottone, Leppard chooses a baritone, Harnoncourt,
preferably, a counter-tenor. As for the Nurse, at Glyndebourne she is a mezzo and played straight; at Zurich she is
sung by a tenor and rather guyed.

Hall's staging is predominantly naturalistic; Ponnelle's is
more stylised and artificial. Glyndebourne places the piece in
the Renaissance period of the work's composition, setting it
in simple decor and clothing. Zurich and Ponnelle go for the
Court of Louis XIV with fanciful dresses, wigs, strong
make-up and elaborate wigs and headdresses. Similarly Hall
concentrates on the inner emotions of the characters: Ponnelle prefers bold gestures and pictures with an element of
caricature.

The two casts faithfully fulfil their respective director's
wishes. As with *Orfeo* above, the Zurich cast is totally dedicated to Ponnelle's way and performs with great panache.
Ewing conveys both Poppea's sensuality and vulnerability.
Yakar, chief victim of Ponnelle's florid ways, is merely a sex-
kitten. On the other hand Bailey is a cipher as Nero beside
Tappy's obsessed, almost psychotic emperor, keenly sung.

Clarey is a deeply moving, dignified Ottavia, Schmidt more of a tragedy queen, but she sings magnificently. Salminen's forceful, sonorously sung Seneca is the still centre of the Decca version – at least until his premature death. Lloyd portrays a more placid, philosophical figure. Esswood makes an affecting Ottone for Ponnelle; Duesing seems too modern for Hall.

The sound on the Decca is infinitely preferable to that on Castle, but the latter provides subtitles, Decca none, at least on VHS. While sad to put aside Ewing's magnetic Poppea (some may not be able to do so if they have a chance to sample her interpretation), the Decca is the better buy, with many potent images, arrestingly filmed, from Ponnelle.

Antonio Vivaldi (1678–1741)

Orlando furioso
Susan Patterson (Angelica), Marilyn Horne (Orlando), Kathleen Kuhlmann (Alcina), Sandra Walker (Bradamante), Jeffrey Gall (Ruggiero), William Matteuzzi (Medoro), Kevin Langan (Astolfo). Chor and Orch of San Francisco Opera/Randall Behr. Dir: Pier Luigi Pizzi; video dir: Brian Large. Virgin VHS VVD 1090.

Vivaldi wrote some fifty operas, but only fifteen are preserved and few of those are ever staged. They show his considerable flair for vocal writing allied to his well-known gifts as an orchestrator, but as a creator of characters through music he was not in the same class as Handel (qv). Orlando furioso is no match for Handel's Alcina which derives from the same tale based on an epic poem by Ariosto (1516). The work dates from 1727 in Venice. It is a story of loves lost and found on Alcina's magic island owned by the nymphomaniacal sorceress Alcina. This foreshortened version was given at the San Francisco Opera in 1989 when it was a success. Vivaldi's arias are by turn scintillating, tender, terrifying.

Pizzi's attempt at staying faithful to baroque style and gesture results in a stilted, garish staging, and Behr's conducting has more pace than sensitivity. Horne, though past her best days, remains an impressive interpreter of this kind of music and has a high old time in Orlando's mad scene. Kuhlmann is positive and inveigling as the enchantress Alcina. Patterson is an elegant Angelica. Counter-tenor Gall, a mellifluous Ruggiero (as in Handel), has the work's most memorable aria – here a sensuous love-song accompanied by a flute.

Picture and sound are no more than adequate. The audience laughs at lines provided in a translation (on surtitles) not offered to a home audience but, in spite of its drawbacks, the video will become a historic document as one of the few surviving souvenirs of Horne in action.

John Gay (1685–1732)

The Beggar's Opera
Carol Hall (Polly Peachum), Rosemary Ashe (Lucy Lockit), Isla Blair (Jenny Diver), Patricia Routledge (Mrs Peachum), Stephen Daltrey (Macheath), Stratford Johns (Peachum), Peter Bayliss (Lockit). English Baroque Soloists/John Eliot Gardiner. Dir: Jonathan Miller. Philips LD 070 408–1.

The Beggar's Opera is really more like the first musical than an opera, more often than not given by operatic forces: here we have a nice combination of singers, a hero from the pop world and actors. The work had its premiere on 28 January 1728, a collaboration between John Gay, a poet and playwright, and actor-manager John Rich. It was a runaway success, a popular alternative to the serious operas of Handel (*qv*), concurrently running in London. It consisted of short airs adapted to Gay's lyrics from all kinds of musical sources (these are all usefully listed in this set's booklet), and including songs derived from Purcell and Handel. In its picture of London low life it ridiculed and satirised a whole range of targets in British society.

The original instrumentation was provided by a German composer called Pepusch. In more recent times there have been versions by Frederick Austin at the Lyric, Hammersmith

(1920, highly successful) and an almost complete rewrite by Britten for Aldeburgh (1948), which turns the work almost into another opera by Britten. For this staging, first seen on BBC Television in 1990, Stephen Barlow and John Eliot Gardiner have attempted to return to an authentic eighteenth-century style using period instruments imaginatively in a wholly successful act of re-creation, alertly conducted by Gardiner himself.

Jonathan Miller, the director, has avoided any attempt at updating or sending a social message inappropriate to the piece; rather he has succeeded in reproducing the milieu of 1728, including the nefarious activities of the denizens of the city, at once money-orientated, immoral and opportunist and allowed the moral for our own times to be there for all to see. Everyone looks a shade too clean, no dirt on the boots as it were, but the close-ups hold nothing back as regards the crime and debauchery of the day.

Stephen Daltrey makes a notable Macheath, suggesting the man's sex appeal, his bravado and his vulnerability. Daltrey's singing seems remarkably apt for the ballad songs. As the main objects of his desire, Polly and Lucy, Carol Hall and Rosemary Ashe, both professional sopranos, are nicely differentiated, the former rosy-cheeked and honest, the latter a slattern but attractive. The actors who play Peachum and Lockit are also well contrasted. Stratford Johns is earthy and sly as the first, Peter Bayliss magnificently drunken and scheming as the second – his growling delivery of his songs is irresistible. Isla Blair turns in a nice vignette as the deceiving whore, Jenny Diver.

The video is admirably directed by Miller himself in David Myerscough-Jones's well-observed sets. The picture and sound quality are up to Philips's highest standards.

George Frideric Handel (1685–1759)

Giulio Cesare
1. Valerie Masterson (Cleopatra), Della Jones (Sextus), Sarah Walker (Cornelia), James Bowman (Ptolemy), Janet Baker (Julius Caesar), David James (Nirenus),

Christopher Booth-Jones (Curio), John Tomlinson (Achilla), Chor and Orch of English National Opera/ Charles Mackerras. Dir: John Copley. Virgin VHS VVD 383. In English.
2. Susan Larson (Cleopatra), Lorraine Hunt (Sextus), Mary Westbrook-Geha (Cornelia), Jeffrey Gall (Julius Caesar), Drew Minter (Ptolemy), Cheryl Cobb (Nirenus), James Maddalena (Achilla), Hermann Hillebrand (Curio). Dresden Staatskapelle/Craig Smith. Dir: Peter Sellars. Decca VHS 071 408-3; LD:—1. Subtitles.

No doubt because it depicts events well documented in history, this was the first piece to restore Handel's reputation in the opera house. Its popularity is well deserved as it shows the ardent, wilful nature of the eponymous hero and the voluptuous, minxish character of the seductive, scheming Cleopatra in a number of varied and wonderfully apt arias, while at the same time giving music of appropriate character to loyal Sextus, vicious, spoilt Ptolemy and grieving, put-upon Cornelia.

These two productions, both deriving from the opera house, could not be more different. The first, faithful to Handel, is a pleasure to see and hear; the second is a hateful travesty of his intentions. John Copley's long-running production, recorded in 1984, has Janet Baker as Julius Caesar. A Handelian of long standing, she handles this trousers role as to the manner born and learnt. This emperor is, as Handel predicates, at once commanding, amorous, self-willed. Baker's singing is vibrant, fleet and, where needed, as in the touching recitative mourning Pompey's ashes, deeply eloquent.

Masterson is an apt Cleopatra for this Caesar, voluptuous, flighty, pleasing to the eye, and her singing of Cleopatra's many arias conveys the differing moods of each unerringly. Della Jones is a properly concerned and impetuous Sextus; as his grieving mother Cornelia, Sarah Walker sings and acts with noble dignity. Bowman is as imperious and nasty as Ptolemy should be and John Tomlinson is a rightly vicious Achilla. Mackerras conducts a lithe, vital reading of the many-faceted score. Copley's staging may by now seem a shade dated but it is never less than in sympathy with the music and keeps well within the bounds of Handelian style.

By contrast Sellars, in updating the piece to the modern Middle East, altering the plot (of course) to make Caesar a visiting American President, only succeeds in belittling Handel's music and also makes its formal dimensions seem the more inappropriate for the modern stage. Some of the staging is as unpleasing as it is crude, and all the main characters look as awful as they are unreal. The results are at best cheaply smart, at worst ludicrous and an insult to Handel.

Nor do the singers do much to redeem things. The most accomplished is Lorraine Hunt, who does her best to overcome the staging's limitations, and makes much of the indecisive yet eager Sextus. Gall sounds overparted and harsh as Caesar, Minter, the other counter-tenor, is better suited as Ptolemy. Larson, a somewhat thin-toned soprano, is the worst victim of Sellars's idiotic conceits. The conducting is decent rather than inspired; at least it observes Handelian verities. Those who must have a 'different', modern approach to their operas may be entertained. True Handelians must surely prefer the Copley/Mackerras approach.

Xerxes (Serse)

Valerie Masterson (Romilda), Lesley Garrett (Atalanta), Ann Murray (Xerxes), Jean Rigby (Amastris), Christopher Robson (Arsamanes), Christopher Booth-Jones (Elviro), Rodney Macann (Ariodates). Chor and Orch of English National Opera/Charles Mackerras. Dir: Nicholas Hytner; video dir: John Michael Philips. Philips LD: 070 414—1. In English.

This set makes it almost worthwhile on its own acquiring a laserdisc player. As a performance of a Handel opera it is near-perfect, justifying it as a winner of the Laurence Olivier Opera Award. As a piece it represents Handel at the peak of his achievement. It is a comic opera with more than an underlay of emotional seriousness where the passions of the principals are concerned. Although the central character is the Persian king Xerxes, lover of a plane tree (the so-called Largo, so often recorded on its own, is a paean to the tree at the beginning of the work) and a bridge over the Hellespont, here represented in miniature, the story is almost entirely fictional, relating the infatuation of Xerxes for Romilda, daughter of his general Ariodates. At the same time she is in love with Arsamanes, Xerxes's brother, who is secretly adored by Romilda's sexy sister Atalanta. Meanwhile Amastris, Xerxes's true beloved, returns in disguise as a man to find Xerxes enamoured of Romilda. As can be imagined there is room here for a deal of deception, scheming and misunderstanding, although all ends happily.

Handel clothed the story in music of the greatest charm, flexibility and, where needed, serious import. Under the musical direction of such an experienced Handelian as Charles Mackerras, the score is lovingly sung and played, and the members of the original cast, recorded here in 1988, are without exception perfect in their roles – and how often can one say that? Ann Murray has done nothing better than this authoritative portrait of the preening, self-willed monarch, her singing in the bravura class. Masterson projects Romilda's many feelings with clear, steady tone and flexible line, and she acts superbly. Counter-tenor Christopher Robson makes Arsamanes into a man of many emotions, all keenly expressed. As Atalanta, Garrett is all wheedling charm. Rigby portrays the faithful, distressed Amastris in firm alto tones. Macann's military man is properly ridiculous.

All are directed by Hytner with loving care within a highly ingenious framework, featuring deckchairs, a statue of the composer and a vista of ancient Persepolis, in the decor of David Fielding. The English translation, Hytner's own, is faultless and draws an immediate response from the audience, who applaud (perhaps too readily). Indeed we are sharing in a true evening of unalloyed pleasure at the London Coliseum. The picture and sound quality are first-rate.

Christoph Willibald Gluck (1714–87)

Orfeo ed Euridice
1. Elisabeth Speiser (Euridice), Elizabeth Gale (Amor), Janet Baker (Orfeo). Glyndebourne Festival Chor and

Orch/Raymond Leppard. Dir: Peter Hall; video dir: Rodney Greenberg. Castle VHS CVI 2035. Subtitles.
2. Gillian Webster (Euridice), Jeremy Budd (Amor), Jochen Kowalski (Orfeo). Chor and Orch of Royal Opera House, Covent Garden/Hartmut Haenchen. Dir: Harry Kupfer; video dir: Hans Hulscher. Virgin VHS VVD 986; Pioneer LD PLMCB 00621.

Gluck's most famous opera, a setting of the Orpheus legend, exists in various forms stretching from the original, lean version with an alto castrato hero (the version used on the Pioneer set) composed for Vienna in 1762, through the longer version in French, with ballet, dating from 1774, to Berlioz's conflation devised for Pauline Viardot in 1859 (used on the Glyndebourne set). In all Gluck moved away from the long arias and strict formality of his predecessors towards a style based on the essentials of dramatic continuity and direct expression.

The Glyndebourne performance was staged as a part of Janet Baker's farewell to the stage in 1982, and she rewarded her many admirers and Glyndebourne's tribute with an interpretation that evinced her many gifts as a singing actress, suggesting all Orfeo's conflicting emotions: loss at Euridice's death, resolution as she determines to search for her, terror at the cavortings of the Furies (here seen as a monkey pack cavorting at the gates of Hades), wonder in the Elysian Fields (the solo 'Che puro ciel' there serenely delivered), and torment when Orfeo is forbidden to look back at his beloved. When he does finally yield to her pleadings for just one glance, Orfeo-Baker is disconsolate at losing her again – the famous aria 'Che farò senza Euridice' is sung with an impassioned intensity typical of Baker. And it is sung as Orfeo cradles Euridice in his arms, just one marvellous moment in Peter Hall's finely judged, perceptive staging, lamed only by the treatment of Amor as a pink-clad figure with wings and by the final tableaux of celebratory dances (after Orfeo's constancy has won Euridice a reprieve), treated in too homespun a fashion.

John Bury's sets are based on a central path along which Orfeo progresses at the start of each act. The Elysian Fields are suggested as a Wedgwood-like never-never land. Speiser makes a vulnerable, desperate Euridice, Gale a somewhat hard-edged Amor. Leppard, observing some period practice while using modern instruments, conducts a vital reading, a sympathetic backdrop to the central interpretation of Baker, who is at her trenchant best in 'Addio mio sospiro', the bravura aria later added by Gluck and restored here to end Act 1. Baker's voice may by this date have lost some of its lustre but the artistry and conviction are more than ever in evidence. Dame Janet introduces the performance with some pertinent thoughts on the piece. Picture quality and sound unfortunately leave something to be desired.

The Covent Garden staging of a Berlin production by Kupfer offers a very different experience. Eveything seems conceived in the mind rather than coming from the heart, the reverse of Hall's concept. The kaleidoscope of revolving mirror panels, in Hans Schavernoch's decor (not too visible on video), reveals a labyrinth of railway lines, platforms, corridors, hospital waiting-rooms, call boxes, internal organs, although these are dimly perceived on this laserdisc version. Kupfer's movement shows Orfeo in a time warp, a double persona of leather-jacketed lover with guitar and evening-dressed concert artist.

The action is updated (naturally) to today. Euridice is killed in a car accident after she and Orfeo have watched a concert during the overture. After that Orfeo seeks out her body in an impersonal hospital, then goes in search of her soul. No Furies are seen on stage; Orfeo implores the choir, in evening dress, to let him by. Elysium is hardly represented; Euridice's image is placed on a TV screen dragged around the stage by Orfeo. She, for some reason, changes from white into black, then gets into a plastic mac. Amor is mimed by a very young boy, sung side stage by a treble, again in evening dress. The final trio is delivered in evening dress by the principals, their scores in hand.

The musical edition is that of the Vienna premiere, therefore lasting only some eighty minutes. This spare, direct version has notable impact even in such an oddball staging. Haenchen conducts with more brio than feeling. Kowalski is a wonderfully fluent and personable Orfeo, his counter-tenor appropriately other-worldly, and he at least brings passion to his role. His excessive decoration of the line of 'Che farò' is however questionable. Webster is an attractive Euridice but obviously uncomfortable with much of what she is asked to enact. As Amor, the boy soprano sings sweetly. The sound and picture are first-rate, but absence of subtitles is a drawback.

Wolfgang Amadeus Mozart (1756–91)

Mitridate
1. Yvonne Kenny (Aspasia), Joan Rodgers (Ismene), Massimiliano Roncato (Arbate), Ann Murray (Sifare), Anne Gjevang (Farnace), Gösta Winbergh (Mitridate), Peter Straka (Marzio). Concentus Musicus Wien/Nikolaus Harnoncourt. A film by Jean-Pierre Ponnelle. Decca VHS 071 407–3; LD:–1.
2. Luba Organosova (Aspasia), Lillian Watson (Ismene), Jacquelyn Fugelle (Arbate), Ann Murray (Sifare), Jochen Kowalski (Farnace), Bruce Ford (Mitridate), Justin Lavender (Marzio). Chor and Orch of Royal Opera House, Covent Garden/Paul Daniel. Dir: Graham Vick; video dir: Derek Bailey. Pioneer LD PLMCC 00941.

Written when Mozart was fourteen, _Mitridate_ is an astonishing work disclosing his genius as a composer of emotional understanding at a precipitately precocious age. He depicts with unerring sensibility the feelings of the thwarted lovers, Aspasia and Sifare, the indignant fury of the ruler Mitridate as he thinks all around him are conspiring to undermine his will, and the machinations of the evil Farnace.

The film, dating from 1988, is worthy of the work's achievement. Ponnelle makes masterly use of his chosen venue, the highly atmospheric Teatro Olimpico in Vicenza, with his camerawork, close-up and distanced, unusual angles that help project the drama, and he makes profitable use of the da capo tradition of _opera seria_ to underline the thoughts and emotions running through the minds of the principals. Ponnelle's own sets and Pet Halmen's costumes, heavily

_13_

─────────────

embroidered eighteenth-century, and the lighting are entirely apt to the piece and also in harmony with the setting.

Harnoncourt leads a performance that excises a couple of arias and, mercifully, pares away the recitative to a minimum, allowing the drama to proceed at a compelling pace. So does his direct, severe reading and the superlative playing of his Concentus Musicus. This is the basis of a convincing act of authenticity all round with tempi perfectly judged and textures clear.

Kenny as Aspasia and Murray as Sifare give eloquent portrayals, as they have since done in these roles at Covent Garden. Kenny is particularly moving in her Act 3 aria, 'Pallide ombra', which looks forward to Countess Almaviva's music. Murray is magnificent in Sifare's long Act 2 aria as he takes his farewell of Aspasia, a central point in the opera with Kenny's Aspasia reacting touchingly to her beloved's words. Both use coloratura to project feelings. Harnoncourt rightly prefers a contralto to a counter-tenor as the vicious, later remorseful Farnace: Gjevang is vivid in looks and voice.

Winbergh's Mitridate, lordly, impetuous and yet sensitive, is an involved and involving interpretation. Rodgers acts and sings with an easy grace appropriate to youthful Ismene. A treble as Arbate is a questionable choice. Although sound and vision are post-synchronised, the process has been so well supervised as to silence criticism.

Vick's direction, for Covent Garden, is perhaps even more persuasive than Ponnelle's at Vicenza and has the advantage over its rival in being a record of a real occasion in the theatre. Considered a triumph at its first appearance in 1991, it rightly won the Evening Standard Award as opera production of that year. This video derives from the 1993 revival which is, if anything, more arresting. Fusing ideas culled from various traditions in the theatre of the East and eighteenth-century European practice, it creates a tour de force of what was called by one critic 'cultural synthesis'. Paul Brown's panelled, eminently mobile sets provide the sympathetic backcloth of the clearly defined, closely articulated movement to which Brown's extravagantly panniered costumes add a gesture of welcome flamboyance. Yet all this visual daring never dwarfs the singers, who are allowed to perform with insight and character.

They are a superb team, superbly conducted by Daniel, who has every tempo just as it should be and emphasises how the young Mozart managed to transcend the conventions of *opera seria*. Organosova rivals Kenny in moving expression and matches the technical demands of the role even more confidently. Murray repeats her dignified, compassionate Sifare, although the voice has lost a little of its earlier ease and focus in the meantime. Farnace, cast here with a counter-tenor, is given a really devious, vicious profile by Kowalski, who delivers his imprecations with great éclat. Ford sings the taxing title role as if it had been written with his incisive, flexible tenor in mind. Watson is an enchanting Ismene.

Bailey's visual direction is exemplary and the sound is faultless. Subtitles would have been useful, but the booklet has a detailed synopsis that signposts the arias. Cuts are also made here; they can be borne in the cause of a swifter-moving drama. Either version is recommendable.

La finta giardiniera
Ann Christine Biel (Serpetta), Britt-Marie Aruhn (Sandrina), Eva Pilat (Arminda), Annika Skoglund (Ramiro), Richard Croft (Belfiore), Stuart Kale (Don Anchise), Petteri Salomaa (Nardo). Chor and Orch of Drottningholm Court Theatre/Arnold Östman. Dir: Göran Järvefelt; video dir: Thomas Oloffson. Virgin VHS VVD 616; LD: Philips 070 418–1. Subtitles.

In this work the nineteen-year-old composer announced his genius as a composer for the stage, writing music that was far more advanced than any of his contemporaries' in terms of dramatic development and harmonic daring. Indeed the music looks forward, more than the succeeding works of his youth, to the maturity of *Figaro* and *Giovanni*, most notably in the long scenes for Belfiore and Sandrina in Acts 2 and 3, and in the extended finales to Acts 1 and 2. Indeed Sandrina's scenes, lost in the woods, use an expressive range that pre-echoes the music of the Countess and Elvira. Then the orchestration could only have come from Mozart's hand, particularly in the use of woodwind instruments as in the duet of reconciliation for Sandrina and Belfiore in Act 3. The plot, which involves a series of lovers' quarrels and mistaken identities, is of little consequence, but wherever there is a chance for depth of characterisation the young Mozart eagerly seizes it.

Järvefelt, in this 1988 Drottningholm performance, sometimes resorts to artificiality and farce in a mistaken belief that this will make the opera palatable to modern tastes. Zany sight gags and mugging by an army of unnecessary extras sometimes deflect from the real emotions and dark undertones being enacted by the principals and in the orchestra, but in the most heartfelt passages Järvefelt's gifts as a discerning director mercifully come to the fore. Cuts include several arias (regrettable) and a deal of recitative (not so regrettable). Östman gives a lucid and mellow account of what remains, eliciting beguiling sounds from his period-instrument orchestra.

The cast is, in most respects, excellent. Aruhn is at first too reserved a Sandrina, but she recovers to sing affectingly. Biel's tart, teasing Serpetta is a pertinent characterisation. Pilat is a confident, tonally warm Arminda: it is not her fault that the character is depicted as a silly-billy. In the castrato role of Ramiro, Skoglund's mezzo is stirring. Croft is a fleet and manly Belfiore, though again the florid reading sometimes imposed on the part is a liability. Kale is an amusing Don Anchise, Salomaa an attractive Nardo. Sound, picture and camerawork are of exemplary standard.

Il re pastore

Angela Maria Blasi (Aminta), Sylvia McNair (Elisa), Iris Vermilion (Tamiri), Jerry Hadley (Alessandro), Claes Hakan Ahnsjö (Agenore). Academy of St Martin in the Fields/Neville Marriner. Dir: John Cox; video dir: Brian Large. Philips LD 070 129–1. Subtitles.

This *serenata* finds the fledgling Mozart in charming mood. The pastoral idyll is here presented in traditional eighteenth-century dress as it might have been given in the composer's day. The decor is modest. The singers sit listening attentively on the side of the stage as their colleagues perform. Nothing is taken out of the bounds of the work's original intentions as an entertainment for a royal household.

As ever with Marriner, everything is musically smooth and effective but the depths of the score, such as they are, remain unexplored. At the harpsichord, a bewigged John Constable, acting as *maestro di capella*, smiles benignly on his charges.

McNair sings a typically sweet and charming Elisa. As her lover Aminta, Blasi is a bland, endlessly smiling lightweight, but she sings nimbly. Hadley does the little required of him as the Emperor Alexander with aplomb but is not always secure in his runs. Vermilion projects the feelings of a princess down on her luck with real conviction. Best of all is the veteran Ahnsjö, a Mozartian stylist, who sings Agenore's music as to the manner born. All in all, a pleasing though anodyne experience, finely directed and in excellent sound.

Idomeneo

1. Yvonne Kenny (Ilia), Carol Vaness (Elettra), Jerry Hadley (Idamante), Philip Langridge (Idomeneo), Thomas Hemsley (Arbace). Glyndebourne Festival Chor and Orch/Bernard Haitink. Dir: Trevor Nunn; video dir: Christopher Swann. Castle VHS CVI 2019. Subtitles.

2. Bozena Betley (Ilia), Josephine Barstow (Elettra), Leo Goeke (Idamante), Richard Lewis (Idomeneo), Alexander Oliver (Arbace). Glyndebourne Festival Chor and Orch/John Pritchard. Dir: John Cox; video dir: David Heather. Pickwick VHS SL 2003.

3. Anne Christine Biel (Ilia), Anita Soldh (Elettra), David Kuebler (Idamante), Stuart Kale (Idomeneo), John-Eric Jacobsson (Arbace), Chor and Orch of Drottningholm Court Theatre/Arnold Östman. Dir: Michael Hampe; video dir: Thomas Olofsson. Virgin VHS VVD 946.

Mozart's *opera seria* was for long almost entirely neglected as a static and therefore unperformable opera about characters of classical antiquity with no relevance to life in the nineteenth or twentieth century. When it was given in Vienna or Salzburg it was usually in an edited version (one of these was by no less a composer than Richard Strauss). It was only returned to something like its original form when

Glyndebourne first presented it in 1950. Since then it has been regularly given there, and two of these performances derive from different productions there, the first (by Trevor Nunn) from 1983, the second (by John Cox) from 1974.

While received opinion has it that Nunn's effort was a success and Cox's a failure, I tend to the opposite view, but unfortunately the Cox derives from a dimly recorded Southern Television transmission that ruthlessly abbreviated Act 1. None the less the stark perspectives of the concentric hoops leading to various vistas and tableaux were and are a highly imaginative answer to the work's admittedly slow-moving action and restrained nature. Within it Cox directs a performance that goes to the heart of the matter where the key relationship between father and son is concerned. Leo Goeke's sad eyes convey all Idamante's sorrow when he believes he is to be killed on account of his father's oath to sacrifice the first person he sees when rescued from a storm, that person being his son, and the experienced Richard Lewis is a moved and moving Idomeneo throughout as he attempts to thwart the will of the gods. Elettra's conflicting emotions are brilliantly conveyed by the young Barstow, showing all the woman's jealousy and incipient madness, and Bozena Betley is all sweetness and light as the gentle Trojan princess Ilia whom Idamante prefers to the stronger-willed Elettra.

Nunn's first attempt at opera is notable for its attempt at creating the Cretan milieu with screens showing suitable motifs. Nunn attempts a marriage of Minoan vigour with oriental delicacy of movement and gesture, but something of Mozart's emotional pulse is lost along the way in the spare setting. The projections of storm and calm work well as far as they go. The cast is a variable quantity. Vaness offers a properly fiery, richly contoured Elettra although one that misses the crazed element Barstow so electrifyingly conveys. Kenny sings warmly and keenly as Ilia, but is a trifle wooden in her portrayal. Similarly Hadley's Idamante is blankly presented though his tenor is pleasing on the ear. That cannot be said for Langridge's voice, but he compensates for sometimes grating tone by his portrayal of the tormented monarch, always telling and involving.

Both Haitink and Pritchard have the measure of the piece,

serious, lyrical, forward-moving, though neither quite pierces to its core as John Eliot Gardiner has done on CD. Neither version has very good sound, but the Castle is markedly superior to the Pickwick (mono). In spite of the insights of Cox's staging, the more recent version is the one to have.

By comparison with both Glyndebourne directors, Michael Hampe in the Drottningholm performance skates over the surface of the music. In an effort to preserve the *opera seria* verities, he offers a dullish staging conventionally set and conventionally enacted. Stuart Kale sings firmly but with little sense of Idomeneo's torment. As Ilia and Elettra, Biel and Soldh both create real characters but are betrayed by moments of vocal fallibility. As is the case with Hadley at Glyndebourne, Kuebler is given most of the music Mozart wrote for his tenor Idamante in the Munich version (the Vienna premiere had a soprano castrato in the part) and sings it in splendid style. Östman is, as ever, concerned with making Mozart as vividly and dramatically effective as it may have been at its first performances and as always is worth listening to. Picture and sound are no more than average.

Die Entführung aus dem Serail

1. Edita Gruberová (Konstanze), Reri Grist (Blonde), Francisco Araiza (Belmonte), Norbert Orth (Pedrillo), Martti Talvela (Osmin), Thomas Holtzmann (Pasha Selim). Chor and Orch of Bavarian State Opera/Karl Böhm. Dir: August Everding; video dir: Karlheinz Hundorf. DG VHS 072 406-3; LD:−1.

2. Aga Winska (Konstanze), Elisabet Hellström (Blonde), Richard Croft (Belmonte), Bengt-Ola Morgny (Pedrillo), Tamás Szüle (Osmin), Emmerich Schäffer (Pasha Selim). Chor and Orch of Drottningholm Court Theatre/Arnold Östman. Dir: Harald Clemen; video dir: Thomas Olofsson. Virgin VHS VVD 848; Philips LD: 070 417−1. Subtitles.

In this work Mozart elevated the *Singspiel* (a play with music, the numbers divided by long stretches of dialogue, in this case drastically reduced these days) to something much more substantial than merely ephemeral entertainment. He invested the main characters, including – indeed particularly – the speaking part of the Pasha Selim with deep feelings. Selim worships the captive Konstanze who, true to her name, is constant to her beloved Belmonte, who arrives at Selim's castle to rescue her. The lighter side of the story concerns the Pasha's lascivious overseer Osmin, who lusts after Konstanze's English maid Blonde, herself in love with Pedrillo, Belmonte's servant. Lively music for the comic characters contrasts with extended and complex arias for Konstanze and Belmonte, and a superb quartet for the reunited lovers at the end of Act 2 (of three). After a moving duet for Konstanze and Belmonte, as they await death after their escape is foiled, all ends happily when Selim proves benign and forgiving.

These two performances couldn't be more different in concept; neither is an ideal representation of the piece. Everding's 1980 Munich staging is set in Max Bignens's attractive decor, sliding panels that unobtrusively alter the setting and provide a simple backcloth to Everding's traditional staging. This employs sight gags that are sometimes more facetious than funny, but Everding is thoughtful and probing in dealing with the serious side of the work: the frustrated desire of the Pasha for Konstanze and the reciprocal love of Belmonte and Konstanze. He is helped inestimably by Holtzmann's strong, tormented acting and speaking as the Pasha Selim, an object lesson in how to project this difficult role.

Gruberová's Konstanze, faultlessly sung, is nicely balanced vocally between the lyrical and the heroic and she has no trouble with the awkward coloratura of the part, but her acting is expressive in only the most conventional way. Araiza sings mellifluously but is also a staid actor. Grist was by 1980 a somewhat mature Blonde who has dulled what was once an irresistible portrayal. Orth is a conventionally effective Pedrillo. Talvela is a towering, dark-voiced Osmin, paradoxically threatening and cuddly at the same time. In the pit is the eighty-six-year-old Böhm in one of the last new productions he conducted. His masterly reading, finely balanced, unerringly phrased, will be a lasting souvenir of his powers as a Mozartian.

Böhm's pacing is stately and poised. Östman, at Drottningholm in 1990, using period instruments, adopts swift, sometimes unstable tempi in a much more buoyant, energetic interpretation which marches with the simple, telling direction of Clemen predicated by the small stage. This is certainly closer to what one would have seen in Mozart's day. Carl Friedrich Oberle's sets give a pleasingly ochre colour to the action. The overall result is unfussy, unpretentious, a shade homespun, but in sum enjoyable for its modesty.

Winska is an appealingly youthful and vulnerable Konstanze. Although her singing sometimes sounds untutored, she rises to the challenge of the long, showpiece aria, 'Martern aller Arten', in which Konstanze shows courage and defiance in the face of the Pasha's threats of torture unless she submits to his advances. Croft makes a handsome Belmonte in voice and demeanour, well up to the demands of Belmonte's taxing part. He is granted Belmonte's third aria, 'Ich baue ganz', omitted by Böhm on the rival version.

Hellström is a proudly tall Blonde with keen-edged soprano to match, altogether a lively portrayal, fitly partnered by Morgny's eager, athletic Pedrillo. Szüle offers an unexaggerated, slightly dull Osmin, whose bass is a bit short at the bottom. The Selim is conventional when compared with Holtzmann's arresting portrayal on the other set. The German dialogue, often indifferently accented, is altered and foreshortened. In spite of some reservations, this is a fair representation of Mozart's intentions although there is room for something more imaginative.

Le nozze di Figaro

1. Alison Hagley (Susanna), Hillevi Martinpelto (Countess), Constanze Backes (Barbarina), Pamela Helen Stephen (Cherubino), Susan McCulloch (Marcellina), Francis Egerton (Basilio, Curzio), Bryn Terfel (Figaro), Rodney Gilfry (Count), Carlos Feller (Bartolo), Julian Clarkson (Antonio). Monteverdi Choir, English Baroque Soloists/John Eliot Gardiner. Dir: Jean Louis Thamin; video dir: Olivier Mille. DG Archiv VHS 072 439–3; LD:−1. Subtitles.

2. Marie McLaughlin (Susanna), Cheryl Studer (Countess), Yvetta Tannenbergerova (Barbarina), Gabriele Sima (Cherubino), Margarita Lilowa (Marcellina), Heinz Zednik (Basilio), Franz Kasemann (Curzio), Lucio Gallo (Figaro), Ruggero Raimondi (Count), Rudolf Mazzola (Bartolo), István Gáti (Antonio). Chor and Orch of the Vienna State Opera/Claudio Abbado. Dir: Jonathan Miller; video dir: Brian Large. Sony VHS SHV 46406; LD:S2LV 46406.

3. Mirella Freni (Susanna), Kiri Te Kanawa (Countess), Janet Perry (Barbarina), Maria Ewing (Cherubino), Heather Begg (Marcellina), John van Kesteren (Basilio), Willy Caron (Curzio), Hermann Prey (Figaro), Dietrich Fischer-Dieskau (Count), Paolo Montarsolo (Bartolo), Hans Kraemmer (Antonio). Vienna Philharmonic Orch/ Karl Böhm. A film by Jean-Pierre Ponnelle. DG VHS 072 403–3; LD:—1.

4. Georgine Resick (Susanna), Sylvia Lindenstrand (Countess), Birgitta Larsson (Barbarina), Ann Christine Biel (Cherubino), Karin Mang-Habashi (Marcellina), Torjbörn Lilliequist (Basilio), Bo Leinmark (Curzio), Mikael Samuelsson (Figaro), Per-Arne Wahlgren (Count), Erik Saedén (Bartolo), Karl-Robert Lindgren (Antonio). Chor and Orch of Drottningholm Court Theatre/Arnold Östman. Dir: Göran Järvefelt; video dir: Thomas Olofsson. Philips LD: 070 421–1. Subtitles.

All these versions have something significant and singular to offer as a commentary on what remains Mozart's most accessible and popular opera, depicting the follies and amours in a close-knit aristocratic household of the eighteenth century. Da Ponte's libretto based on Beaumarchais's classic comedy evinces insights into human behaviour still valid today. Three of the sets emanate from stage productions. The fourth, the Böhm/Ponnelle version, is one of several Unitel videos directed by Ponnelle expressly as a film and adopting the post-synchronisation of voices and as such it is *sui generis*, employing many tricks of the cinema, such as voice-overs as in the Count's and Countess's arias, and much canny and sometimes gimmicky camerawork. The singers, a highly distinguished group, are made to work hard for their money, acting and reacting voraciously at their director's behest. Ponnelle's own sets, while opening up the action, never stray far outside the stated milieu of the work and are glorious to view.

In most respects this is already a historical document, although made as recently as 1976. Director and conductor are dead. The singers have either retired or else given up the roles assigned them here. By and large the vocal performances are as alluring as those on any of the other versions, most notably in the case of Freni's enchanting, saucer-eyed Susanna, ideally sung in creamy tones, and Ewing's fetching, androgynous Cherubino. Ewing's amazingly expressive face, mobile body and vibrant voice have never been heard since to such advantage. Te Kanawa, as the Countess, was then in her prime. The smooth, refined singing is seconded by the soprano's appealing presence but she looks awkward having to act to her own singing. So, to an extent, does Fischer-Dieskau. This Count is a dominating figure in his own household, almost cruelly aggressive and very much at odds with his servant Figaro, here sung and acted strongly by Prey, who is more at home here than as Figaro's earlier incarnation in Ponnelle's film of Rossini's _Barbiere (qv)_. The smaller parts are played more as caricatures than genuine characters. Basilio and Marcellina lose their Act 4 arias.

The Sony set derives from a 1991 performance at the Vienna Festival, specifically designed for the Theater an der Wien. It is a joy from start to finish. Miller has had an intimate rapport with Beaumarchais and Mozart since he staged the former's play at the Old Vic for the National Theatre in the 1960s. After that his production of the opera for English National Opera was much enjoyed. Here it has been refined and perfected into a rewarding fusion of text and music, a reading based on the work's own time but full of insights into the motivation of the characters and wholly realistic in its projection of an enclosed society with all its loves, hate, jealousies and intrigues. Nothing is exaggerated yet everything is made clear and pointful, and happily contained in the period theatre for which Peter G. Davison has designed a revolving set that suggests a lived-in chateau, just right in colour and character.

Abbado's conducting nicely complements Miller's interpretation. It is fleet without being superficial, serious without being hard-driven, always aware of Mozartian verities. All the details tell using a reduced VPO in a small house. McLaughlin's Susanna is a quick-witted, no-nonsense portrayal adaptable to every situation in demeanour and vocal accent, her solos finely shaped. Gallo is a nimble, amiable Figaro with a voice of just the right weight to match – listen to the variety he brings to the well-worn 'Non più andrai' – and he happily avoids the extremes of excessive charm or militant rebellion when confronted with Raimondi's saturnine, at times neurotic Count, an ageing, uncertain ruler of his rocky domain. As the Countess, Studer may look a shade matronly, but she acts convincingly and with wit. Her singing is at once rich and delicate. Sima's Cherubino is delightful: creamy tone, adorable personality, acute acting. Of the comprimario roles, Mazzola deserves special praise for his precise but formidable Bartolo and Zednik for his hilarious Basilio. He and Margarita Lilowa's broad Marcellina are deprived of their Act 4 arias but all the recitative is included. Large's video direction shows his experienced hand. The sound is first-rate.

Both the other versions employ period instruments. That from Drottningholm, dating from 1981, is uniform with the other recordings from this source, attempting in visual and aural terms to recreate a performance of Mozart's day. Järvefelt's staging is wittily observant in a fairly conventional way and a shade homespun when compared with its rivals, the decor decidedly old-fashioned. Östman's reading is swift and light of weight, less arresting than his CD-only version, which employs a more experienced group of singers. Here, although the emphasis is on ensemble, there are at least four ingratiating, unfussy portrayals, offering a suitable antidote to Ponnelle's way with his principals. Resick's Susanna is pleasing, straightforward and attractive in terms of singing and acting, and Samuelsson is a bustling, down-to-earth Figaro with an agreeable baritone. Lindenstrand, lacking the vocal resources of Te Kanawa or Studer, is in a way the most touching and genuine Countess on video. Biel, very much a soprano Cherubino and all the better for that, makes a nicely vulnerable, impulsive portrayal. The rest are more ordinary.

Neither the picture nor sound quality is very clear, but the musical reading has the advantage over its rivals in presenting the score absolutely complete (Basilio's and Marcellina's arias restored in Act 4), and in offering a modicum of appoggiaturas and decorations as would have happened in Mozart's time.

The Gardiner/Thamin version, stemming from performances at the Châtelet Theatre in Paris in 1993, is a much more sophisticated affair than its Drottningholm counterpart, although it is set in very spare and not always convincing scenery. As is common these days, Thamin emphasises the political and sexual connotations of the piece, the former too blatantly with peasants and servants far too rebellious.

Thamin's *Personenregie* and Mille's video direction project the erotic vibes passing from Figaro and the Count to Susanna, and from Cherubino to the Countess, which works well when you have such a formidable Figaro as Terfel, a Susanna as personable and as expressive as Hagley and a Count Almaviva as lecherous and dominating as Gilfry. All three sing truly and firmly. The method is less successful when Cherubino is so obviously a girl play-acting and the Countess is so phlegmatic. The blatant guying in Cherubino's 'Voi che sapete' and Egerton's unconvincingly farcical Basilio and Curzio are also unwelcome, but McCulloch and Egerton make a wittily amusing pair of Marcellina and Basilio (both denied their arias).

Gardiner conducts a typically direct, swift account of the score, free of routine, alive to every nuance. It is in the best tradition of period Mozart interpretation today, but the re-ordering of numbers in Act 4 is questionable. Sound is excellent; so is the picture apart from the black spaces at the top and bottom, which betray the fact that the film has been made for High Definition Television, already popular in Japan but virtually unavailable as yet in Britain.

Anyone wanting the opera done with modern instruments and directed with insightful clarity should opt for Abbado/ Miller. Those seeking a period-instrument version will choose Gardiner/Thamin. Both offer enjoyable and challenging experiences. As an extra, Böhm/Ponnelle is a naughty, high-powered extravagance while Östman/Järvefelt is truly authentic.

Don Giovanni

1. Anna Tomowa-Sintow (Donna Anna), Julia Varady (Donna Elvira), Kathleen Battle (Zerlina), Gösta Winbergh (Don Ottavio), Samuel Ramey (Don Giovanni), Ferruccio Furlanetto (Leporello), Alexander Malta (Masetto), Paata Burchuladze (Commendatore). Chor of Vienna State Opera, Vienna Philharmonic Orch/Herbert von Karajan. Dir: Michael Hampe; video dir: Claus Viller. Sony VHS SLV 46383; Sony LD SLV 46383.

2. Edita Gruberová (Donna Anna), Ann Murray (Donna Elvira), Susanne Mentzer (Zerlina), Francisco Araiza (Don Ottavio), Thomas Allen (Don Giovanni), Claudio Desderi (Leporello), Natale de Carolis (Masetto), Sergei Koptchak (Commendatore). Chor and Orch of La Scala, Milan/Riccardo Muti. Dir: Giorgio Strehler; video dir: Carlo Battistoni. Castle VHS CVI 2061. Subtitles.

3. Helena Döse (Donna Anna), Birgit Nordin (Donna Elvira), Anita Soldh (Zerlina), Gösta Winbergh (Don Ottavio), Håkan Hagegård (Don Giovanni), Erik Saedén (Leporello), Tord Wallström (Masetto), Bengt Rudgren (Commendatore). Chor and Orch of Drottningholm Court Theatre/Arnold Östman. Dir: Göran Järvefelt; video dir: Thomas Olofsson. Virgin VHS VVD 342; Philips LD: 070 419–1. Subtitles (LD only).

4. Edda Moser (Donna Anna), Kiri Te Kanawa (Donna Elvira), Teresa Berganza (Zerlina), Kenneth Riegel (Don Ottavio), Ruggero Raimondi (Don Giovanni), José van Dam (Leporello), Malcolm King (Masetto), John Macurdy (Commendatore). Chor and Orch of Paris Opera/Lorin Maazel. Dir: Joseph Losey. Artificial Eye VHS Op2.

Mozart's *dramma giocoso* remains one of the most fascinating works in the regular repertory, open to so many different interpretations and often adapted to the ethos of a particular time. For those who want shock value at all costs the Decca version directed by Peter Sellars (not listed above) may have some relevance, but as ever his concept is so way out as to destroy the thing he is trying to make accessible to a new, untutored audience. Mozart and *Don Giovanni* need no such spurious patronising. Sellars has done the same to Shakespeare: *vide* his rightly vilified *Merchant of Venice*. Deborah Warner's Glyndebourne staging (soon to be on video) is almost as lamentable in misconstruing Mozart and Da Ponte as is Sellars's effort.

That a modern director can throw new light on a piece without destroying its own validity is shown by the late, lamented Järvefelt in his 1979 Drottningholm reading of the work, which chimed perfectly with Östman's period-instrument interpretation of the score. It shows one individual, Giovanni, living his life in eighteenth-century society and testing himself to destruction. The action concentrates on this wilful roué's final days on earth as he declines from sensual, foppish seducer to manic, drunken wreck. Giovanni finally discards his wig to reveal a cropped pate reminiscent of Hogarth's Rake. Järvefelt makes the effect all the more arresting by placing Giovanni's demonic behaviour within a pastoral setting.

Hagegård carries out his director's wishes to the letter in a magnetic portrayal of Giovanni that shows a man possessed by his own demon. The supercilious figure seen at the start gradually disintegrates before our eyes, becoming debauched and dissolute by the supper scene. Hagegård's singing is light and/or pointed as the situation demands. By his side Saedén presents a down-at-heel, earthy Leporello. Döse is a suitably neurotic yet moving Anna, the part just occasionally straining her resources at the top of her register. Nordin, on the other hand, is an unsuitably contained, chill Elvira. As Östman prefers the version of the Prague premiere she is denied her Act 2 aria, no great loss in the circumstances. By the same token Ottavio's 'Dalla sua pace' is excluded, a shame when Winbergh sings the role so fluently (but see below). Soldh's charmingly artless Zerlina is a delight; the rest of the cast is uneven.

Östman's tempi are, as ever, controversial: 'Là ci darem la mano' quicker than usual, 'Madamina' (Leporello's aria) and

Giovanni's so-called Champagne aria slower. They undoubtedly work well within the context of the small-scale staging, period instruments and a baroque theatre. The reservations lie in only moderate picture and sound quality in both mediums.

The interpretations of both Muti and Karajan could hardly be more different from Östman's. They look back at *Giovanni* from a nineteenth-century perspective with a full-blown modern orchestra, speeds predominantly on the slow side, which is not to say either is dull or ill-considered. Far from it: with directors and casts carefully chosen, both offer valid and interesting views of the work.

Strehler has always been an imaginative director and this *Giovanni*, staged at La Scala in 1987, is no exception. The scale of his production in Ezio Frigero's grand, atmospheric, architectural sets is well conveyed by astute camerawork with the singers, as is Strehler's wont, often seen in silhouette. Allen's Giovanni, as it was elsewhere, most memorably at Glyndebourne in 1982, is a possessed, saturnine, almost psychotic creature with a frightening leer when under pressure. The eyes tell all. Desderi's Leporello, as directed by Strehler, is a quick-witted cynic who is ruthlessly treated by his master and endures many pratfalls.

Gruberová's Anna is efficient, haughty, little more. By contrast Murray's Elvira, unflatteringly costumed and coiffured, is a distraught, impassioned figure. As Ottavio, Araiza is slightly negative but he phrases with distinction. Mentzer ravishes every sense as Zerlina and is suitably partnered by Carolis's warm-voiced, personable Masetto.

By and large, Karajan's final Salzburg Festival *Giovanni* in 1987 is more impressively staged and sung. For once Karajan abjured producing himself and called in the experienced Michael Hampe from Cologne. His then-regular designer Mauro Pagano provided Spanish renaissance, balustraded galleries on either side of the stage with arched arcades under them. Huge proscenium screens slide silently to stage centre for quick changes of location, revealing the red bas-relief rooftops of Seville, a central white rotunda in Giovanni's castle garden, the low wall of the cemetery and so on.

A thrilling dénouement is achieved when the Stone Guest

arrives at the dissolute banquet: all earthly accoutrements disappear to disclose a nocturnal background of planets and asteroids, a notable *coup de théâtre*. The universe itself has called Giovanni to account for his misdemeanours. It is a valid and exciting close to a visually unified staging that for once uses the huge spaces of Salzburg's large theatre intelligently. Hampe's direction is always telling and well motivated, and – unlike many modern stagings – it isn't relentlessly dark in feeling: comedy is well served.

The orchestra is the Vienna Philharmonic at its most burnished and inviting. Karajan offers a traditional reading with traditional tempi as conceived for the half century preceding the move towards 'authentic' performance. Zerlina's aria 'Batti, batti', the mask trio and 'Il mio tesoro' may be too slow for their or the singers' good, but the weight and import of the reading cannot be denied when so finely executed and nuanced, and given a cast of really impressive artists, even if most look at least ten years too old for the roles they are allotted.

Ramey's bass-baritone lacks variety of colour and his facial expressions are virtually non-existent, perhaps to suggest a stony-hearted seducer, but he is always a presence and sings securely throughout. He is partnered by Furlanetto's amusing Leporello, the one singer who looks too *young* for his part. Much better suited by the *buffo* range than in serious roles, Furlanetto's authentic Italian and eager personality sit nicely on the part. The *donne* are formidably enacted and exactly sung by Tomowa-Sintow and Varady, the former a truly tragic heroine, the latter a compact, stylish, tortured soul – it would be hard to imagine Elvira better done except from the point of view of physical appearance. Exactly the same can be said of Winbergh's Ottavio, here given both his arias, which he sings with light and shade, a technical finesse any Mozartian tenor, past or present, would be proud to emulate. Battle's sweetly sung Zerlina is a shade self-conscious and wooed by too eupeptic a Masetto. Burchuladze's Commendatore is too gravelly for aural comfort but his is an impressive presence.

With impeccable sound and picture this is the safest recommendation, but some may prefer the much leaner

Drottningholm interpretation or perhaps the famous Losey film set in Vicenza with Raimondi's conventionally dark-hued, handsome Giovanni and Te Kanawa at her peak as Elvira, Berganza an enchanting Zerlina. But unresponsive conducting from Maazel, a poor soundtrack and feeble lip-synch are serious drawbacks to what in the end proves artificial, just the effect the film set out to avoid, but it does all look quite ravishing.

Paul Czinner's film of the 1954 Salzburg staging has just been republished by DG (072 440–3). It looks woefully dated, but is distinguished by Elisabeth Grümmer's Anna, Lisa della Casa's Elvira and Furtwängler's grandly dramatic reading.

Così fan tutte

1. Amanda Roocroft (Fiordiligi), Rosa Mannion (Dorabella), Eirian James (Despina), Rainer Trost (Ferrando), Rodney Gilfry (Guglielmo), Claudio Nicolai (Don Alfonso). Monteverdi Choir, English Bach Soloists/John Eliot Gardiner. Dir: Gardiner; video dir: Peter Mumford. DG Archiv 072 436–3; LD:—1.

2. Ann Christine Biel (Fiordiligi), Maria Höglind (Dorabella), Ulla Severin (Despina), Lars Tibell (Ferrando), Magnus Lindén (Guglielmo), Enzo Florimo (Don Alfonso). Chor and Orch of Drottningholm Court Theatre/Arnold Östman. Dir: Willy Decker; video dir: Thomas Olofsson. Virgin VHS VVD 475; Philips LD: 070 416–1. Subtitles (LD).

3. Daniela Dessi (Fiordiligi), Delores Ziegler (Dorabella), Adelina Scarabelli (Despina), Josef Kundlák (Ferrando), Alessandro Corbelli (Guglielmo), Claudio Desderi (Don Alfonso). Chor and Orch of La Scala, Milan/Riccardo Muti. Dir: Michael Hampe. Castle CV1 2062. Subtitles.

4. Edita Gruberová (Fiordiligi), Delores Ziegler (Dorabella), Teresa Stratas (Despina), Luis Lima (Ferrando), Ferruccio Furlanetto (Guglielmo), Paolo Montarsolo (Don Alfonso). Vienna Philharmonic Orch/Nikolaus Harnoncourt. Dir: Jean-Pierre Ponnelle; video dir: Wolfgang Treu. Decca 071 424–3; LD:—1.

The first three of these versions, taken from opera-house performances, fulfil the stringent demands, vocal and histrionic, of the most probing and fascinating of the three Mozart/Da Ponte operas. Formally faultless, musically inspired throughout, _Così fan tutte_ appeals to modern taste in its exploration of emotional and erotic relationships among a quartet of lovers. No one performance can encompass every facet of this fascinating libretto and score, but these readings are, in their different ways, greatly satisfying.

The Gardiner, recorded at the Châtelet Theatre in Paris in 1992, is set in Carlo Tommasi's ravishing decor conjuring up the time and place (eighteenth-century Naples) of the original. Gardiner's own direction makes very clear the emotions uncovered by Don Alfonso's cynical plans to test the constancy of the ladies. It is at all times responsive to the music, but does employ a couple of questionable devices: members of the cast occasionally march through the stalls and/or sing from there, and Gardiner makes certain scenes more sexually explicit than would have been possible or wanted in Mozart's own day.

The principals are of the right age for their roles. Roocroft's Fiordiligi is intrepidly sung, her tone always firm and gleaming, and the role is expressively acted. She is properly partnered, as Mozart intended, by a soprano rather than a mezzo Dorabella: Mannion proves an apt foil for Roocroft and is deliciously flighty when falling for her Albanian lover (Guglielmo in disguise). Her singing is fresh and true. Rainer Trost is a young, fluent tenor who makes light of most of Ferrando's taxing music; however, he is denied the second and most florid of the character's three arias (which is in fact included on Gardiner's studio-made CD-only version). His vulnerable-looking Ferrando is a nice foil to Gilfry's more macho Guglielmo, which is sung in firm, rounded tones. The voices of all four blend perfectly in the many ensembles. Eirian James is a sparky, knowing Despina, Nicolai a laid-back, smooth Alfonso, both well integrated into the action. Gardiner's direct, big-scale conducting is the engine-room of the performance, superbly sustained by his period-instrument orchestra. Subtitles are missed.

The Drottningholm reading of 1984, surely comes closer

even than Gardiner to what Mozart must have envisaged. Not only is the baroque theatre akin to the size of those he would have known, but the slim, alert account of the music seems truly eighteenth century in tempo and feeling. Yet the lightness of the interpretation does not preclude depth of emotion, far from it: this is a sensuous, subjective performance that goes to the heart of the matter; it does without the touch of over-pointing that sometimes lames the Gardiner; and the recitative is taken at a quicker, more natural pace. The inclusion of many appoggiaturas enhances the vocal line.

None of the singers is known outside Sweden yet all six coalesce into à coherent, well-disciplined ensemble. No voice is particularly individual in timbre but each is more than adequate and well-schooled in Mozartian style, and the youthfulness of the principals makes their emotional predicaments that much more palpable. So, as a whole, this account is a viable alternative to the Gardiner. The girls, dressed in virginal white, are credible sisters. The men are personable and athletic. Despina is rightly earthy, Alfonso unobtrusively in command. Ferrando loses his second aria, just as well as Tibell's technique might not have been up to it, but the exclusion of Guglielmo's 'Donne miei le fate a tanti' is inexplicable and to be deplored.

Willy Decker's direction in Tobias Hoheisel's simple but effective sets is neatly observed, drawing out the paradoxes of the relationships and the agony and ecstasy of love. The overture is illustrated – amusingly – with shots of the singers travelling to the theatre and preparing for the performance, and showing the lovers in mufti, disillusioned, at the close. Excellent subtitles are provided.

The La Scala performance, dating from the 1988–9 season, enshrines a straightforward, wittily observant staging by Hampe in Mauro Pagano's traditional sets. Muti draws ravishing sounds from his own orchestra and paces the whole work with a nice blend between brio and subtlety (but is given too much prominence in the pit by the video director). He is always kind to his singers and encourages them to phrase with the utmost distinction.

Dessi is the main beneficiary of Muti's caring attitude, singing with steady, warm, pliable tone throughout and proves fully equal to the exigent demands of both Fiordiligi's arias, showing the passion and emotional stress that lie not far below the surface of her protestations. She ideally conveys the character's increasing perturbation of mind and heart, so that the capitulation to Ferrando, sung in such a hushed tone, is that much more moving. Ziegler makes a fresh, eager, uncomplicated Dorabella.

Kundlák's lyrical and ardent Ferrando is sung with alternating vigour and sensitivity, always sweet of tone, but like Trost denied his second aria. As an actor he is eclipsed by Corbelli's personable Guglielmo, a persuasive interpretation delivered in a mellow, even baritone. Scarabelli's very Italianate Despina is truly sung and enunciated. Desderi's Alfonso, in spite of his short stature, commands the stage and keenly stresses the experienced man's cynical philosophy.

The Decca version, a Unitel film of 1984, suffers from a number of disadvantages. Ponnelle's direction and designs are fussy and artificial. The action often borders on farce. The acting is superficial with a deal of ogling and exaggeration. The sound is post-synchronised. Much of the action is set outdoors, inimicable to this (and most) operas. Nor has the musical performance much to commend it beyond Harnoncourt's distinguished conducting. Most of the principals are too old for their roles, at least when caught in close-up as here, and none gives a reading that isn't equalled or surpassed in the sets discussed above. This is a version, then, to appeal only to those unlucky ones who find Mozart boring and must have him tarted up in, as it were, fancy dress and comic business.

Die Zauberflöte

1. Edita Gruberova (Queen of Night), Lucia Popp (Pamina), Francisco Araiza (Tamino), Norbert Orth (Monostatos), Wolfgang Brendel (Papageno), Jan-Hendrik Rootering (Speaker), Kurt Moll (Sarastro). Chor and Orch of Bavarian State Opera/Wolfgang Sawallisch. Dir: August Everding; video dir: Peter Windgassen. Philips VHS 070 405–3; LD:−1. Subtitles.
2. Luciana Serra (Queen of Night), Kathleen Battle

(Pamina), Francisco Araiza (Tamino), Heinz Zednik (Monostatos), Manfred Hemm (Papageno), Andreas Schmidt (Speaker), Kurt Moll (Sarastro). Chor and Orch of Metropolitan Opera, New York/James Levine. Dir: John Cox/Guus Mostart; video dir: Brian Large. DG VHS 072 424–3; LD:−1.

3. Birgit Louise Frandsen (Queen of Night), Ann Christine Biel (Pamina), Stefan Dahlberg (Tamino), Magnus Kyhle (Monostatos), Mikael Samuelsson (Papageno), Petteri Salomaa (Speaker), László Polgár (Sarastro). Chor and Orch of Drottningholm Court Theatre/Arnold Östman. Dir: Göran Järvefelt; video dir: Thomas Oloffson. Virgin VHS VVD 663; LD: Philips 070 422–1. Subtitles.

4. Luciana Serra (Queen of Night), Margaret Price (Pamina), Peter Schreier (Tamino), Robert Tear (Monostatos), Mikael Melbye (Papageno), Theo Adam (Speaker), Kurt Moll (Sarastro), Leipzig Radio Chor Dresden Staatskapelle/Colin Davis. Animator: Rens Groot. Philips VHS 070 429–3; LD:−1.

Mozart's fairy-story-cum-moral-fable has fascinated directors and musicians throughout its life, one of the few works by Mozart for the stage to have remained in the repertory practically since its inception. Directors love to exercise their imagination in suggesting the various levels of physical and spiritual existence depicted by the composer and his librettist Schikaneder. All four of these versions offer, in their differing ways, valid views of the piece.

The Bavarian State Opera performance of 1983 finds the Munich audience generally appreciating a production and musical reading that matches the vision of the piece. Indeed Everding's staging was so much admired that it later transferred to London's Covent Garden in a slightly less successful incarnation. Here at its original home, magic is present in the way the three Boys move along the breadth of the stage on a basket in mid-air, backcloths unfurl seemingly endlessly in one direction while Pamina and Papageno walk in the other, the Queen of Night appears in an eerily lit moonscape and so on. Jürgen Rose's sets are by and large inspired by the work's own spirit. By contrast Sarastro and his priests are shown against a severer background as exponents of idealism in the Age of Reason, an idea also adopted by Jonathan Miller, and one that works well. Windgassen captures on screen most of the sets' colour and fascination. Just occasionally the otherwise amusing treatment of Papageno becomes too cute as when his and Papagena's bevy of children arrive in the scene where they at last find each other.

Sawallisch's conducting is warm, finely balanced and phrased, truly Mozartian in feeling. The video enshrines the late Lucia Popp's truthful, moving Pamina for posterity, a portrayal sung with conviction allied to secure, well-etched phrasing that culminates in an eloquent account of her G minor aria. Future generations will be able to see and hear why she was so loved by her contemporaries. Though not on that level of achievement, Araiza's Tamino looks convincing and sings with a deal of sensitivity in a suave, well-groomed tenor. Moll presents a noble but placid Sarastro, Gruberová a commanding Queen of Night, Orth a suitably malicious Monostatos. Ladies and Boys (from the Tölz Boys Choir) are uniformly excellent, and Rootering is a notable asset as a gravely eloquent Speaker. Brendel's Papageno is gawky and surprisingly charmless, the set's single disappointment and an important one.

If only Hemm had been Papageno in the Munich cast, it would have been near-ideal. As it is, he is the main asset of the 1991 Met set, done for the Mozart bicentenary. He is a vital, cheeky, truly Viennese birdcatcher, a naughty boy who has never quite grown up. Battle's slender-voiced but sweet-toned and smoothly acted Pamina is pleasing enough. Araiza is not in as easy voice as he was in Munich but his reading of the role has deepened appreciably. Moll's Sarastro has become more fatherly. Serra's famed Queen of Night is past its sell-by date (see page 37 for a better performance from her). Zednik is an even better Monostatos than Orth. Boys are far superior to Ladies. Schmidt's beautifully sung Speaker misses the spiritual aspect of the character. Levine's somewhat unstable, nervous conducting is no match for that of Sawallisch, although the Met orchestra plays wonderfully well.

David Hockney's famous sets, huge, painted, swiftly

changing flats, are suitably colourful and fantastic. Yellow, violet and midnight blue conjure up the different milieux of the work, often to arresting effect. Originating at Glyndebourne they are here successfully expanded to fit the Met's vast stage and the cameras manage to overcome the possible disadvantage of the decor dwarfing the singers: Large's video direction is, as ever, virtually faultless. The animals magicked from the woods by Tamino's flute are much more endearing here than in the Munich show. This is an enjoyable performance if not quite on the elevated level of the Everding/Sawallisch and lacking the subtitles provided on that alternative.

Östman once again presents an altogether other experience. After the large scale and visual display of the Munich and New York performances, it is a particular pleasure to encounter the unfussy, unforced simplicity of this Drottningholm production of 1989. The period style of staging the work is here effortlessly achieved. Järvefelt's solutions to the work's difficulties seem so natural and inevitable in the right surroundings that one never wishes to see a more complex 'interpretation' again. Here when a scene change is needed, the backdrop flies unobtrusively away to be replaced by another produced by the old theatre's original machinery. Within the small confines of this tiny theatre, the work and the music blossom easily. One feels transported back to the period of composition.

The cast, with one exception, is Swedish. That exception is the Sarastro of Polgár, who offers supple, mellow singing and a sensitive presence that makes Moll seem ordinary. Dahlberg restores all the wonder to Tamino's part through his expressive singing and acting, and he has the ideal tenor, sweet but with a touch of metal in it, for the part. Biel's straightforward, heartfelt, purely sung Pamina is in the Popp class. Samuelsson's Papageno is an engaging peasant, full of earthy humour, quite natural in his deportment and singing. Salomaa's Speaker is solemn yet eloquent, just right. Smaller roles are taken with true, unexaggerated character. A squeaky Queen of Night is the only drawback.

Östman's unponderous, flowing, rhythmically alert interpretation is a balm after too many portentous readings.

Sound and picture are superior to those on the other sets from this source discussed above. Applause is a trifle obtrusive, but not so much as to spoil pleasure in an utterly delightful experience.

Finally there is the interesting curiosity of Groot's animated film, produced for the bicentenary in 1991. This consists of imaginative paintings and drawings that are constantly moved in time (literally) to the score. The illustrations evolve continually in an attempt, mostly successful, to catch the mood and action of the opera. On this often-inspired backcloth are superimposed the characters, who move in a more stilted way and never quite come to life except in crude caricature. Groot seems happier creating mood and atmosphere than in painting expressive figures. None the less the total effect is never at odds with the score and often illuminates the piece in a thoroughly entertaining way. Children would probably love it.

The recording used is Colin Davis's Philips set of 1984, a stately, deeply thought-through reading, a shade lacking in lightness of touch in Papageno's music, but offering finely shaded playing from the Dresden Staatskapelle. Price is a rich-voiced, slightly distanced Pamina, Schreier an ardent Tamino, Melbye a delightful Papageno, Moll (again!) in peak form as Sarastro, and Serra here superbly fiery as Queen of Night.

Intermittently available has been the famous 1973 Ingmar Bergman film. The score is treated cavalierly, the opera is sung in Swedish and the voices are post-synchronised, but the version – if you can find it – has childlike magic only a genius of a director could provide and the cast, particularly Håkan Hagegård's lovable Papageno, is generally excellent, as is Eric Ericson's conducting.

Ludwig van Beethoven (1770–1827)

Fidelio

1. Elizabeth Gale (Marzelline), Elisabeth Söderström (Leonore), Anton de Ridder (Florestan), Ian Caley (Jaquino), Robert Allman (Pizarro), Curt Appelgren

(Rocco), Michael Langdon (Don Fernando). Glynde-bourne Opera Chor and Orch/Bernard Haitink. Dir: Peter Hall; video dir: David Heather. Pickwick VHS SL 2004. Subtitles.

2. Marie McLaughlin (Marzelline), Gabriela Benackova (Leonore), Josef Protschka (Florestan), Neill Archer (Jaquino), Monde Pederson (Pizarro), Robert Lloyd (Rocco), Hans Tschammer (Don Fernando). Chor and Orch of Royal Opera House, Covent Garden/Christoph von Dohnányi. Dir: Adolf Dresen; video dir: Derek Bailey. Virgin VHS VVD 951.

Beethoven's single opera elevated the *Singspiel* tradition to the status of romantic opera. While retaining the old tradition of set numbers interspersed with dialogue, he adapted the set-pieces to his own needs and style, so that he could adequately relate the tale of Leonore's heroic and successful attempt to save her wrongly imprisoned husband, Florestan, from being murdered by the evil prisoner governor Pizarro. He had three tries at the opera until he was satisfied with its form; even so it remains hard to bring off in the theatre because of the demands of the main roles and the difficulty of finding singers who can speak dialogue convincingly.

Neither video, one taken from Covent Garden in 1990, the other from Glyndebourne in 1979, provides an ideal solution, but the latter is much to be preferred to the former. Dresen's dull staging, in Margit Bardy's unit set for the Royal Opera, is staidly, almost pedantically conducted by Dohnányi: the per-formance plods where it should take off. Then Benackova conveys little or nothing of Leonore's desperate plight: for all its technical assurance and firm tone, there's no inner ten-sion, not enough warmth in her singing. Pederson does little more as Pizarro than provide a strong voice so that his impre-cations count for nothing. McLaughlin doesn't look happy or sing comfortably as Marzelline. There remain Lloyd's well-thought-through Rocco, Protschka's sincere, involving but too eupeptic Florestan and – in the final scene – a touch of real class from Tschammer's sonorous, authoritative Don Fer-nando, the benign minister who arrives in the nick of time to save his old friend Florestan.

Matters are hardly helped by Dresen's rewriting of the original dialogue which succeeds only in removing well-considered (by Beethoven) leads into his musical numbers in favour of a sprawling, unfocused text, none too convincingly spoken by a non-German cast (its one German constituent has no speech!). The real parrot in the opening scene wholly destroys the spiritual aspect of the great canon quartet. Altogether there is nothing here to draw people into one of opera's most moving music-dramas.

Hall's Glyndebourne production, much praised on its first appearance, is another matter. Avoiding all modern glosses on the piece, Hall returns it to the milieu and stage directions of the libretto with arresting results. Hall and his designer John Bury actually enhance the timeless message of the piece by placing it in its ordinary background, suggesting a lived-in prison where heroism is all the more telling as it grows out of a domestic background with washing lines and a vegetable patch in view. Bury faithfully adopts the libretto's idea of a central gateway at the back with village women trying to make their food offerings. Pizarro's troops aren't the usual military automatons but ordinary soldiers doing their reluctant duty. The sunlit tree overhanging the courtyard is the symbol of the Prisoners' longing for freedom. Colour appropriately comes in the final scene in the form of flags and bunting.

As ever Hall directs his principals faultlessly. Marzelline is paradoxically quite tough yet totally besotted with Fidelio-Leonore. Jaquino is a roughish yet likeable oaf. He is made all the more sinister by Allman's grey, staring look, hinting at a dangerous psychopath. Best of all is the inner suffering of the courageous Leonore – but then the role is taken by that superb singing actress Söderström – as she depicts the effort needed to assume the role of a tramp-like youth and gradually learns the fate of her husband. The emotional tension extends to the Swedish soprano's singing although her voice isn't quite firm or strong enough for Beethoven's demands on it, possibly because she has come to the part a shade late in her career: she also looks too old for it.

It may be because Glyndebourne realised the fact that it surrounded her with other experienced singers. De Ridder rightly looks emaciated by his solitary confinement but his singing lacks that extra dimension of intensity the role needs. Similarly Allman's Pizarro is vocally one-dimensional. Gale, visibly pregnant, a fact emphasised in close-ups, isn't in her most fluent voice. Most vocal pleasure comes from Appelgren's puzzled Rocco, a venal but forgivable gaoler and a bass with a pleasing, warm tone. Caley's Jaquino is also well sung.

Haitink comes closer to the heart of the piece than Dohnányi and makes the most of its inner workings, but misses the tense fervour that has informed the best interpretations of his predecessors. Neither he nor the cast are helped by the confined, mono recording, but the video direction is excellent, bringing to the fore Hall's subtle and focused groupings of his charges.

Carl Maria von Weber (1786–1826)

Der Freischütz
Caterina Ligendza (Agathe), Raili Viljakainen (Aennchen), Toni Krämer (Max), Wolfgang Schoene (Ottokar), Wolfgang Probst (Caspar), Roland Bracht (Hermit). Chor and Orch of Württemberg State Opera/ Dennis Russell Davies. Dir: Achim Freyer; video dir: Hartmut Schottler. Castle CVI 2039. Subtitles.

For those unaware of its pleasures, Weber's forward-looking score could be an eye-opener. It combines melodies of flowing, individual cut contrasted with music representing evil which, for its time, evinces harmonic daring of an arresting kind. The arias for the heroine Agathe and her friend Aennchen express the burgeoning romantic spirit at its most attractively ardent. Brutish Caspar, who has sold his soul to the devil (represented by the speaking part of Samiel) and seeks to ruin depressed Max, represents the world of superstition and magic encapsulated by the supposed free-bullet of the title. As a natural background we hear lusty choruses from the local huntsmen.

Not all this may be made manifest in this, the only video version available, in many ways a perversion of the work: in his effort to make the piece somehow relevant for audiences today Achim Freyer resorts to the questionable ploy of sending up the story. When the production first took to the boards at Stuttgart in 1980, it was followed by ten minutes of booing and cheering as rival factions were either disgusted or delighted by Freyer's efforts, which also provokes during the course of the performance gales of unwanted and inappropriate laughter.

The staging resembles a performance by marionettes, thereby at a stroke destroying the human context of the piece. Soloists and chorus employ angular, stereotyped movements as if they were puppets on a string. The extensive dialogue is spoken in stilted form. The Wolf's Glen, that frighteningly original scene in which the magic bullets are forged, is peopled by Breughelesque monsters, one acting in a blatantly obscene manner. The Bridesmaids' Chorus is a parody, the Huntsmen's Chorus resembles a barber-shop choir. Only the grave, moralising Hermit, the story's *deus ex machina*, is treated seriously. The sets are crude and gaudy.

The result represents a deliberate attempt to sabotage Weber and his librettist Friedrich Kind by making fun of them. Instead of a simple, rural society rocked by supernatural events beyond its collective ken, we get a jokey show. That said, there is a kind of horrible pleasure to be derived from seeing what lunacy will next be inflicted on the poor opera and also to see it all done with the evident compliance, indeed delight of the cast.

Musically things are only marginally better. Davies conducts a lithe, disciplined but not very loving account of the score with speeds that are often too fast for the reflective passages. Ligendza tries her best, against almost insuperable odds, to inject some emotion into her music, but her Wagnerian voice has difficulty getting around Weber's more athletic writing. Viljakainen is an awkward Aennchen whose poor German is revealed in the extensive dialogue (the score and text are given virtually uncut). Krämer is a hangdog, wooden Max with a tolerably heroic voice and sensitive intentions. Probst's Caspar is unconvincing, mainly the fault of the production, but Bracht is an imposing Hermit and as the aristocrat Ottokar, Schoene sings firmly.

The video direction is singularly unimaginative, the cameras just set in the stalls and moved backwards or forwards from time to time. The sound quality offers a reasonable opera-house acoustic. One must hope this seminal work will soon be more worthily represented in this medium.

Giacomo Meyerbeer (1791–1864)

Les Huguenots
Joan Sutherland (Marguerite de Valois), Amanda Thane (Valentine), Suzanne Johnston (Urbain), Anson Austin (Raoul), John Pringle (Nevers), Clifford Grant (Marcel). Chor and Orch of Australian Opera/Richard Bonynge. Dir: Lotfi Mansouri; video dir: Virginia Lumsden. Pioneer LD PLMCD 00181.

Meyerbeer, a German Jew whose real name was Jakob Liebmann Beer, provides one of the most curious examples of declining reputation in musical history. Having written successful operas in German and Italian, he went to Paris, where he studied French opera and became its most successful exponent. In 1831 he produced the much-admired *Robert le Diable*, now almost entirely forgotten. It was followed in 1835 by *Les Huguenots*, which proved even more popular, appealing to the French taste for the grand and decorative. Within its own terms of reference, *Les Huguenots*, which deals with the abiding and mutual hatred of Catholics and Huguenots in sixteenth-century France leading to the Massacre of St Bartholomew's Day, works well enough, an appreciable achievement provided it is taken seriously and there are singers around who can cope with Meyerbeer's inordinate demands on them. The lack of such has been one reason for Meyerbeer's eclipse this century.

This 1990 revival of Mansouri's production for Australian Opera was put on as Sutherland's farewell to the house. Only sentiment or indiscriminating loyalty to a great singer can hide the fact that she is no longer able adequately to sustain the demands of the Queen's music, although one may marvel that a soprano in her mid-sixties can still manage the part at all. As the impulsive Huguenot Raoul, Austin has the notes, but they reach us in ear-splittingly harsh tone and the tenor's technique isn't up to Meyerbeer's demands. As his unhappy and doomed love, Valentine, Thane is technically better equipped for her role, but her tone is unappealing. The bass Clifford Grant, like Sutherland, bade his adieu to the stage with this Marcel, another case of a voice being only a shadow of its former self. Johnston, as a spry Urbain (the Queen's page) provides the only vocal consolations in the performance.

Bonynge conducts with some flair. The production is dim stock. The video direction is no more than adequate, but the sound is excellent. Meyerbeer's cause is better served by _L'Africaine_ (see below).

L'Africaine

Ruth Ann Swenson (Sélika), Shirley Verrett (Inéz), Placido Domingo (Vasco da Gama), Justino Diáz (Nelusko). Chor and Orch of San Francisco Opera/Maurizio Arena. Dir: Lotfi Mansouri; video dir: Brian Large. Virgin VHS VVD; LD: Pioneer PLMCD 00601.

Meyerbeer's final opera, given its premiere a year after his death, deals – with a glance at history – in Vasco da Gama's explorations of Africa, the opposition from his conservative superiors, and his love for two women, the African slave, Sélika and his fiancée Inéz. It is written with Meyerbeer's usual skill in conveying atmosphere and drama. Immensely long, it is almost always cut these days in performance (as it is here). It covers a storm at sea, love in the tropics and death beneath a manzanilla tree. The scenes in the council chamber, prison, on board ship, in temple and garden call for lavish staging, which it receives in this 1988 revival of a 1972 staging at the San Francisco Opera. Conventional it may be, but it remains true to a piece that is really superior hokum, and is performed with a will, including strong contributions from the company's chorus and ballet. Arena conducts convincingly.

But the success of any performance depends almost entirely on the singers: after its first performance it was undertaken by many of the great artists of the day. The cast here is headed by Domingo in cracking form. Vasco is a strenuous role: Domingo fulfils all its demands with heroic, fearless attack and, where needed, as in the love duet with Sélika, a deal of liquid tone. He also looks his part and acts with involvement as the courageous explorer, probably one of his best parts.

Verrett was undoubtedly better suited to the part of Sélika in 1972. Here she looks a deal too matronly, but overcomes that disadvantage with her dignified acting and she still finds vocal resources to convey much of the put-upon girl's agony of the heart. Her death scene, having breathed the poisoned leaves, is eloquent indeed. In the role of Inéz, the sweet, simple woman who is Vasco's true love, Swenson sings her two sensuous solos with ravishing tone, refined accents and deft phrasing, and looks lovely. Diáz does what he can with the somewhat conventional Nelusko, fellow countryman of Sélika and in love with her. Large's video direction is as sympathetic as ever.

Gioacchino Antonio Rossini (1792–1868)

La cambiale di matrimonio

Janice Hall (Fanny), Amelia Felle (Clarina), David Kuebler (Edoardo Milfort), Alberto Rinaldi (Slook), John del Carlo (Sir Tobias Mill), Carlos Feller (Norton). Stuttgart Radio Symphony Orch/Gianluigi Gelmetti. Dir: Michael Hampe; video dir: Claus Viller. Teldec VHS 9031–71479–3; LD:—6.

La scala di seta

Luciana Serra (Giulia), Jane Bunnell (Lucilla), David Kuebler (Dorvil), Alberto Rinaldi (Blansac), Alessandro Corbelli (Germano). Stuttgart Radio Symphony Orch/Gianluigi Gelmetti. Dir: Michael Hampe; video dir: Claud Viller. Teldec VHS 9031–73828–3; LD:—6.

L'occasione fa il ladro

Susan Patterson (Berenice), Monica Bacelli (Ernestina), Robert Gambill (Conte Alberto), Stuart Kale (Don Eusebio), Natale de Carolis (Don Parmenione), Alessandro Corbelli (Martino). Stuttgart Radio Symphony Orch/ Gianluigi Gelmetti. Dir: Michael Hampe; video dir: Claus Viller. Teldec VHS 4509–92170–3; LD:−6.

Il signor Bruschino

Amelia Felle (Sofia), David Kuebler (Florville), Alberto Rinaldi (Bruschino), Alessandro Corbelli (Gaudenzio). Stuttgart Radio Symphony Orch/Gianluigi Gelmetti. Dir: Michael Hampe; video dir: Claus Viller. Teldec VHS 9031–71482–3; LD:−6.

These are four of Rossini's so-called *farse*, one-act burlesques that he wrote at the start of his career between 1810 and 1813 at Venice's Teatro San Moise. They show the genius and style that soon propelled him to the top of the league among Italian composers, in demand everywhere for his wares. Of these four, the last three are superior in invention, melodic and harmonic, to the first, and reveal Rossini well on the way to his mode of writing comic operas that teem with high-spirited inspiration tempered by a vein of elegiac sentiment. All four performances stem from an ensemble gathered at the Schwetzingen Festival in north Germany, productions shared with the Cologne Opera, whose director, Hampe, staged all four, the first and last in 1989, the second in 1990, the third in 1992, using several of the same singers and the same conductor. The ensemble nature of all four offers rewarding results, as does the uniform idea of having each piece set against a backcloth of the relevant city.

La cambiale di matrimonio, the earliest of these pieces (1810), shows Rossinian promise rather than fulfilment. It tells a tale familiar in *opera buffa* of a father (here Sir Tobias Mill) wanting to marry off his daughter (Fanny) to a rich suitor (Slook, a Canadian merchant) while she is secretly engaged to an eligible younger man (Edoardo). It is set in London, St Paul's very visible in the distance. There are plenty of opportunities for Rossini to project *buffo* humour taken eagerly by the amusing del Carlo as Mill and Rinaldi as Slook. As Fanny, Janice Hall is no more than competent. Kuebler, an experienced Rossini tenor, sings seamlessly. Amelia Felle as the maid Clarina reveals a pretty presence and voice. Gelmetti conducts with his customary brio.

So he does in *La scala di seta* (1812), another piece of amorous intrigue not amounting to much from the point of view of plot but full of delightful music, most of it in the ensembles, although the heroine Guilia's cavatina and cabaletta show Rossini already advanced in his writing for the soprano voice. It is sung with style and relish by Serra. Bunnell, as the *seconda donna*, has what Richard Osborne describes in his essential book on Rossini (J.M. Dent, 1986) as a 'blithe and folksy' aria. Kuebler turns in another accomplished performance as her secret husband, and Corbelli is the soul of good cheer as the perplexed servant Germano. Hampe's direction stays the right side of extravagant comedy. Here is another innocent hour's pleasure.

L'occasione fa il ladro (1812) is a sophisticated intrigue in which the confusions and misunderstandings attendant on changes of identity among two pairs of lovers are legion. This is ideal Rossini territory and he makes the most of it in music that is well varied in tone and character. Hampe's direction is alert but here he sometimes overdoes the artificial gesture. Gelmetti conducts with his accustomed brio. As the two lovers, Gambill and de Carolis, tenor and baritone, sing with a sure sense of style and warm tone. As Berenice, Patterson is efficient but hard-toned. Her companion Ernestina is sung with Italianate cut by Bacelli. Best of all is Corbelli as Alberto's servant Martino, a model of the *buffo* manner at its most authentic. Kale is a nicely fussy Don Eusebio, Berenice's uncle and guardian.

The delights of *Bruschino* (1813) are manifold and it has a tougher profile than the other *farse*. Tomassini's set is sundrenched. Hampe's direction is pointed without ever being overdone. Gelmetti is at his lively best. And here the cast is ideal. Felle makes a seductive, perky Sofia, the ward of Gaudenzio, here played and sung to perfection by Corbelli; their duet, where he guides her into the wiles of marital bliss, is young Rossini at his most beguiling. As her secret lover Florville, Kuebler sings as fluently as ever. He pretends to be the son of Bruschino, a local bigwig sung and acted with nice pomposity by Rinaldi. The sense of team-play is palpable throughout: everyone makes the most of a delightful score. If you want to acquire just one of these sets make it this one.

The sound and picture on all four issues are excellent. It is a pity there are no subtitles in either format, but the synopses that come with the folder are reasonably helpful.

Il barbiere di Siviglia

1. Maria Ewing (Rosina), Max-René Cossotti (Almaviva), John Rawnsley (Figaro), Claudio Desderi (Bartolo), Ferruccio Furlanetto (Basilio). Glyndebourne Festival Chor and Orch/Sylvain Cambreling. Dir: John Cox; video dir: David Heather. Castle VHS CVI 2016.
2. Kathleen Battle (Rosina), Rockwell Blake (Almaviva), Leo Nucci (Figaro), Enzo Dara (Bartolo), Ferruccio Furlanetto (Basilio). Chor and Orch of Metropolitan Opera, New York/Ralf Weikert. Dir: John Cox; video dir: Brian Large. DG VHS 072 414–3. LD:−1.
3. Teresa Berganza (Rosina), Luigi Alva (Almaviva), Hermann Prey (Figaro), Enzo Dara (Bartolo), Paolo Montarsolo (Basilio). Chor and Orch of La Scala, Milan/Claudio Abbado. Dir: Jean-Pierre Ponnelle. DG VHS 072 404–3; LD:−1.
4. Cecilia Bartoli (Rosina), David Kuebler (Almaviva), Gino Quilico (Figaro), Carlos Feller (Bartolo), Robert Lloyd (Basilio). Cologne Opera Chor, Stuttgart Radio Symphony Orch/Gabriele Ferro. Dir: Michael Hampe; video dir: Claus Viller. RCA VHS 09026–61217–3; LD:−6.
5. Nelly Corradi (Rosina), Ferruccio Tagliavini (Almaviva), Tito Gobbi (Figaro), Vito De Taranto (Bartolo), Italo Tajo (Basilio). Chor and Orch of Rome Opera/Giuseppe Morelli. A film by Mario Costa. Pickwick VHS 1057.

This has always been the most popular, by far, of Rossini's

operas, loved and performed for its high spirits, melodic invention and zippy rhythms. For years it virtually represented the composer alone in the repertory. Times have happily changed in that respect, but the rediscovery of Rossini's other operas has not lessened the appeal of the consistently inspired *Barber*.

The Glyndebourne staging of 1981 is a source of almost unalloyed delight. Cox's direction is full of life and pertinently observed detail without ever tipping over into unwanted farce. Dudley's painterly sets are a feast for the eye with Seville very much the location. Romantic Spain is conjured up foreground and background. We spy Figaro's shop in the first scene, tailor as well as barber apparently. In the second act we are in a canopied penthouse with a telescope for the inquisitive Bartolo.

Against this engrossing background we meet a delightful group of principals. Ewing, as Rosina, gives an apposite display of *jolie laide* charm with an engaging, naughty smile playing around her capacious mouth, a whole heap of pouts and a general sense of fiery insubordination. This is a veritable dynamo of a Rosina, every gesture and expression acutely timed. Her tone may not be ideally full or warm, but the touch of resin in her voice is not inappropriate. She uses runs and decorations as a legitimate chance to make her verbal points.

Rawnsley's Figaro is equally alive with invention, facial and vocal, beginning with a subtly rethought 'Largo al factotum' avoiding clichés. His voice is in pristine condition, nimble in fioriture, never under pressure at the top. His is a swaggering interpretation, but never one to hog centre-stage. Cossotti offers an Almaviva of lyrical delicacy in his set-pieces and witty acting in his disguises, an altogether winning performance. Desderi is a younger Bartolo than usual, a more plausible candidate for Rosina's hand and one who reveals a touch of steel behind the comic façade. Here's a man in the prime of life, at once conceited and insensitive. He delivers his patter aria, 'A un dottor', with virtuoso aplomb. Nothing here of the tired old *buffo* routines. Furlanetto's Basilio is also younger than most. With his long fair hair, open sandals and straw shovel hat he looks as if he were, as one contemporary critic had it, an 'eighteenth-century hippy', an eccentric reading but not wholly implausible. Even Berta and Ambrogio are for once kept from being caricatured.

Cambreling's conducting is on the sober, measured side which allows the musical inspiration, instrumental and harmonic, of the score to make its mark, enhanced by a care over sonority that imparts an unexpected breadth to the piece well caught in the recording. Heather's video direction captures the spirit and the physical exuberance of this highly enjoyable performance.

For the wide spaces of the Met in 1990, Cox's direction has, perhaps inevitably, coarsened. The effects are now drawn with a broader brush, the characters less firmly focused. Nor is Robin Wagner's dull set a match for Dudley's pictorial touch. As Rosina, Battle, a soprano rather than the required mezzo, sings neatly, acts knowingly. Nucci's Figaro, strongly sung, is drawn from stock. Blake's basically unglamorous voice has all the notes and more: he even executes Almaviva's fiendish last-scene aria with technical fluency. Dara's Bartolo, the traditional old codger, is nimbly sung but better heard some years earlier under Abbado (see below). Furlanetto's Basilio has by now become more conventional. Weikert's conducting is routine.

La Scala's effort is one of Ponnelle's lavish, hyperactive films of an opera made in 1972 following stage performances of a similar production with a similar cast given in many centres. Director/designer Ponnelle is constantly inventive and never allows the eye to become bored as his camera moves ceaselessly from jape to jape, face to face, but in the end so much movement proves counter-productive and one longs for the camera to stay in one place for a few bars at a time. It reaches its apex (or nadir?) of larking in the crazy chemistry laboratory of Basilio's calumny aria, explosions and all. The all-smiling and/or mugging cast look a shade dated in their approach: nowadays, we have gone beyond such caricature and pointless bonhomie, but given the style it is expertly executed by a cast in sympathy with Ponnelle's ways. Abbado's disciplined, high-powered conducting is sometimes a shade overbearing for the good of Rossini's effervescent score.

Berganza, with long experience of her role, is a delightful Rosina, singing smoothly and in agile manner, but even in 1972 a shade mature-looking for teenage Rosina. By contrast Alva looks amazingly young for one who already had many Almavivas to his credit. His voice remains fresh but his aspirating of runs is tiresome. Dara is again the conventional *buffo*, excellent of his kind and his aria 'A un dottor', taken by Abbado at a whizzing pace, is a tour de force of patter singing. As Basilio, Montarsolo carries facial and body movements to the limits of tolerance – and sometimes beyond. The sound is exemplary and the post-synchronisation expertly done. Subtitles are missed.

Hampe's staging on the RCA version may be conventional, but he does make real characters out of the principals and the action is clearly delineated. Taken live from the 1988 Schwetzingen Festival, this production was the second collaboration with Hampe and the Cologne Opera that later provided the successful revival of one-act works from Rossini's youth (see above). Bartoli is an exuberant, vocally inventive Rosina, videoed just before she was turned by Decca into a superstar. In her enthusiasm to project her reading she is inclined to overdo the pouting. Kuebler is a dapper Almaviva and amusing in his two disguises but not an individual vocalist. Once past a rather forced 'Largo al factotum', Quilico is a resourceful Figaro. Feller presents Bartolo as a real person rather than a caricature and, in spite of being a veteran, manages to get his tongue and tone around 'A un dottor'. Cast against the grain, Lloyd is a self-conscious Basilio. Ferro, a seasoned Rossinian, gives the score plenty of verve.

The 1946 film is important for preserving two singers in noted assumptions: Gobbi as Figaro, revelling – almost too ebulliently – in the plenitude of his youthful powers, and Tagliavini as Almaviva, singing sweetly. The action looks dated; the score is woefully cut; the lip-synch is appalling; the sound is abrasive. But Tagliavini and Gobbi are lively enough. Better still are the old-style *buffos* – Taranto and Tajo – both giving an object-lesson in outrageous comedy and verbal acuity. The Rosina is comic in the wrong way, constantly being fey and flirtatious like a third-rate 1930s film actress. This is altogether a fascinating period-piece.

La Cenerentola

1. Margherita Guglielmi (Clorinda), Frederica von Stade (Cenerentola), Laura Zannini (Tisbe), Francisco Araiza (Don Ramiro), Claudio Desderi (Dandini), Paolo Montarsolo (Don Magnifico), Paul Plishka (Alidoro). Chor and Orch of La Scala, Milan/Claudio Abbado. Dir: Jean-Pierre Ponnelle; video dir: David Watkin. DG VHS 072 402–3; LD:—1.
2. Marta Taddei (Clorinda), Katherine Kuhlmann (Cenerentola), Laura Zaninni (Tisbe), Laurence Dale (Don Ramiro), Alberto Rinaldi (Dandini), Claudio Desderi (Don Magnifico), Roderick Kennedy (Alidoro). Glyndebourne Festival Chor, London Philharmonic Orch/ Donato Renzetti. Dir: John Cox; video dir: John Vernon. Castle CVI 2053.

In many ways this is Rossini's most attractive work, a culmination of his early work in its happy marriage of his ebullient *buffo* style with a welcome vein of sentiment. Based on the Cinderella legend, it presents the downtrodden Angelina, known as Cenerentola (Cinderella), in appealing terms, her music at once tender and warm-hearted in contrast to the brittle music written for her sisters and father. At the same time, the singer of the central role must have the vocal facility to encompass Rossini's roulades in which the part abounds.

The DG version is another of Ponnelle's extravagant soufflés (see *Barbiere*, above). This 1981 film, loosely based on his 1970s staging for La Scala which travelled the operatic world, exploits Rossini's quirky rhythms for all they are worth in balletic movement: hardly a note is left unillustrated. According to your mood this can be exasperating or exhilarating. It is without question extravagantly inventive within Ponnelle's own equally extravagant decor. Magic play with a statue of Rossini and an ensemble shown in silhouette are just the most telling of Ponnelle's many creative ideas.

His singers enter into the fun with a will, particularly Desderi as the Prince's servant Dandini, disguised as his master to test out the ugly sisters. With his chubby presence and glinting eyes, matched by his mobile voice (though the aspirates in his runs are overdone), he makes a pleasing meal of the role. Montarsolo, even more experienced in the Ponnelle style, ogles and pouts his way through the *buffo* bass part of Magnifico, the girls' egregious father. The ugly sisters are deliberately overdressed and over the top. As Rossini's idea of a fairy godperson, the Prince's mysterious tutor, Plishka, makes his mark, and he is imaginatively directed.

The serious side of things is equally well managed. Von Stade's charismatic presence and keen-edged coloratura mask the fact that her tone isn't really quite substantial enough for the part. Araiza makes an ideal partner. Here, in his original incarnation as a finely equipped Rossinian tenor (he has since essayed, with less success, heavier repertory) he sings with fluent style and mellifluous tone. As ever Abbado takes his Rossini very seriously, missing some of the music's wit but none of its brio: the playing of La Scala's orchestra is superb. Picture and sound are faultless.

John Cox's Glyndebourne staging of 1983 is a sad disappointment after his delightful *Barbiere* (see page 48). Here his cute, pantomime treatment of what is after all a gentle, human comedy is quite misconceived, indulging in the worst pantomime tradition of knockout wheezes: false noses, funny underwear, model horses, and a toy theatre moved by child extras in the storm. This is all facetious beyond redemption. So are Allen Charles Klein's Stuart-period scenery and costumes, character being subsumed in overdressing.

It's a wonder, in all this flummery, that Kuhlmann manages to convey much of the feeling and sentiment of Cinderella's role, looks the part and sings it with smooth tone and virtually immaculate fioritura. Dale sings with reasonable fluency but looks stiff and unconvincing as Prince Ramiro. Rinaldi is a forceful rather than amusing Dandini. Desderi catches the nastiness as well as the ridiculous side of Don Magnifico, though his voice, more baritone than bass, is better suited to Dandini (see page 51).

Renzetti conducts a swift, crisp account of the score, wanting in Rossinian wit and humanity. Vernon's video direction is discerning. The sound is reasonably faithful to the original Glyndebourne acoustic, clear but dry. For some reason, Castle for once omits subtitles.

L'Italiana in Algeri

Nuccia Focile (Elvira), Doris Soffel (Isabella), Susan Maclean (Zulma), Robert Gambill (Lindoro), Enric Serra (Taddeo), Rudolf A. Hartmann (Ali), Günther von Kannen (Mustafá). Bulgarian Male Chor, Stuttgart Radio Symphony Orch/Ralf Weikert. Dir: Michael Hampe; video dir: Clause Viller. LD: RCA 9026–61218–6. Subtitles.

After *Barbiere* and *Cenerentola*, this has been the most performed of Rossini's comic operas in recent times. Although the story of the Algerian Bey (Mustafá) falling in love with an Italian girl of the title is far-fetched, it inspired Rossini to one of his most effervescent and witty scores, the comedy leavened by the tender love music for Isabella and her lover Lindoro held captive by the Bey.

This version, made in 1987, was the first collaboration between the Schwetzingen Festival, the Cologne Opera and Stuttgart Radio with Hampe as regular producer. Here, in the traditional and colourful decor of Mauro Pagano, Hampe manages a lively, pointed staging without stepping over into farce or artificiality except in the case of an actor in monkey costume as Mustafá's constant – and irritating – companion. Weikert keeps the score on a tight rein that doesn't exclude exuberant touches in the many ensembles.

Soffel is very much the performance's star. Her grainy mezzo, skill in *fioriture* and sparky acting dominate the stage whenever she is on it, and she obviously revels in both the range and technical demands of the role. She brings the appropriate sensuality to 'Per lui che adoro' and the touch of heroic called for by 'Pensa all patria' when Isabella rallies her Italian compatriots before they successfully attempt an escape from Mustafá who has been virtually hypnotised into the mysteries of 'Papataci'. Gambill's tenor is efficient rather than beguiling, but he makes an enthusiastic Lindoro. Von Kannen's Mustafá is a shade Teutonic in timbre, but he creates a real character, not merely a *buffo* caricature out of the Bey. Yet it is Serra, as Isabella's quasi uncle-cum-lover, an equivocal role (derived from that other Taddeo in *commedia dell'arte*) who demonstrates the advantage of having Italian as a native tongue in this kind of piece.

Viller's video direction is, as always, perceptive and the sound brings us into the small, baroque theatre to share in the fun.

La gazza ladra
Ileana Cotrubas (Ninetta), Elena Zilio (Pippo), Nucci Condò (Lucia), David Kuebler (Giannetto), Alberto Rinaldi (Podestà), Brent Ellis (Fernando), Carlos Feller (Fabrizio). Chor of Cologne Opera, Gürzenich Orch/ Bruno Bartoletti. Dir: Michael Hampe; video dir: José Montes-Baquer. Virgin VHS 0700293.

Following the success of *La Cenerentola* at Rome early in 1817, Rossini wrote this *opera semiseria* for Milan where he enjoyed another triumph. The story is based on a historical event involving the trial and execution of a French girl for theft later found to be the work of a thieving magpie (*gazza ladra* of the title), though Rossini contrives a happier ending. He composed a score that managed to keep in balance comedy, pathos and near-tragedy, marking a transition from the earlier comedies to the later grand operas written for Paris. There are more extended and complex numbers as befits the subject, among them a superb sextet in the second scene during the course of which the guilt for stealing silver seems unerringly to point to the hapless Ninetta, a magnificent trial scene that anticipates Verdi, and a march to the scaffold that Berlioz must have known.

This Cologne staging of 1984 is well worthy of the work, one of the most successful of Hampe's lengthy list of Rossini productions, and yet another graced by Mauro Pagano's beautiful, realistic decor and costumes. Hampe manages to suggest both the homely, happy milieu in which Ninetta works as a servant of Fabrizio and Lucia Vinogradito and where she has fallen in love with Giannetto, who is just returning from war service as the opera begins. Into this apparent idyll Rossini – and Hampe – subtly introduce the lecherous, deceitful Podestà, the local mayor. As Ninetta brusquely rejects his advances, he ruthlessly pursues her over the seeming theft, throws her into prison and has her tried and convicted. Hampe clearly delineates all the conflicting emotions.

Cotrubas makes a suitably vulnerable victim, her desperate looks when accused speaking volumes, and she sings, given a rather too vibrant tone, with her usual sensibility. Rinaldi makes a properly lustful mayor, and Ellis does well as Fernando, engineer of the subplot as a deserter whom his daughter Ninetta is trying to keep from the law's clutches. Kuebler sings with his customary fluency in Rossini as the rather wet Giannetto. Zilio is an almost too lively Pippo, who's the one to discover the erring magpie in the nick of time to save Ninetta's neck. Veterans Condò and Feller do well as the Vinograditos.

Much of the performance's success derives from Bartoletti's alert sensitivity in the pit. Both sound and picture are first-rate. In place of absent subtitles, the story is told on screen during the overture.

Guglielmo Tell
Cheryl Studer (Matilda), Amelia Felle (Jemmy), Luciana D'Intino (Edwige), Chris Merritt (Arnold), Giorgio Zancanaro (Tell), Giorgio Surian (Furst), Luigi Roni (Gessler). Chor and Orch of La Scala, Milan/Riccardo Muti. Dir: Luca Ronconi; video dir: Giulio Bertola. Castle VHS 6063/4–3 (two videos). Subtitles.

Tell, which proved to be Rossini's last opera, looks forward into the romantic era of the mid-nineteenth century, and subtly combines French and Italian style (it was written for Paris). Conceived on the grandest scale and lasting almost four hours when given complete as on this video (ballet music and all), it tells of the struggles of the Swiss cantons in the fourteen century to free themselves from their hated Austrian oppressors, here epitomised by the ruthless dictator Gessler. The rural bliss of the early scenes is rudely disrupted by internal struggles that involve personal loss and a striving for liberty from the jackboot, led by the heroic Tell. A subplot involves the love of Arnold, Swiss patriot, for the Austrian Matilda who eventually throws in her lot with the Swiss who, after many vicissitudes, overcome the invaders. It ends with a paean to freedom, a kind of apotheosis of the Rossinian crescendo. It is a truly epic work that deserves to be heard in its entirety as here, when Rossini's noble if flawed vision comes into its own. Without this work, much that followed might not have developed as it did.

This 1988 performance at La Scala, the brainchild of Muti, played the score in an edition specially prepared for the autograph, using a revised form of the traditional Italian translation. Muti manages to encompass every aspect of the many-faceted score, its innate lyricism, its panoply of superb ensembles, its dramatically apt episodes, such as the famous apple-shooting scene. He paces every bar unerringly, never allowing the piece to hang fire as it can in lesser hands, papers over the cracks of the in-filling passages where Rossini's inspiration occasionally flags, and obtains wonderful playing, attentive to dynamics and precision, from his La Scala Orchestra.

The singers are more notable for their vocal than for their histrionic powers. There's a rugged honesty of purpose about Zancanaro's Tell that lets one overlook some staid acting, and he shapes Tell's affecting solo with all his familiar and welcome management of line and words. Studer is at her considerable best in the grateful music Rossini wrote for his final heroine, summation of so much that had gone before in his writing for the female voice. Her contribution to solos and ensembles benefits from her rich, warm tone allied to her sensitivity of phrase and control of fioriture. She is partnered by Merritt, as Matilda's tenor-lover Arnold, in his most ingratiating form. On this occasion he seems in fresh and untroubled voice, tireless even in the furthest reaches of his role above the stave and delicate in Arnold's quieter music. His acting is rudimentary but is quite touching in its simple sincerity. Roni is suitably implacable as the evil Gessler. Tell's family are well represented by D'Intino as his sympathetic, trenchant wife Edwige, and by Felle, firm-voiced as son Jemmy. Smaller roles are variably taken.

Ronconi's production is dominated by three huge screens on which are projected, in the outer acts, photos and moving pictures of alpine landscapes, mountain tops, woods pierced by sunlight, and rushing waterfalls. For the other acts we see buildings appropriate to those predicated in the libretto. In the theatre these were said to dwarf the singers, which I can well believe, but on video the cameras can of course concentrate the eye on individuals and the film images work rather well. In front of the screens is an arrangement of pews on which the chorus are assembled in various configurations. Vera Marzot's costumes are a shade sombre. Ronconi's direction of the principals is minimal and there's not enough suggestion of a people up in arms against their despicable rulers. Still, enough is done to allow the singers to project their feelings and that is, after all, the most important element in opera whatever overweening directors may think: Rossini here speaks clearly to us through the voice and the orchestra.

The video direction is so-so, and the sound, at least on the copies sent for review, is sometimes muzzy. Neither of these drawbacks is sufficient to prevent recommendation, as the merits of Rossini's late masterpiece come across so strongly from this dedicated cast and conductor. Subtitles here are very useful at unravelling the complexities of the plot.

Gaetano Donizetti (1797–1848)

Lucia di Lammermoor
Joan Sutherland (Lucia), Richard Greager (Edgardo), Robin Donald (Normanno), Malcolm Donnelly (Enrico), Clifford Grant (Bide-the-Bent). Chor of Australian Opera, Elizabethan Sydney Orch/Richard Bonynge. Dir: John Copley; video dir: Peter Butler. Virgin VHS VVD 779; Pioneer LD: PLMCC 00641.

Donizetti's work based on Sir Walter Scott's *The Bride of Lammermoor* is the most commonly heard of his serious operas because the title role with its challenges for the soprano voice has always attracted prima donnas. During the early years of the twentieth century it became largely the province of coloratura sopranos who tended to prettify the music at the expense of its dramatic and emotional strengths. Maria Callas and, after her, Joan Sutherland restored it to its true stature as a piece for a lyric-dramatic soprano with the agility to encompass its more florid aspects. Indeed Sutherland made her breakthrough on to the international stage when she first attempted the part in a now-legendary evening in 1959, while she was at Covent Garden in a Zeffirelli staging designed for her. From then on she made it very much her own and recorded it twice in audio-only recordings when in her prime.

By the time Sutherland's portrayal was filmed in 1986, in the Sydney Opera House, she was in her sixtieth year. Although the technical facility remains intact, the lovely voice now sounds sadly tarnished and the higher notes effortful. Inevitably the previous drawbacks in her singing, muzzy diction and excessive sliding into notes, are now emphasised. Under the all-revealing gaze of the camera she hardly looks credible as Scott's and Donizetti's forlorn young heroine. Clips of her earlier performances (see Recital section, page 244) only go to prove the decline here.

None of the other principals does much to improve matters. As Edgardo, Greager's efficient but tight and unattractive tenor lacks Italianate timbre. Donnelly's forceful Enrico is compromised by unsteady tone. Grant, in the sympathetic role of Lucia's tutor, is perhaps the best of the bunch, though his vibrato has loosened with the passing years. Bonynge is to be congratulated for conducting a full version of a score too often cut in the theatre and doing so with such Donizettian flair.

Copley's well-managed production in Henry Bardon's traditional decor is too often enshrouded in gloom. On the whole even Sutherland enthusiasts may rest content with one of Sutherland's CD Lucias.

Mary Stuart
Rosalind Plowright (Elizabeth I), Janet Baker (Mary Stuart), David Rendall (Leicester), Alan Opie (Cecil), John Tomlinson (Talbot). Chor and Orch of English National Opera/Charles Mackerras. Dir: John Copley; video dir: Peter Butler. Castle VHS CVI 2038. In English.

Mary Stuart (Maria Stuarda), was the second of Donizetti's operas based very loosely on Tudor history (preceded by

Anna Bolena). Indeed the librettist here (Giuseppe Bardari) culled his text from Schiller's tragedy of the same name, treating the events concerned very freely, and including a wholly fictitious but arrestingly dramatic confrontation between the two Queens in which Mary, goaded by Elizabeth's insults at a meeting in the park at Chatsworth, denounces her rival as a royal bastard. In this scene, as throughout the work, Donizetti evinces his gift for writing swiftly moving drama within the formal means current then (1836) in Italian opera. It is among the best of his serious works.

It was staged at the ENO in 1976 as a vehicle for Janet Baker as Mary, using a later version of the score in which Donizetti adapted the title part for the mezzo Malibran. Dame Janet returned to the role for her farewell to the stage in 1982 when this recording was made at a live performance. It remains one of her most arresting portrayals as she enacts Mary's change from her carefree, youthful entry at Chatsworth (aria and cabaletta nicely turned) through that scene where she humbles Elizabeth to the long, dying fall (in every sense) in the last act that climaxes in an intimate prayer before she goes to her execution. Baker's careful colouring of her warm tone, her subtle treatment of the text and her deeply felt acting are all the mark of a singer at the peak of her powers. We are lucky to have this interpretation preserved so faithfully for posterity.

She is fittingly partnered by Plowright as an Elizabeth who is seen at once as haughty, wilful and vulnerable, a reading projected with imposing presence and dramatic fire by a large and exciting voice that just occasionally sounds strained at the top. Rendall is fiery yet concerned as a Leicester torn between duty to his Queen and love for Mary. Opie's persuasive Cecil and Tomlinson's wily Talbot complete a performance that shows the ENO at the height of its corporate achievement under Mackerras's firm and enlivening beat.

Copley's direction neatly exposes the tensions among the characters while handling the big ensembles in masterly fashion within Desmond Heeley's traditional, evocative sets. Peter Butler's video direction is exemplary in having cameras always at the right spot at the right time. Both picture and sound are of high quality.

Roberto Devereux

Beverly Sills (Elizabeth I), Susan Marsee (Sara), John Alexander (Robert Devereux, Earl of Essex), Richard Fredericks (Nottingham). Wolf Trap Company Chor, Filene Center Orch/Julius Rudel. Dir: Tito Capobianco; video dir: Kirk Browning. VAI VHS 69080.

This later work of Tudor history might well have been called *Elizabeth I* as the Queen takes centre stage and is presented in a more rounded form than in *Maria Stuarda*. Here she is depicted as furiously jealous of Essex, whom she suspects (rightly) of loving another – Sara, Duchess of Nottingham, wife of Essex's best friend. There is a wonderful opportunity here for Donizetti to develop his gift for extended duets, which he eagerly seizes.

At the New York City Opera, Sills undertook Maria Stuarda, Anna Bolena and Elizabeth I in this opera, which was adjudged perhaps her most successful assumption, a well-known critic acclaiming her portrayal as 'unforgettable' when she first undertook it in 1970. She is caught in the part here in 1975 in the NYCO staging transferred to Wolf Trap in Virginia. She certainly has the part in her voice where technique is concerned, but her tone is sadly one-dimensional and fluttery, not that of a commanding ruler and, to match, her portrayal is merely petulant. She lacks the regal authority of bearing and demeanour shown by Plowright (see page 59) and as a result her performance, for all its considerable artifice, remains unconvincing.

She receives committed support from the firm-voiced and handsome Alexander as Essex, the appealing Marsee as Sara and the capable Fredericks as Nottingham. In the pit Rudel does little more than go through the paces; Capobianco's direction is conventional in the worst sense, turning the opera merely into costume drama. The comparison with Copley's perceptions in the ENO *Mary Stuart* shows just what can be done, within tradition, for Donizetti. Here gestures, costumes, make-up all go to make the suspension of disbelief difficult.

The video direction is no more than adequate and the same can be said for the mono sound. Although Sills was noted in serious roles, she is better represented on video by her account of the title role in *La fille du régiment (qv)*, where her comic gifts are on display.

L'elisir d'amore
Kathleen Battle (Adina), Luciano Pavarotti (Nemorino), Juan Pons (Belcore), Enzo Dara (Dulcamara). Chor and Orch of Metropolitan Opera, New York/James Levine. Dir: John Copley; video dir: Brian Large. DG VHS 072 432–3; LD:−1.

This delightful work, poised nicely and equably between comedy and sentiment, is the less sophisticated country cousin of *Don Pasquale*, not so spruce and witty perhaps but full of engaging melodies and rustic charm. The shy, ingenuous hero is lovesick Nemorino, a peasant pining after minxish Adina, who drives him to distraction by proposing to marry the Sergeant Belcore. The quack doctor, Dulcamara, a *basso buffo*, visiting the rural village where Adina and Nemorino live, persuades Nemorino to buy the elixir of the title, really a bottle of cheap Bordeaux, which gives him a false confidence. After many alarms and excursions, true love wins the day.

This version derives from a 1991 Metropolitan performance featuring Pavarotti, the most engaging Nemorino of his time. His boyish, cheeky nature and burly presence serve the role well, as he has shown many times on stage. Despite his size, he manages to suggest all Nemorino's inhibited, retiring nature and at the same time the passion that lies within him. His distinctive tone and phrasing are near-ideal for Donizetti, and he sings nimbly through the taxing ensembles.

Battle is well suited by Adina, suggesting her fickle, teasing yet not unfeeling nature to perfection and singing with sweet tone and refined sensibility, particularly in her Act 2 solo. Dara is a lively, properly ridiculous Dulcamara, deft in his big patter song and always a presence even though his voice wants some depth of tone. Pons's unwieldy baritone as Belcore is the only drawback, but even he enters into the fun in a performance that everyone on stage and in the audience is obviously enjoying. Levine conducts with brio but the orchestra sound is sometimes too heavy.

Copley's staging in Beni Montresor's pastel-shaded, multi-layered decor is a larger-scale replica of their Covent Garden production dating from 1976. Movement is well managed, only occasionally descending into the merely cute. It has been discerningly directed for video by Large. The sound picture is exemplary. Unfortunately no subtitles have been provided to complete pleasure in a most recommendable issue.

La fille du régiment
1. Joan Sutherland (Marie), Heather Begg (Marquise de Berkenfeld), Anson Austin (Tonio), Gregory Yurisich (Sergeant Sulpice). Australian Opera Chor, Elizabethan Sydney Orch/Richard Bonynge. Dir: Sandro Sequi; video dir: Peter Butler. Virgin VHS VVD 829.
2. Beverly Sills (Marie), Muriel Costa-Greenspon (Marquise de Berkenfeld), William McDonald (Tonio), Spiro Malas (Sergeant Sulpice). Wolf Trap Company Chor, Filene Center Orch/Charles Wendelken-Wilson. Dir: Lotfi Mansouri. VAI 69071. In English.

This, the sixtieth of Donizetti's seventy-five operas, is an *opéra-comique* written for Paris in 1838. It tells of the love of the peasant Tonio for the supposedly orphaned girl Marie who has become a regiment's mascot and drummer-girl. He joins up to win her hand. Donizetti revels in the chance to write a light-hearted score packed with good, easy-on-the-ear tunes and military rhythms that set the feet stamping, but the whole needs careful handling if it is not to decline from witty, Gallic humour into Anglo-Saxon farce. The Sydney staging, by Sandro Sequi, mounted in the pleasing decor of Henry Bardon and Michael Stennett as a vehicle for Sutherland's tomboyish, larger-than-life Marie, never quite steps over the mark that divides comedy from slapstick but comes near it.

A great time is had by all on both sides of the footlights and, in a benign mood, one might enjoy the whole thing un-critically, but truth to tell, Sutherland, who made such an effect in the part in 1966 at Covent Garden, looks twenty years too old for the part, frankly somewhat grotesque. Her voice sounds worn, though the technique stands up reasonably well to the demands placed on it. At Covent Garden, and on the Decca records made thereafter, Pavarotti scored one of his first successes. Except that he actually looks the part of the shy Tonio, Anson Austin is no suitable replacement for his noted predecessor as his singing is hard-edged and unpleasing. Yurisich, who has gone on to greater things, is an ideal Sulpice, ridiculous but not guying his role. Bonynge, in his element, conducts an authentic version of the score that restores it to its original, French forms. What a pity, in an opera containing so much dialogue, there are no subtitles.

They aren't needed for the open-air performance from Wolf Trap Park (Virginia) given in 1974 as the opera is given in English and all the singers make their diction clear. This version may have an element of improvised charade about it but in its direct way it probably comes a deal closer than the Sydney set to Donizetti's original concept. Lotfi Mansouri's staging in Beni Montresor's cardboard cutout decor has the conscious intention of creating a 'let's pretend' theatre without slipping over too often into farce or artificiality.

Sills's gawky, bonhomous Marie and her direct, uncomplicated vocalisation, vital in joyful passages and poignant when Marie thinks she has to give up her Tonio, is just what's wanted for the regiment's delightful mascot and adopted daughter. Sills, a real trouper, misses no opportunity to woo her captive audience. McDonald sounds far easier and more natural in the high-lying tessitura of Tonio's music than Austin and presents the naïvety of the character attractively. Malas, an experienced Sulpice, is suitably fatuous. The conducting is more energetic than subtle. Picture and sound are only just adequate but this video has historic importance in offering a permanent record of Sills in one of her most engaging portrayals. It is well worth any trouble in locating it.

Giuseppe Verdi (1813–1901)

Nabucco
Ghena Dimitrova (Abigaille), Bruno Baglioni (Fenena),
Ottavio Garaventa (Ismaele), Renato Bruson (Nabucco),

Dimiter Petkov (Zaccaria). Chor and Orch of Verona Arena/Maurizio Arena. Dir: Renato Giaccheri. Castle VHS CVI 2003. Subtitles.

Nabucco (1842) was Verdi's first success, immediately placing him in the forefront among composers in Italy. In it he articulated the desire of his people for liberty and independence. That is expressed through the aegis of the oppressed Hebrews under the heel of the Babylonians as shown in the famous 'Va pensiero' chorus. But it also deals with the overweening ambitions of Nabucco's daughter Abigaille and her attempt to overthrow her crazed father. Both are unerringly characterised in Verdi's score. Though modest in harmonic and rhythmic invention, the work has an abundant store of melody and a deep sense of humanity, a harbinger of what was ahead in Verdi's output.

This is an archetypal opera for the Arena at Verona, and its vast stage is used cleverly (1981) to suggest, in monolithic structures, a view of the Biblical setting. The costumes are of a grandeur to match, larger than life but so is the whole effort. Bruson is ideal casting for Nabucco. His keenly focused baritone and his gifts for projecting an unstable yet formidable character are a match for Verdi's concept. He brings out all the different facets of this complex character, his violence, sense of terror and finally love, and offers an unforgettable account of his 'Dio di Giuda' solo. Dimitrova matches him decibel for decibel and gesture for gesture in her big-scale portrait of Abigaille, probably her best performance on video, bel canto and power finely balanced.

Petkov is a poor, insecure Zaccaria, and the subsidiary but important roles of Fenena and Ismaele are no more than adequately cast. Arena leads a clear, well-adjusted account of the score and gives his singers secure support. The chorus sings with heart and soul.

I Lombardi

Ghena Dimitrova (Viclinda), José Carreras (Oronte), Carlo Bini (Arvino), Silvano Carroli (Pagano). Chor and Orch of La Scala, Milan/Gianandrea Gavazzeni. Dir:

Gabriele Lavia; video dir: Brian Large. Castle VHS CVI 1027. Subtitles.

This episodic, ramshackle score, dating from 1843, did not repeat the success of *Nabucco*. Its complex, dense plot about feuds among Crusaders in eleventh-century Milan, then Antioch, is partially redeemed by glimpses of the great Verdi to come such as the put-upon heroine Viclinda's 'Salve Maria' and the noble third-act trio.

This La Scala staging of 1984 is traditional to a fault. Lavia's production has its moments, especially in the numerous choral scenes where the tableaux are impressive, particularly in the notable 'O Signore dal tetto natio', but the principals are under-directed and none shines with any particular radiance. Dimitrova has a certain grandeur of manner that carries her through passages where her technique is sorely pressed and she acts with some conviction at a rudimentary level. As Oronte, the Moslem in love with Viclinda, Carreras sings his aria 'La mia letitzia infondere' with coarse-grained tone but improves thereafter, especially fine in the aforementioned trio after which Oronte expires. Carroli as the equivocal Pagano is unsatisfactory, singing crudely and with poor intonation. The veteran Gavazzeni gives a youthful, dynamic and richly contoured account of the score. The video picture is hampered by poor lighting. The sound is adequate.

Ernani
Mirella Freni (Elvira), Placido Domingo (Ernani), Renato Bruson (Don Carlos), Nicolai Ghiaurov (Don Silva). Chor and Orch of La Scala, Milan/Riccardo Muti. Dir: Luca Ronconi; video dir: Preben Montell. Castle CVI VHS 2047. Subtitles.

This splendid piece, based on a drama by Victor Hugo (Sarah Bernhardt starred in the original play) is imbued with the youthful brio of Verdi's early work. The music is closely tailored to Piave's well-crafted libretto. The plot concerns Ernani, a young aristocrat-turned-bandit, and his love for Elvira, soon to be wedded to her kinsman Don Silva, a much older man. Don Carlos, the future Emperor Carlos V, is also in love with Elvira. Verdi lavished on this strong story of love and conspiracy in sixteenth-century Spain his maturing gift for drama through music.

This performance, recorded at La Scala in 1982, is one of the most satisfying versions of a Verdi opera on video. Most of the faults of Ronconi's production, such as having an 'audience' on stage, are simply ignored by the video director who rightly concentrates on the superb acting and singing performances of the distinguished principals, who are well directed by Ronconi. Freni may look a shade fazed by her famous and taxing aria in Act 1, but once past that test, in which she acquits herself well, she sings and acts vividly as Elvira, pouring out warm tone unstintingly. Domingo gives a convincing portrayal as the fiery and ardent Ernani, filling his music with golden tone and well-etched phrasing.

But the most arresting performance of all comes from Bruson in the juicy baritone part of Don Carlos, to whom Verdi gave some of his most inspired solos. With his mellow, evenly produced voice, innate sense of Verdian style and gifts as an actor, his reading is in a class of its own. Gruff old Silva is sung and portrayed sombrely, movingly by Ghiaurov. Muti is fully in sympathy with Verdi's rhythmic impetus and his melodic invention in an interpretation that is at the same time keenly accented and yielding to the singers. The sound and picture are above average.

I due Foscari
Linda Roark-Strummer (Lucrezia), Alberto Cupido (Jacopo Foscari), Renato Bruson (Francesco Foscari). Chor and Orch of La Scala, Milan/Gianandrea Gavazzeni. Dir: Pier-Luigi Pizzi; video dir: Brian Large. Castle VHS CVI 2060. Subtitles.

This melodrama based on Byron's play of the same name, takes place in fifteenth-century Venice and concerns itself with the predicaments of the Foscaris: the elderly doge Francesco is torn between allegiance to the state and his love for his son Jacopo, who has been unjustly accused of murder. It is a dour story played out on a historical plane. The portrait of Francesco is the first in Verdi's gallery of concerned fathers, and he has much rewarding music to sing. Bruson's noble, tormented performance of the role in this 1988 La Scala staging is its chief raison d'être. He is particularly eloquent in the finale where he relinquishes the trappings of power and lets us see the character's deep disillusionment with humanity. The part is sung with Bruson's customary attention to the vocal verities, another object-lesson from this distinguished baritone in Verdian interpretation.

Unfortunately the other two principals are unworthy of him. Roark-Strummer's tight vibrato and strident tone strike the ear uncomfortably and her acting is rudimentary and/or hysterical. Cupido's hard tone, ill-tuned singing and crude acting hardly do justice to Jacopo's prison scene, one of the most original pieces of writing in early Verdi. Gavazzeni, in his eightieth year, conducts with all his old energy and understanding of the Verdian idiom. Pizzi's production and designs stress the omnipresent and crushing curse of power, symbolised by the oppressive throne high above an ornate staircase that dominates the action. This and Pizzi's carefully designed, sombre costumes are well caught in the exemplary video direction. The sound balance catches the atmosphere of La Scala.

Giovanna d'Arco
Susan Dunn (Giovanna), Vincenzo La Scola (Carlo VII), Renato Bruson (Giacomo). Chor and Orch of the Teatro Comunale, Bologna/Riccardo Chailly. Dir: Werner Herzog; video dir: Keith Cheetham. Teldec VHS 9031 – 71478 – 3; LD:–6.

This is an uneven, transitional work (1845) that shows Verdi experimenting with fresh forms but also tied to some old concepts. Based loosely on Schiller's tragedy, *Die Jungfrau von Orleans*, it has Joan in love with Charles, the Dauphin, but resisting fleshly delights through the intervention of her heavenly voices. She is accused on the flimsiest of evidence – by her own father, Giacomo – of being a witch. He denounces his daughter at Charles's coronation but she is freed from prison to lead the French army against the English when she dies from battle wounds. The score is most notable for an early example of Verdi's writing for a father and daughter.

This performance, dating from 1989, has film director Herzog working with his usual designer, Henning von Gierke. It may have worked better on the Bologna stage than it does here, where the angels and demons hardly seem to be adequately represented. There's much use of emblems such as brightly coloured sheets, crosses, rocks, and chains. From a film director the movement is strangely static. Not surprisingly the experienced Bruson fares better than his less-experienced colleagues. Dunn does little but look elated or frightened, although her simplicity of approach has its own validity. La Scola merely stands and sings.

Dunn sings beautifully, particularly in her Acts 1 and 2 arias and her duet with Bruson's Giacomo. Her tone and phrasing are authentically Verdian and apt in their own right. She is wonderfully partnered by Bruson in the duet where he realises she is not sullied as he supposed. Listen to how Dunn phrases so eloquently 'Amami ma un solo istante' and then how Bruson answers with his sad, forgiving phrase, 'Ella innocente e pura'. Here and in his Act 1 solo, Bruson offers perfection in moulding line, tone and text into an integrated whole. This is all seconded by his imposing presence. Beside these two extraordinary readings, La Scola's Carlo is ordinary – but so is his music. Chailly keeps a nice balance between raw energy and lyrical poetry. Sound and picture are of high quality.

Attila

Maria Chiara (Odabella), Veriano Luchetti (Foresto), Silvano Carroli (Ezio), Yevgeny Nesterenko (Attila). Chor and Orch of Verona Arena/Nello Santi. Dir: Giuliano Montaldo; video dir: Brian Large. Castle VHS CVI 2055. Subtitles.

One of the most inspired of Verdi's early successes, *Attila* (1846) is fired by the energy and ebullience of his so-called 'galley' years. It has no true heroes or villains. Indeed even Attila, who sacked Italy in the fifth century, is half tyrant, half guilt-ridden ruler. He is shown as all too trusting of the conquered Romans and is eventually murdered by the machinations of the fiery Odabella, who pretends love for the Hun, and of Ezio, emissary of the Roman emperor. Ezio offers Attila the whole world if he will leave Italy to the emperor. Verdi presents the earthy melodrama in primary colours with a series of rousing arias, duets and ensembles, tempered by more reflective solos for Odabella and her tenor-lover Foresto.

This video, filmed at the Verona Arena in 1985, has all the raw excitement of the best offerings in that vast venue. Montaldo's staging in Luciano Ricceri's grand sets may not be very inspired but it does what it intends to do, project the drama to the thousands below, with a rude simplicity. Nor is subtlety the strong suit of the performers, who adopt the semaphoring style so long the habit in Italian houses. That doesn't prevent Chiara from conveying all Odabella's single-minded purpose, namely to slay Attila with her own hands, and her tender love for Foresto, expressed so eloquently in her Act 1 aria. Hers is the voice of the authentic Italian *spinto*, so rarely heard over the past twenty years, and apart from some discolouring in extremis at the top she sings gratifyingly and in the right style. So does Luchetti as Foresto, another idiomatic Italian who delivers his role in a spirited fashion that never oversteps the bounds of musicality.

Attila and Ezio aren't so well served. As Attila, Nesterenko sounds hollow and/or rusty much of the time, though he has his moments of conviction and visually he is properly dominating. There is no redeeming feature in Carroli's off-key, stretched singing and wooden acting as Ezio. Chorus and orchestra perform well under Santi's experienced hand. Large is sometimes too keen to home in on the personal confrontations at the expense of the larger view of events.

Macbeth
1. Josephine Barstow (Lady Macbeth), Keith Erwen (Macduff), Kostas Paskalis (Macbeth), James Morris (Banquo), Glyndebourne Chor, London Philharmonic Orch/John Pritchard. Dir: Michael Hadjimischev; video dir: David Heather. Pickwick SLL 7017. Subtitles.

2. Mara Zampieri (Lady Macbeth), Dennis O'Neill (Macduff), Renato Bruson (Macbeth), James Morris (Banquo). Chor and Orch of Deutsche Oper, Berlin/Giuseppe Sinopoli. Dir: Luca Ronconi; video dir: Brian Large. Virgin VHS VVD 384; Pioneer LD: PLMCC 00121.
3. Shirley Verrett (Lady Macbeth), Veriano Luchetti (Macduff), Leo Nucci (Macbeth), Samuel Ramey (Banquo). Chor and Orch of Teatro Communale, Bologna/Riccardo Chailly. A film by Claude D'Anna. Decca VHS 071 422–3; LD:−1. Subtitles.

Verdi's lifelong veneration of Shakespeare resulted in three operas based on his plays. *Macbeth*, the first, originally written in 1847, was substantially revised in 1865. For long it was criticised for being un-Shakespearean, which hurt Verdi deeply. In recent times, the opera has rightly been praised for following the ideas and atmosphere of the play in a score that concentrates on the Macbeths and on the Witches (all marvellously delineated). As a result of the advocacy of the director Carl Ebert at Berlin and later at Glyndebourne (where it was first staged in 1939 and thence frequently after the war), it has become virtually part of the regular repertory.

It is the Glyndebourne performance of 1973 that deserves pride of place here. Emanuele Luzzati's grey-green, mist-enshrouded decor, a unit set at an angle, is a fit backcloth for the evil deeds of the principal schemers, who are intelligently directed. There are some arresting images straight from the start when the Witches spring up from seemingly nowhere. The movement and costumes may be traditional but they are worked with so convincingly on all sides, with Glyndebourne's standards of ensemble and dedication evident throughout, that the results are constantly enlivening. The intimacy of the old Glyndebourne theatre seems to enhance the sense of a tense, claustrophobic world.

Pritchard surpasses himself in a taut, gripping interpretation, timing all numbers unerringly and belying his reputation for being a slack conductor. Paskalis's black-browed acting and singing made him famed in this role, justifiably so on this evidence, a riveting interpretation that stands the test of time, catching the tensions and horror of

Macbeth doing things against his inner nature. He is led to evil deeds by Barstow's devilish, wheedling, almost erotic Lady Macbeth sung with unflinching attack and reaching its vocal and histrionic climax in a haunted account of the famous sleepwalking scene. This all-in portrayal is a fit souvenir of this diva's singular art. The pity is that so little else remains of her repertory on video or CD. Morris sings firmly as Banquo, but fails to create a definite character. Erwen is a trenchant Macduff.

For its day the picture and sound (mono only) are remarkably faithful to the original production.

The 1987 Berlin performance is hampered by monochrome, monolithic sets that can hardly be seen in the dreary lighting. Colour is provided by the scarlet costumes for the Macbeths. Ronconi rather leaves his singers to their own devices. His treatment of the Witches is ludicrously tame. Hasn't he bothered to listen to Verdi's revolutionary music for these covens? And where's the blood on the Macbeths' hands when they speak of it? Even the appearance of the eight kings, for which the composer wrote some of the most original music in nineteenth-century opera, goes for little.

As is his wont, Sinopoli's conducting oscillates between the frenetic and the dangerously slow, but in compensation he sees Verdi's writing for the orchestra from the point of view of a fellow composer and draws much wonderful detail from his accomplished Berlin players. But the main enjoyment in this performance comes from the singing of the Macbeths. Bruson's tormented, weak-willed Thane is sung with an intensity that matches that of Paskalis. Guilty before and after Duncan's murder, terrified at the appearance of Banquo's ghost, fatalistic in his last-act aria, superbly sung, his is a justifiably famous Macbeth, not as trenchant or single-minded as that of Paskalis but just as valid as a reading.

As his Lady, Zampieri looks suitably crazed and single-minded from the beginning. She sings with a curiously fruity, open tone that can become strident, giving her all in the cause of a vivid portrayal. Strangely she omits the high D flat at the end of a blood-curdling Sleepwalk. Morris is again a bland, unperturbed Banquo, O'Neill a provincial-sounding Macduff. The now well-known Sharon Sweet appears briefly as the Gentlewoman attending Lady Macbeth and announces a formidable voice in her few utterances. The choral contribution is excellent. Even Large seems defeated in trying to get something out of nothing when filming this production.

The 1987 Claude D'Anna film ought to sweep the board, considering the forces and expense involved. Made on location at the fortified castle of Godefroy le Bouillon in the Belgian Ardennes, it opens up the action on to a realistic plane. Opera is already an exotic art. If you take it away from the proscenium arch and put it in such a naturalistic setting, with the added problems of post-synch, you are asking people to suspend disbelief even further than in the theatre. What are these people doing dressed up in a field or on a mountain pass or in the castle's dungeon singing their hearts out? It can work (see Delius), but here more problems are posed than solved.

D'Anna certainly has a lively, imaginative mind. The idea of having Macduff and the exiles perform their scene at the funeral of Macduff's family is truly inspired, but too often the antics of Monty Python are recalled, as in the treatment of the Witches at the Macbeth banquet: at any moment you expect a bearded Palin or Jones to pop up on the screen. D'Anna goes into overkill to make our flesh creep in his lopsided view of the scenery. The Witches are nubile but seemingly crazed dancers. A dagger appears to Macbeth from nowhere. Banquo sings his aria at the burning of corpses after an execution. All very cinematic but not always appropriate to Verdi, let alone Shakespeare.

Then, as already suggested, the miming of actors to singers' voices is sometimes troublesome. When most of us have a clear idea of Ramey's features, it is disorientating to have his voice emerge from another's features (was Ramey, who can act reasonably well, unavailable for the filming session, or didn't he like the way his part was conceived?). The lip-synch is well managed except in the case of Verrett, a noted Lady Macbeth, who cannot have taken kindly to the process, nor does she here seem to have her heart in the business, hardly ever suggesting her character's fanatical zeal in achieving her ambitions. Although Nucci sometimes forces his voice out of focus, he makes a reasonably effective Macbeth, though not one in the Bruson or Paskalis class.

Chailly is good at exploring the extreme originality of the score and his reading imposes a unity on to the disparate pictures. The recording, also available on CD, is a shade reverberant, having been made in a Bologna church. So much for dramatic verities. Still those unused to attending performances in the theatre may find this film more credible than will seasoned opera-lovers. At least it is all done with considerable enthusiasm and éclat, even if these are sometimes misplaced.

Luisa Miller

June Anderson (Luisa), Susanna Anselmi (Frederica), Taro Ichihara (Rodolfo), Eduard Tumagian (Miller), Romuald Tesarowicz (Wurm), Paul Plishka (Walter). Montpelier Opera Chor, Chor and Orch of Lyon Opera/ Maurizio Arena. Dir: Jacques Lassalle; video dir: Claus Viller. Pioneer LD PLMCC 00711.

This important predecessor (1849) to Verdi's great middle-period operas shows him stretching forward to a more lyrical, refined style of writing, most notably in Luisa's music, and dealing with the interior feelings of his principals. The libretto, based on Schiller's drama, *Kabale und Liebe*, takes place in eighteenth-century Tyrol. Its involved plot ends in tragedy with the death of the lovers Luisa and Rodolfo, victims of the evil, saturnine Wurm.

This video emanates from a production at the Lyon Opera in 1988. The sets are penny-plain, unfussy almost to a fault, etching in the Tyrolean background, against which the singers move naturally and easily with no attempt at a 'concept' or interpretation other than the composer's. That leaves the soloists very much to their own devices. Two of the principals have no difficulty in projecting their characters, the admirable father-daughter combination of Anderson's Luisa and Tumagian's Miller who in solo and duet suggest their loves and cares with an appealing directness in firm, unsullied tones and shapely phrasing. Plishka, as Rodolfo's guilty father Walter, offers generous singing lamed by an incipient wobble. Some moments of questionable intonation apart, Ichihara interprets Rodolfo's music, including his famous aria, 'Quando le sere al placido', a Pavarotti favourite, with keen tone but dramatically he is a cipher. The villain Wurm is undercast.

As is his wont, Arena gives a straightforward, unexaggerated account of the score in hand with excellent playing from the Lyon orchestra. Viller's video direction and the sound quality are both faultless.

Stiffelio
Catherine Malfitano (Lina), José Carreras (Stiffelio), Robin Leggate (Raffaele), Gregory Yurisich (Stankar), Gwynne Howell (Jorg). Chor and Orch of Royal Opera House, Covent Garden/Edward Downes. Dir: Elijah Moshinsky; video dir: Brian Large. Covent Garden VHS CGP 03; Pioneer LD PLMC 80061. Subtitles.

Censored and shunned when first given because it dealt with the then frowned-on subject of the adultery of Lina, the priest Stiffelio's wife, with a parishioner, this interesting, off-centre piece with a somewhat Ibsenesque libretto (by Piave) has recently had its reputation rescued. Indeed its story of intimate relationships in a close-knit community, and their consequences, quite new for opera at the time, has more relevance today than most of Verdi's early opera and as such is an apt successor to *Luisa Miller* with which it has several resonances. Besides, Verdi, having just started to cohabit with Giuseppina Strepponi, had his heart in the score.

This Covent Garden staging of 1993 is a fit response to Verdi's probing ideas. Elijah Moshinksy creates the right claustrophobic atmosphere in his exemplary direction, projecting the near-tragedy taking place in the confines of a religious community isolated from the outside world: the setting somewhere in mid-nineteenth-century USA being an inspired idea. Downes seconds the production with the fervour of his interpretation, and his orchestra plays with verve and consistent distinction.

None of the singers may be quite ideal for their roles but the sum is greater than the parts given the sense of teamwork evinced all round. Malfitano's voice hasn't the weight of a true Verdian soprano, but her trenchant singing combined with her detailed acting out of Lina's terrified guilt occasioned by her illicit love could hardly be bettered, and her singing gains in confidence as the performance progresses. Stiffelio himself may call for a more stentorian delivery and a more committed response than Carreras offers, but his appealing voice carries most of the overtones essential to the role, and for the most part he is in excellent voice. Though a formidable presence, Yurisich lacks the vocal bite for vengeful Stankar's music: he finds his best form in his set-piece aria. Howell is well cast as the upright Jorg.

Large's screen direction is faultless, cameras always at the right place at the right time. The sound in both formats is well balanced and wide in range. This is one of the most satisfying Verdi sets on the market.

Rigoletto

1. Edita Gruberová (Gilda), Victoria Vergara (Maddalena), Luciano Pavarotti (Duke of Mantua), Ingvar Wixell (Rigoletto), Ferruccio Furlanetto (Sparafucile). Vienna State Opera Concert Chor, Vienna Philharmonic Orch/Riccardo Chailly. A film by Jean-Pierre Ponnelle. Decca VHS: 071 401–3; LD:—1.

2. Marie McLaughlin (Gilda), Jean Rigby (Maddalena), Arthur Davies (Duke of Mantua), John Rawnsley (Rigoletto), John Tomlinson (Sparafucile). Chor and Orch of English National Opera/Mark Elder. Dir: Jonathan Miller; video dir: John Michael Philips. Thames Video VHS TV 8013. In English.

3. Lina Pagliughi (Gilda), Anna-Maria Canali (Maddalena), Mario Filippeschi (Duke of Mantua), Tito Gobbi (Rigoletto), Giulio Neri (Sparafucile). Chor and Orch of Rome Opera/Tullio Serafin. Dir: Carmine Gallone. Pickwick VHS SL 1056.

This is the first of Verdi's great mid-period masterpieces that established him beyond doubt as the leading composer of Italian opera in the nineteenth century. It is based on Victor Hugo's play *Le roi s'amuse*, which – like the opera – ran into censorship difficulties over depicting a corrupt ruler: the only character with moral strength at a licentious court, here ruled by the libidinous Duke of Mantua, is his jester Rigoletto. Verdi's fluent score unerringly depicts the obsession of the Duke with women, the haunted character of Rigoletto himself, a bitterly mocking fool at court, a worried, loving father at home, where he unduly protects his innocent daughter Gilda from the outside world, which makes the Duke's virtual rape of Gilda the more heinous. Verdi's score is consistently inspired, most tellingly so in the two long duets for Gilda and Rigoletto.

These three video versions could not be more starkly contrasted. Ponnelle's 1983 film, shot on location at Mantua, is one of his most imaginative achievements in the medium, full of atmosphere and colour yet intelligently concentrating on the principals. It is also frank. The first scene is an explicit orgy. Gilda's seduction by the Duke is made (almost) manifest. Her relationship is given an almost incestuous touch (appropriate word). Altogether the visual aspect, both as regards scenery and camerawork, has a startling immediacy that makes one think anew about the characters' relationships and Verdi's reaction to them.

In Wixell's Rigoletto (which he arrestingly doubles with that other wronged father, Monterone) it has a dominating, intense protagonist, an interpretation that goes well beyond the usual convention of operatic acting. Wixell may not have the Italianate bite in his tone the role ideally calls for but everything else, vocal and dramatic, is right in this stunning performance. His realistic portrayal makes the posturing and vocal grimaces of Pavarotti as the Duke seem faintly ludicrous, but Pavarotti consoles us with the generosity of heart and vocal brio of his singing well tailored to the Duke's music.

Gruberová's Gilda comes somewhere in between. With her Pre-Raphaelite curls and pure vocalisation she is quite touching, but she isn't convincing as the protected virgin of Verdi's imagining though she goes to her death with true feeling. You also sense her agony in the great Quartet as she sees the Duke, whom she still loves, wooing Maddalena, and here Ponnelle shows his skills as Gilda and Rigoletto look through a window at the flirtation of Maddalena and the Duke. Veteran Fedora Barbieri makes something of Giovanni with her venal eyes as she colludes with the Duke entering the Rigo-letto establishment. Chailly conducts a strongly limned, unfussy performance (every bar included). The picture and sound are first-rate.

The 1982 ENO video enshrines the now-famous and long-running Jonathan Miller staging (which he introduces on screen) transferring the action to 1950s mafia New York. The Duke is 'Duke', Rigoletto a barman attending the mafioso, Gilda a repressed, unsure girl. The concept is carried out with complete consistency from the Little Italy nightclub where 'Duke' holds sway down to the notorious juke-box in Spara-fucile's down-at-heel diner. Each character looks convincing; even the old wheeze of a curse doesn't seem inappropriate. With James Fenton's translation adding another touch of authenticity, this is one updated staging that works perfectly.

Miller also draws well-integrated, individually convincing performances from his principals. None is more vivid than Rawnsley's imperious Rigoletto, a composition of bile, scorn and tenderness in about equal parts and exploding with ele-mental force after he has discovered his daughter's fate. Rawnsley's singing is equal to all Verdi's appreciable demands on his baritone. As Gilda, McLaughlin exactly catches Miller's idea of an insecure, slightly neurotic girl. She is not vocally happy in a part that lies about a third too high for her fundamentally lyric voice, but as with her Violetta in *Traviata (qv)*, she is forgiven any vocal shortcomings by the conviction of her performance as a whole. Davies makes a credible spiv of 'Duke', at once bully and charmer, with a leering smile. His singing is forthright and strong. Tomlinson is a sinister, still Sparafucile, Rigby a luscious Maddalena. Elder's conducting is surprisingly lacklustre until Act 3. Pic-ture and sound are no more than adequate.

Of course they seem better than that beside the primitive black and white and occasionally crackly sound of the 1947 film, enacted on the stage of the Rome Opera, but neverthe-less dubbed, probably because Pagliughi's figure was considered unsuitable for Gilda and she sings to a young actress's miming of the part. Given the out-of-date conven-tions of the acting and the old-fashioned sets, this version has a deal to commend it, not least Serafin's classically shaped interpretation, yielding and exciting by turns. Then Gobbi's Rigoletto, although dramatically somewhat stilted by modern standards, sets vocal parameters hard to equal: he uses his flexible, expressive baritone to create all Rigoletto's cynicism, love, anger and sorrow in a compelling portrayal of the hunchback that employs Gobbi's superb gifts in colouring, a note or word to enhance meaning, all the more remarkable in a baritone only thirty-four at the time.

Pagliughi's Gilda is accurately and sweetly sung but with little of the emotional content we now expect in the part. Filippeschi's elegant, old-style Duke is sung with fine-grained tone and authentic Italianate attack, though his acting is rudimentary. Neri's black bass is ideal for Sparafucile. So, providing you are prepared to indulge the poor picture, there is much to please the ear, but the dubbing is all too obvious. The formerly traditional and disfiguring cuts in Verdi's closely wrought score are made.

Il trovatore
1. Rosalind Plowright (Leonora), Fiorenza Cossotto (Azucena), Franco Bonisolli (Manrico), Giorgio Zancanaro (Luna). Chor and Orch of Verona Arena/Reynald Giovaninetti. Dir: Guiseppe Patroni Griffi; video dir: Brian Large. Castle CVI 2005. Subtitles.
2. Eva Marton (Leonora), Dolora Zajick (Azucena), Luciano Pavarotti (Manrico), Sherrill Milnes (Luna). Chor and Orch of Metropolitan Opera, New York/James Levine. Dir: Frank Melano; video dir: Brian Large. Decca VHS 072 213—3; LD:—1.

Superficially this blood-and-thunder work is a throwback to early Verdi, but on closer examination it is much more tautly constructed than any of the operas of his galley years. A dark-hued score, mostly in the minor, its complex plot speaks of dark, primitive passions in primary, exciting colours and with a seemingly endless fund of vigorous melody; it seldom fails to make its mark if there are four singers available to fulfil the exigent demands of their roles. Happily the Verona Arena performance of 1985, a full-blooded interpretation, just about does the trick.

The decor is designed by the sculptor Mario Ceroli, well-known for his intricate work in unpainted wood. Here his grand-scale artefacts and emblems hurried around the stage make an apt background in the Arena to a vital, inspiriting performance, though their relevance one to another is hard to determine. Griffi's direction of the principals is minimal and he has his chorus running from side to side for no very evident reason. But the sum is greater than the parts.

Plowright's warm soprano apparently carried easily into the Arena's wide spaces as may be judged even on video. Hers is a generous, well-schooled performance, ably acted and marred only by uncertainty and some strain at the top in the earlier acts. Once past her Act 4 aria, she begins to throw caution to the winds (a bit late perhaps?) and viscerally to excite her audience. Bonisolli, with his macho voice and presence, does that throughout and even indulges in an encore of 'Di quella pira', his fearsome high Cs more secure the second time round. His sense of Verdian style is variable, but he often evinces more intelligence than he is sometimes given credit for. His acting is something else.

But the vocal star has to be Zancanaro who rightly stops the show with his 'Il balen', sung with impeccable style in that firm vibrant baritone of his, and he continues in the same vein throughout, a Verdian baritone of compelling authority tempered by elegance of phrase. Cossotto knows how, through long experience, to throw out her voice into the Arena and milk an audience for applause. If her voice isn't as secure as it once was it still rings with authentic fire and passion: she duly brings down the house with her wealth of voice and commitment. Giovaninetti controls events with reasonable success, keeping his four thoroughbreds just about in harness. It's all fun – and thrilling – in excellent sound and vision.

By its side, the 1987 Met version is tame. To be sure Pavarotti is there as Manrico with his involvement, his basic appeal to the heart, but – as he freely admits – Manrico is a role one size too big for his basically lyric tenor. He is best in the fiery nobility of the Act 3 recitative and aria. 'Di quella pira' is down a semitone. In what was her Met debut, Zajick makes an understandably nervous start but, her youthful looks apart, develops the character with some skill and increasing vocal confidence. Marton neither looks nor sings Leonora convincingly, the tone harsh and over-vibrating, its colour unvaried. Milnes, sadly declined in voice, sings in an effortful, unfocused manner. Levine's conducting is coarse-grained and he sanctions the cutting of Leonora's cabaletta 'Tu vedrai', which Plowright makes so convincing on the other version. The staging is weak, traditional and poorly coordinated. Not recommended despite good sound and picture.

La traviata

1. Tiziana Fabbricini (Violetta), Roberto Alagna (Alfredo), Paolo Coni (Giorgio Germont). Chor and Orch of La Scala, Milan/Riccardo Muti. Dir and video dir: Liliana Cavani. Sony VHS SHV 48 353; LD: S2LV 48 353.

2. Marie McLaughlin (Violetta), Walter MacNeil (Alfredo), Brent Ellis (Giorgio Germont). Glyndebourne Chor, London Philharmonic Orch/Bernard Haitink. Dir and video dir: Peter Hall. Pickwick VHS SL 2006; Pioneer LD: PLMCC 00291.

3. Angela Gheorghiu (Violetta), Frank Lopardo (Alfredo), Leo Nucci (Giorgio Germont). Chor and Orch of Royal Opera House, Covent Garden/Georg Solti. Dir: Richard Eyre; video dirs: Humphrey Burton and Peter Maniura. Decca VHS 071 431–3. LD:−1.

4. Edita Gruberova (Violetta), Neil Shicoff (Alfredo), Giorgio Zancanaro (Giorgio Germont). Chor and Orch of La Fenice, Venice/Carlo Rizzi. Dir: Pier Luigi Pizzi; video dir: Derek Bailey. Teldec LD 4509–92409–3; LD:−6.

5. Anna Moffo (Violetta), Franco Bonisolli (Alfredo), Gino Bechi (Giorgio Germont). Chor and Orch of Rome Opera/Giuseppe Patanè. A film by Mario Lanfranchi. VAI VHS 69069.

6. Beverly Sills (Violetta), Henry Price (Alfredo), Richard Fredericks (Giorgio Germont). Wolf Trap Company Chor, Filene Center Orch/Julius Rudel. Dir: Tito Capobianco; video dir: Kirk Browning. VAI VHS 69079. Subtitles.

The greatest of Verdi's mid-period operas, based on Dumas's *La Dame aux Camellias*, can claim to be the first opera of realism in which Verdi put on the stage a true-to-life story of the day, the courtesan with a heart of gold – and consumption – who sacrifices her new-found love for the sake of hypocritical values of morality. Having himself begun to live out of wedlock with the diva Giuseppina Strepponi, Verdi responded to the subject with music that consistently touches the heart, most especially in the first scene of Act 2, where the elder Germont eventually persuades Violetta to give up his son Alfredo for the sake of the family's reputation and his daughter's honour. It is the culmination of all Verdi's soprano/baritone duets and shows him further developing and expanding the forms of Italian opera for his own and the drama's ends.

The piece is well served on video. Any of the first three choices is eminently worthy of Verdi. Cavani's 1993 La Scala staging, which she has herself directed for video, is an honest, unaffected traditional inscenation in Dante Ferranti's arrestingly beautiful decor, which is all in all a fit background to a musical account of great moment, and she manages at the same time to give us an intimate view of the drama within the context of a big-theatre production.

Fabbricini comes closest to Maria Callas (whom I saw twice in the part at Covent Garden) in catching the very essence of Violetta's character both visually and dramatically. Indeed she must be the most searing, most moving Violetta since that legendary diva. While obviously modelling herself on the reading of her famous La Scala predecessor, Fabbricini is no carbon copy; her personality is different. Fabbricini's Violetta is the more lost, the more vulnerable when assaulted by the Germonts in Act 2: her look at Flora's party when Alfredo denounces her for her seeming betrayal of him says everything, and her final act is filled with poignant expression.

Without quite the coloratura finesse or ease in the *passagio*, she isn't in complete command vocally in Act 1, but certain words – 'palpito', for instance – prepare us for what is to come. In the famous encounter with Germont she is memorable, with a tear in her tone and what the Italians call *morbidezza* to match the scene's great challenges. Here is a fallen woman whose new happiness is wrenched from her, telling it how it is in just the right tone and accent. In the party scene her Violetta is filled with nervous anxiety, in the finale act with tragic phrasing, drained letter-reading, long-breathed, pathetic 'Addio del passato'.

Coni, managing to hide his youth as the elder Germont, appears at once implacable and dignified. His singing has the advantages of warm tone and alert diction. Alagna looks handsome, acts rather sparingly, sings with heady, youthful enthusiasm. Over all presides Muti, the progenitor of this staging, in which he wanted young, malleable principals whom he could mould into a new-minted reading. He succeeds surely beyond even his own expectations. At the same time he and his players support his charges with wonderfully alert, sympathetic playing of the utmost accuracy and refinement. He conducts the score absolutely complete, thus giving his charges a challenge they amply meet. The sound recording doesn't always allow the singers enough presence, but that is a small reservation about a performance that deeply affects all who see and hear it.

That the 1987 Glyndebourne production stands up to this competition is a tribute to Peter Hall's adaptation of the piece to the old Glyndebourne house, where he makes a virtue of the stage's small size by creating an intimate, claustrophobic staging that brings home to us the detail of the drama in John Gunter's closely detailed and well-observed sets. Hall brings out all the aching intensity of Violetta's predicament and tragedy, played out with complete conviction by an excellent cast. McLaughlin's Violetta changes quite arrestingly in Act 1 from showy coquette to infatuated lover, the smallest movement of mind expressed in McLaughlin's expressive features. So it continues with Violetta's noble sacrifice delineated in scrupulously enacted detail.

The soprano gives herself body and soul to the role: her heart-stopping, forlorn eyes evince by turn happiness, vulnerability, distress, fatal acceptance and just about every emotion in between. The attempt to hide her feelings at Flora's party, then the collapse of that façade when accused by Alfredo, finally the desperation and nervous, eager hope of regaining happiness are almost too much to bear. This is the best thing this notable artist has done: perhaps she hasn't returned to the part because it took too much out of her and because a few passages are just beyond her vocally. No matter: the rest is sung with such even, pure phrasing, such subtle shading, such pointed phrasing as to silence criticism.

Ellis's Germont is complacent, interfering bourgeois values personified. It is sung with an eye for obeying Verdi's marks: second verse of 'Di Provenza' sung *piano* for instance. He is allowed both verses of Germont's often excluded cabaletta in a full version of the score that omits only verse two of Violetta's 'Ah, fors è lui'. MacNeil's Alfredo is a credible son of this father, spoilt, shallow, a bit callous, exhibiting real emotion only in the finale. Enid Hartle makes much of little as Annina. A touch typical of Hall's perceptions is her show of delight as she realises it's back to town and normal when Violetta is forced to accept Flora's invite.

Haitink conducts a lived-in, unobtrusive interpretation, favouring deliberate speeds and obtaining excellent playing from the LPO. Hall's own screen direction is imaginative as in the way he superimposes characters when they have the lead in the Act 2 ensemble. The lighting is excellent, the sound faithful to the old house's close acoustics. The supporting material in both formats is unworthy of the superb product.

The latest (1994) version derives from Eyre's traditional staging at the Royal Opera House, conducted by Solti, which disclosed an undoubted star in the ascendant in Gheorghiu, the young Romanian soprano, as Violetta. Indeed it was her arresting assumption that provoked Decca into making not only this video, derived from a BBC telecast arranged at the last moment, but also a CD recording. Gheorghiu's reading is all the better for being seen in close-up; in the theatre she created less of an impression because her physical and facial gestures were somewhat small in scale. The cameras here positively enhance her deeply felt performance, one that obviously comes from the heart and consequently goes to it.

If this Violetta, tall, beautiful, with a definite presence, begins by seeming more like a girl at her graduation party rather than an experienced courtesan, she soon corrects that impression by conveying her vulnerability and fear before

Germont's insistent demands on her and then visibly falls apart emotionally in the later scenes. For all that, I find her less moving than either Fabbricini or McLaughlin but she is better equipped vocally to fulfil all the severe demands of the part, never seeming stretched, as they occasionally can be, by the role. She makes much of the text, moulding phrases through the words, but doesn't provide quite the tonal shades of either of her rivals.

Lopardo is probably the best of the three Alfredos by virtue of his finely varied and honed timbre, his sensitivity over phrasing and his welcome attention to dynamic markings, though he isn't as directly appealing as Alagna in terms of voice or appearance. Nucci is a stiff, straight-backed implacable Germont, effective in a traditional way, but monochrome in his singing. Like the others, he is often hampered by Solti's stodgy way with the score, no match for the much more flexible and involving Muti and Haitink. Like Muti, Solti plays the score absolutely complete. Indeed he made a great hoo-ha about the fact at the time of the production, apparently unaware that anyone else, Muti for instance, had done the same thing in recent times.

Eyre directs his charges sensitively and must take a deal of the credit for his soprano's performance, but as a whole this staging is conventional to the point of dullness – Flora's party particularly so – when set beside its rivals. Bob Crowley's decor is no match for his rivals' work at La Scala or Glyndebourne. Everything happens as and when it should, but you gain no sense of the director having a well-defined view of the piece or seeking to re-interpret it in a meaningful manner. Sensibly the video directors have concentrated on the principals.

Nor is the sound quality anything to be proud of. The music is recessed, with little stereo perspective and even a few signs of distortion. Given the excellence of the CD version, this is a disappointment; even the laserdisc evinces little improvement. Nor have subtitles, included on TV, been provided. Indeed the issue bears the hallmarks of a rushed job. For all that, many will still be interested in the issue for Gheorghiu's interpretation.

After these three revelatory interpretations, Pizzi's 1992

Venice production seems ordinary and dull, Rizzi's conducting lacklustre. Gruberová sings Violetta with efficiency and
some feeling, but her interpretation is no match as regards
interpretative insight for McLaughlin's or Fabbricini's. Shicoff
is conventionally tenorish as Alfredo. Much the most convincing performance comes from Zancanaro, as ever pouring
out strong, firm tone and adding an expressive nuance to his
demands on Violetta.

Mario Lanfranchi's 1968 film shows a deal of imagination in
opening out the story within handsome interiors. Shots taken
from above and from acute angles on the whole enhance the
sense of the sad drama being played out before us. On this
occasion a well-conceived film is partially lamed by the poor
execution of the dubbing. Nobody looks as though they were
actually singing, least of all Moffo as Violetta, who seems to
be deliberately trying to make a virtue of the fact that she
actually is *not* singing, but in the end she defeats her own
object and looks unconvincing. On the other hand she is
quite successful in projecting Violetta's emotions in a fairly
traditional way, very much looks the role, and sings with
steady tone and considerable expressive nuance.

Bonisolli acts stiffly but sings with a fine line, burnished,
Italianate tone and refined phrasing. It is a pleasure to see
and hear the veteran Bechi as father Germont. His tone may
sometimes sound dried out but the voice remains firm, the
phrasing exemplary, and he looks exactly right for his part. In
the cameo role of Dr Grenvil, the sixty-seven-year-old Afro
Poli gives a brief and telling lesson in placing words on tone.
Patanè conducts Rome Opera forces with a deal of energy
and sensitivity. There's much to enjoy here despite some
slow-motion acting, and sound that just occasionally distorts.
(The famous Zeffirelli film, not at present on the market,
went much further in imaginative reinterpretation of the
piece.) All the traditional cuts are made.

The other VAI issue, taken from the 1974 Wolf Trap open-
air Festival, is to be avoided except by Sills fans (incidentally,
she introduces this TV screening). The New York diva looks
far too buoyant, healthy and American to be for a moment a
convincing Violetta and her tone is too shallow and quickly
vibrant for the good of Verdi's music. For once Alfredo really

looks like his father's son. Price is a lightweight, moderately equipped Alfredo. Fredericks is much the best of the singers, his tone warm and steady, his style idiomatic. Rudel conducts a dim, uncommunicative account of the score. The sound and picture are poor to average. This is to be avoided, particularly when so many riches in this work are available elsewhere on video.

Un ballo in maschera
Harolyn Blackwell (Oscar), Aprile Millo (Amelia), Florence Quivar (Ulrica), Luciano Pavarotti (Gustavus), Leo Nucci (Anckarström), Terry Cook (Horn), Jeffrey Wells (Ribbing). Chor and Orch of Metropolitan Opera, New York/James Levine. Dir: Piero Faggioni; video dir: Brian Large. DG VHS 072 425–3; LD:−1.

One of the most abundantly lyrical and attractively varied of Verdi's middle-period works, this score shows him at the peak of his powers, keeping a fine balance between the romantic and the tragic with light relief provided by the high soprano Oscar. Originally set in Sweden and featuring the murder of a monarch (Gustaf III of Sweden), the censor decreed that it had to be relocated in Boston, but modern stagings mostly set it back in Sweden. The unerringly acute characterisation affords wonderful chances for the principals to shine.

The 1990 Met production is set in Sweden (though some Italian names in the libretto are retained!), but unfortunately Faggioni's staging and his own decor are never more than picturesque and superficial, with no attempt to peer into the hearts of the principals or set up the relevant tensions between them. This is all show and no substance, costume drama of the most rudimentary kind all too prevalent at the Met under the Levine regime with no pretence at intellectual rigour. His view seems to be to give the punters what they want – big names and a show. Small attempts at originality in this staging, such as the king having his portrait painted during Anckarström's opening aria and the ceaseless, athletic whirl of the page Oscar as a kind of restless mannequin, only serve to underline the lack of substantial ideas in this all-purpose effort.

Levine's conducting is of a piece with what's happening on stage, over-emphatic, exciting on the surface but wanting true Verdian line and sweep. Mind you, it can't be easy coping with a heap of egos up on stage – the price of relying on star singers – beginning with Pavarotti's Gustavus. Strange to say, despite his girth and his minimal acting, Pavarotti is the one singer to suggest the essence of his role, largely by virtue of his expressive eyes and features. Terrified by Ulrica's prophesy of his death, he laughs off the threat but shows in his looks his fear within. Much more than his soprano partner he attempts a real show of passion in the love duet and pathos at their final meeting, and his death, though stagey, is quite convincing. And he still sings with aristocratic line and sovereign tone, though the top notes are now parcelled out somewhat gingerly. The emotional outburst just before the ball scene has the right heroic charge.

Millo is hampered from the start by being given a wholly inappropriate blonde wig, which only emphasises her static, inexpressive features and movement: this Amelia evinces little or nothing of the woman's conflict of emotions. Vocally she recovers from a strident start to sing with a true Verdian sweep in the love duet, and her Prayer in Act 3 is appealingly phrased.

Nucci, as ever, sings securely but with little sign of light or shade in his over-forceful and marmoreal delivery of this plum among baritone parts in Verdi. His acting appears to be based on one snarling look, and his wig never has a hair out of place. Also unconvincingly wigged, Quivar manages to convey some but not all of Ulrica's strange spells. Blackwell is a ball of energy as Oscar but a little less would mean so much more, and the audience exhibits its collective ignorance by applauding after the first verse of both her arias. The two basses are adequate.

Large concentrates on close-ups, sparing us the worst excesses of the production, although he cannot hide the noise of a scenery change that draws attention away from that aforementioned outburst of Gustavus's in the final act.

The sound is reasonable but not outstanding, catching too

much of the house's barn-like reverberance. Anyone wanting this opera on video ought to wait for something more inspired, but admirers will want the issue for their hero's performance and will not be disappointed by his warm, endearing interpretation, which is most certainly the best reason for acquiring it.

> *I vespri Siciliani (originally Les vêpres Siciliennes)*
> Cheryl Studer (Elena), Chris Merritt (Arrigo), Giorgio
> Zancanaro (Monforte), Ferruccio Furlanetto (Procida).
> Chor and Orch of La Scala, Milan/Riccardo Muti. Dir:
> Pierluigi Pizzi; video dir: Christopher Swann. Castle
> Opera VHS CVI 2228. Subtitles.

Written for Paris, this work relates the story of the occupation of Sicily by the French during the thirteenth century and chronicles the efforts of the Sicilian patriots to dislodge them. Unknown to him at the start, the patriot Arrigo is the son of the French leader Monforte, which presents Arrigo – and his beloved Elena – with divided and ultimately destructive loyalties. The piece shows Verdi spreading his wings on to a larger canvas and occasionally losing his way in attempting to write a French *grand opéra* for Parisian taste, lengthy ballet included. But, at its best, when dealing with private relationships rather than public squabbles, it is a subtle, well-wrought piece. It demands a deal of singing, skill in managing large ensembles and elaborate spectacle.

This performance, which launched La Scala's 1990 season, fulfils almost all the opera's stringent demands yet when it opened it was excoriated by critics and, to an extent, by audiences, possibly because two Americans had been cast in main roles. Pizzi's staging and decor are unimaginative, but they look pleasing and at least have the merit of never coming between us and the music. Muti courageously plays the score complete, ballet and all, and plays it as though he believes in every bar, realising its assets with imperturbable control, easily overcoming any drawbacks, real or imagined. He rouses his forces, solo and concerted, to give of their best, displays all his familiar gifts for energising rhythms and shaping a Verdian line, and draws the best out of what is generally considered Verdi's most telling ballet music. Orchestra and chorus play and sing with the flair of authenticity – as indeed they should – although that authenticity doesn't extend to the use of the original French text: the work is sung, as it has been for most of its chequered history, in Italian translation.

The performance is graced by some superb singing, at least in two of the three most important roles, those of Elena and Monforte. Studer sings with the ring of a true *lirico-spinto* who also has full control in coloratura passages. In public moments her attack is spirited and confident, the tone vibrant and warm, his diction fiery. More reflective sections are sung with innate sensitivity. In her long duet with Arrigo in Act 4, especially the passage beginning 'Arrigo! Ah, parli ad un core', made famous by Callas, she floats her tone appealingly, the line secure, accents delicate and affecting. The Bolero, later, is confidently dispatched with a smile in the voice. She rides effortlessly over the top of the ensembles. All in all she finds what Berlioz called 'the penetrating intensity of melodic expression' of Elena's music.

As Monforte, the work's most interesting character, Zancanaro is equally impressive. His aria, when he realises his predicament as father of a sworn enemy, is sung with the refinement of tone and line and varied dynamics that enhance the strength of his firm baritone and his clarity of diction. He is just as excellent in the succeeding duet, where he reveals to Arrigo that he, Monforte, is his father. His acting is simple but effective. Arrigo is taken by the usually variable Merritt. Even here he doesn't completely convince as a Verdian tenor – tone a shade brittle, technique under pressure – but he delivers all his taxing music with such total conviction and belief in himself that criticism is silenced, and he rises to his high D in Act 5 with confidence. It is not his fault that this Arrigo looks of an age with his father.

Furlanetto's delivery has the advantage, of course, of being Italian and he knows how the music of Procida, leader of the Sicilians, should go, but his voice is not steady or imposing enough to do Verdi justice. Small parts are taken satisfactorily. All in all justice is done to Verdi's noble, innovative if sprawling work. Both video direction and sound recording are worthy of a notable performance that is unlikely to be equalled in the near future.

Simon Boccanegra
Kiri Te Kanawa (Maria Boccanegra/Amelia), Michael Sylvester (Gabriele), Alexander Agache (Boccanegra), Alan Opie (Paolo), Roberto Scandiuzzi (Fiesco). Chor and Orch of the Royal Opera House, Covent Garden/ Georg Solti. Dir: Elijah Moshinsky; video dir: Brian Large. Decca 071 423–3; LD:−1. Subtitles.

Unsuccessful when first presented in 1857, *Boccanegra* was substantially revised by the composer (and the libretto re-drafted by Boito) in 1881 after Verdi had written *Aida* and the *Requiem*. The alterations are carefully melded with the original so that it is hard for anyone but a Verdi specialist to tell what was there originally, what is new. Even so the plot remains opaque, concerning the strife between the patricians, led by Jacopo Fiesco, and the plebeians led by sea-captain Simon Boccanegra in fourteenth-century Genoa. Fiesco's daughter Maria has given birth to a daughter by Boccanegra but dies in childbirth. Twenty-five years later the factions are reconciled when Boccanegra's lost daughter, also called Maria but known as Amelia, comes to light. The story is further complicated by the fact that Amelia is loved by the patrician Gabriele (and she returns his love) and by Paolo, Boccanegra's henchman. When Paolo is denied her hand at the moment when Boccanegra realises Amelia is his daughter, Paolo poisons the Doge. Out of this complex web, Verdi fashioned a dark-hued score that ably contrasts public and private passions, always one of his most sympathetic themes.

Large's video direction of Moshinsky's admirable staging for Covent Garden in 1991 catches the dour, dark mood of the work to perfection within Michael Yeargan's evocative sets, and Peter J. Hall's refined lighting (the same team responsible for the later *Stiffelio*, *qv*). This sensible backcloth allows Verdi's taut drama to unfold in Moshinsky's acute staging where the personal traumas and public feuds are faithfully delineated and executed by a committed cast.

Amelia has always been one of the best of Te Kanawa's roles. She suggests all the girl's innocent radiance both in her acting and singing which, on this night, is full-blooded, even and thoughtfully phrased. As Boccanegra, Agache moves easily through all aspects of this demanding role, and acts it magnificently. His expressive eyes tell us of the Doge's hopes, fears and love for his daughter, and in the Council Chamber scene he shows a dignity and power that dominate the disputants and the stage. He dies with poignant sadness in his tones.

As Boccanegra's antagonist, the formidable, Fiesco, Scandiuzzi evinces classic, *basso-cantante* tones, but in spite of careful make-up, he looks far too young for the role: in any case, it is one drawback to this production, the more noticeable on video, that none of the characters seem to age one jot between the Prologue, in which Boccanegra is acclaimed Doge by the people, and Act 1, although twenty-five years have elapsed. Scandiuzzi sings Fiesco's famous aria in the Prologue with long breath and vibrant tone, then he and Agache's Doge make their confrontations, in the Prologue and the final scene, the moments of superb music-drama they should be. As villain Paolo, Opie offers a keen portrait of a soured, frustrated man. Sylvester suggests all Gabriele's fiery, ardent temperament in his tautly shaped singing.

Solti offers a carefully crafted, well-prepared reading but one that is often stiff-limbed and lacking dramatic propulsion. He is always supportive of his singers and draws some subtle phrasing from the Covent Garden players. Sound and picture are of a high standard, worthy of this engrossing performance.

La forza del destino
1. Leontyne Price (Leonora), Isola Jones (Preziosilla), Giuseppe Giacomini (Alvaro), Leo Nucci (Carlo), Bonaldo Giaiotti (Padre Guardiano), Enrico Fissore (Melitone). Chor and Orch of Metropolitan Opera, New York/James Levine. Dir: John Dexter; video dir: Kirk Browning. DG VHS 072 427–3—1; LD—1.

2. Renata Tebaldi (Leonora), Oralia Dominguez (Preziosilla), Franco Corelli (Alvaro), Ettore Bastianini
(Carlo), Boris Christoff (Padre Guardiano), Renato
Capecchi (Melitone). Chor and Orch of Teatro di San
Carlo, Naples/Francesco Molinari-Pradelli. Legato Classics VHS LCV 0012.
3. Caterina Mancini (Leonora), Cloe Elmo (Preziosilla),
Galliano Masini (Alvaro), Tito Gobbi (Carlo), Giulio Neri
(Padre Guardiano), Vito De Taranto (Melitone). Chor
and Orch of the Rome Opera House/Gabriele Santini. A
film by Carmine Gallone. Pickwick VHS SL 10593.

As the title would suggest, coincidence and destiny play a
strong part in this sprawling but enthralling music-drama. A
blood feud causes an inevitable drift towards tragedy in
which two of the principals, Leonora and Don Carlo, sister
and brother, die. Leonora is killed by Carlo because of her
love for Don Alvaro, a half-caste who has accidentally killed
their father. Alvaro, forced by Carlo to fight for his honour
although he, Alvaro, has retreated to a monastery to avoid
conflict, slays Carlo who murders Leonora as he lies mortally
wounded. In their travels to this tragic dénouement, the principals are given solos and duets of moving character in
Verdi's most noble vein, which need a deal of singing.

The Met performance is on the whole a fair representation
of the piece. The 1984 revival of a production by Dexter is sensible, well lit and unobtrusive in its traditional way, not
attempting any radical re-interpretation. Browning is rather
too reliant on close-ups in his video direction. That is sometimes unkind to singers while they are trying to project their
voices to the furthermost part of a large house.

Those singers are by and large up to Verdi's exigent
demands on their resources. In one of her last stage appearances, Price understandably takes time to find her best form.
Once there she pours out rich tone with a Verdian sweep that
we have seldom heard since. Her acting is dignified rather
than compelling, but her few gestures are telling. One or two
clumsy phrases around the *passagio* apart, Giacomini is a rewarding Alvaro (though not in the Corelli class, see page 93).

He evinces breadth of phrase, security of tone, and confident attack while not omitting restrained touches as in the duets with Carlo.

Beside him Nucci sounds relatively coarse, belting out his music with an eye on the gallery, seldom moderating his forceful voice to the demands of Verdi's many dynamic markings. For all that, it is good to hear a Carlo who is truly Italianate in manner, likewise a Guardiano, the reliable if somewhat rusty Giaiotti, and a Melitone, the compact and amusing Fissore, in a similar mould. Isola Jones sounds as though she is doing her voice no favour by essaying a part as beefy as Preziosilla without the means to encompass it. Even so she makes her mark, looking every inch the sexy campfollower.

Levine has always enjoyed this score and he holds together its extended structure through sensibly related speeds, never allowing continuity to break, in spite of the insistent applause that greets every number. He is to be commended for respecting the composer by giving the score in its entirety. He is supported by shapely playing from the Met Orchestra. Picture and sound are exemplary.

That cannot be said of the two other, venerable performances. The first is however of historic importance. It enshrines a reading from the San Carlo in Naples dating from 1958 with a cast that can seldom have been bettered before and never since. Tebaldi had all the qualities that make a great Leonora: firm, expansive tone, long-breathed line and phrasing, perfect control of dynamics, sensitive feeling for the text. She combines these into an interpretation that confirms her standing as one of the century's leading Verdians and here, as ever in the theatre, she is much more involved than in the studio. Her acting may be limited but she does just enough to second her glorious singing. Corelli, still an underrated tenor, was, like his partner, in his absolute prime in 1958. His trumpet-like, fiery tenor is ideal for Alvaro, and he sings all his music with fearless, brilliant attack, and has the artistry to turn many a memorable phrase. He also looks every inch the tenor hero.

His baritone counterpart is Bastianini, whose macho voice was also an imposing instrument attuned to Verdi's needs.

Although not as sensitive as either Tebaldi or Corelli, he provides a deal of excitement, not least in his Act 3 solo, 'Urna fatale', and his voice blends well with Corelli's in their two duets (the important 'Sleale!' is sadly excised). Guardiano's profound utterances roll off Christoff's granite voice with consummate ease. Dominguez is a mezzo with the wherewithal to fulfil every demand of Preziosilla's music, although she looks a little elderly for *vivandière* duties. Capecchi is a witty Melitone. Molinari-Pradelli is a secure rather than exciting conductor: he hasn't the Verdian fire in his belly.

In this archive recording from Italian Radio and Television (RAI), the sound is more than good enough to judge the outstanding qualities of the singing, but the picture is so poor that the singers' features are often hard to discern, assuming an almost ghostly vagueness. The production is routine. But none of that matters given the importance of this interpretation as a record of the best of 1950s Verdian interpretation. Even at the high asking-price, those interested in great singing would be wrong to overlook it.

The 1949 film by Gallone is no more than a curiosity. Verdi's score is foreshortened, reordered and augmented, and a spoken commentary added in a forlorn attempt to make a swift, intelligible drama. The performances on the film, mostly by actors miming to singing voices, are laughably dated and the outdoor scenes unconvincing, a battle with a sheaf of extras excepted.

As ever, in such cases, there are vocal compensations. In the fourth and last of his participants in such projects, Gobbi sings and acts what remains of Don Carlo's role, curiously one he never attempted in the theatre, with his customary skill and directness of purpose. Masini, who recorded Alvaro with distinction in sound only a few years earlier, still has the authentic ring of a *tenore di forza*, a species now almost extinct. His part is acted, handsomely, by Gino Sinimberghi, himself a tenor, but of a much lighter kind. Mancini's firm, malleable singing as Leonora is mimed by a young actress, who looks out of her element in an operatic milieu.

Perhaps best of the soloists is the grand *basso cantante* of Neri, another kind of voice that seems almost a thing of the past; he is a distinguished Padre Guardiano. The Melitone, who retains much of his contribution, is a lively performer who never overdoes the visual jokes and sings the errant friar's role in a properly rotund tone. Santini is a correct rather than exciting conductor, but then he is burdened with the skeleton of what Verdi wrote. How could Italians have ever perpetrated this mauling of their greatest composer's music?

The film, at least on the copy under review, looks in need of careful restoration. The sound is, considering its age, not unacceptable. Worth sampling for most of the singing.

Don Carlos

1. Daniela Dessi (Elisabetta), Luciana D'Intino (Eboli), Luciano Pavarotti (Don Carlos), Paolo Coni (Rodrigo), Samuel Ramey (King Philip), Alexander Anisimov (Grand Inquisitor). Chor and Orch of La Scala, Milan/ Riccardo Muti. Dir and video dir: Franco Zeffirelli. EMI VHS MVB4 91134–3; LD: LDD4 91134—12. Subtitles.

2. Ileana Cotrubas (Elisabetta), Bruna Baglioni (Eboli), Luis Lima (Don Carlos), Giorgio Zancanaro (Rodrigo), Robert Lloyd (King Philip), Joseph Rouleau (Grand Inquisitor). Chor and Orch of the Royal Opera House, Covent Garden/Bernard Haitink. Dir: Luchino Visconti; video dir: Brian Large. Castle VHS CVI 2033. Subtitles.

3. Fiamma Izzo D'Amico (Elisabetta), Agnes Baltsa (Eboli), José Carreras (Don Carlos), Piero Cappuccilli (Rodrigo), Ferruccio Furlanetto (King Philip), Matti Salminen (Grand Inquisitor). Bulgarian National Chor, Vienna State Opera Chor, Salzburg Concert Chor, Berlin Philharmonic Orch/Herbert von Karajan. Dir: Karajan; video dir: Ernst Wild. Sony VHS S2HV 48312; LD S2LV 48312.

This lengthy work, originally written to a French libretto for the Paris Opéra but later revised in Italian form by the composer, has had a chequered and complex history during which it has been performed in various forms and in varying degrees of completeness. Verdi once again was presenting private tragedy in the midst of public tribulations. The conflicts between state and church, and the attempt by Flanders to free itself from the yoke of Spanish rule, are here the back-cloth for Queen Elisabeth's unhappy marriage to King Philip II of Spain, father of Don Carlos, whom she really loves and to whom she is at first betrothed. Further emotional complications involve the glamorous Princess Eboli, who secretly loves Carlos and has been seduced by the King. In the middle is Rodrigo, Marquis of Posa, friend of Carlos, later confidant of Philip. These travails are set in the context of the superstitious, claustrophobic world of the Spanish Inquisition, the sixth principal being the ninety-year-old Grand Inquisitor. Verdi's genius weaves all the strands into a coherent, compelling whole.

The opera really came into its own in the famous Visconti/Giulini staging of 1958 at Covent Garden which – though sung in Italian – restored the Fontainebleau Act at the beginning. It has been caught for posterity in the 1985 revival, worthy, but not as inspired, particularly as regards the conducting, as some of its predecessors. The other two versions opt for the four-act Italian version, although the 1986 Salzburg performance under Karajan cuts even that drastically. None of these interpretations is wholly satisfactory; each, even the Karajan, has something to commend it.

As a whole the 1992 Muti/Zeffirelli/La Scala must take pride of place mainly because Muti's conducting is so superior to that of his rivals. Those Italian attributes of energy, rhythmic vitality, quick emotions inform the whole reading, enhanced by a feeling for the particular *tinta* (colouring) of this score. Muti has rehearsed his players thoroughly and keeps them on a tight but never stifling rein. Under his direction the music remains consistently tense and alert in a manner the slacker-paced and more ruminative Haitink cannot match, let alone the aged and stiff-limbed Karajan.

Muti also has the advantage of four Italian principals (out of six), headed by the golden-voiced Pavarotti. The experiences of an unhappy *prima* behind him, he sings with his customary ardour, words perfectly on the voice, and exhibiting a line liquid and flowing. Moments such as Carlos's shame in the *auto-da-fé* scene and the tenderness of the final duet are beautifully caught, not least because Pavarotti is willing here to sing quietly. His girth makes him unconvincing as the small, lean, nervous Carlos of history, but he acts with his usual sincerity. By contrast Dessi looks the very image of the wronged, sympathetic Queen but sings with less than ideal steadiness. The timbre and style are right, the technique consistently under siege, spirit willing, flesh weak. Similarly Coni makes an upright, affecting Rodrigo, but under pressure his otherwise warm tone loses true focus as though he, like Dessi, were a shade overparted. On the other hand D'Intino, though fazed by the high cadenzas in the Veil Song, sings most of her role with the brio and attack it calls for, closing with a fearless assault on 'O don fatale' that never descends into melodramatics, and she acts with a deal of credibility.

Ramey is not a mighty-voiced Philip II, but the well-contained focus of his bass is appropriate to Muti's sharply etched performance. He doesn't always probe below the surface to Philip's inner torment: this is a man of action not anguish. Anisimov is a rather ordinary Inquisitor, not frightening enough. The smaller parts are carefully cast, acutely sung.

Zeffirelli's staging is orthodox, evoking the atmosphere of threat and religious bigotry in its dark-hued sets (hard to light for video) and shafts of ceremonial panoply, sacred and secular. It moves easily within the parameters of convention, but isn't as probing as Visconti's was all those years ago. The sound, especially on laserdisc, is astonishingly faithful to La Scala.

Visconti's achievement can still be discerned in the 1985 revival at Covent Garden. Though detail has to some degree lost focus, the rightness of the settings, the grandeur of the concept are still in place as rehearsed by Christopher Renshaw. The Fontainebleau forest is magically evoked, the interiors of San Juste and the Palace have lovely perspectives, Philip's gloomy study becomes even more doom-laden at the entrance of the Grand Inquisitor. Only the *auto-da-fé* looks a shade mingy.

As I have suggested, Haitink's conducting is extraordinarily lacklustre; some scenes seem very long indeed when the rhythmic pulse is so loose. Nor is the playing or choral singing in the class of La Scala. Lima's portrait of Carlos is true to history, presenting him as a neurotic, prone to fits and generally unstable, yet not without Latin charm. Although the voice wants heroic bite at climaxes, and pitch is sometimes a problem, the timbre is right, plaintive and keen-edged. Besides him Zancanaro sings, as ever, with such a firmly delineated line and tone that his occasionally perfunctory acting is quite forgiven: the feeling is all there in the voice. Cotrubas, as was her wont in every one of her roles, suggests appealing vulnerability, a small, forlorn figure of an Elisabeth quite lost in the gloomy caverns of the court. Her voice is a size too small for the part and comes under strain at the top, but many phrases are memorably implanted in the ear and mind.

Lloyd is so keen to project Philip as a Boris-like figure of cares and fear that his king becomes a bit of a caricature. His singing is sensitive but too soft-grained. Rouleau, even with a voice rusting at the edges, remains a frightening Inquisitor with eyes that burn the soul. Smaller parts are no more than adequately sung. The picture and sound are no better than average.

Karajan oughtn't to be your first choice. Alternately limp and overdriven conducting from the grey, tired figure in the pit and Karajan's own, boring production fatally lame the work. Furlanetto is an unsteady, too young Philip. The compensations include an Elisabeth from Izzo D'Amico notable for strong, incisive tone and a sense of Verdian phrasing, nowhere more evident than in 'Tu che le vanità', Elisabeth's long aria of reminiscence in Act 5. Baltsa's Eboli combines dramatic insights with some well-contoured and exciting vocalisation. Cappuccilli, with bags under his eyes and five o'clock shadow on his chin, hardly looks the youthful Posa of Verdi's imagining, but he sings with his old strength and long breath. Salminen makes surprisingly little of the Inquisitor.

The video direction isn't always as prompt as it should be and the sound picture catches too much of the cavernous nature of the Grosses Festspielhaus.

Aida

1. Maria Chiara (Aida), Fiorenza Cossotto (Amneris), Nicola Martinucci (Radames), Giuseppe Scandola

(Amonasro), Carlo Zardo (Ramphis), Alfredo Zanazzo (King). Opera Chor and Orch of Verona Arena/Anton Guadagno. Dir: Giancarlo Sbragia; video dir: Brian Large. Castle VHS CVI 2014. Subtitles.

2. Aprile Millo (Aida), Dolora Zajick (Amneris), Placido Domingo (Radames), Sherrill Milnes (Amonasro), Paata Burchuladze (Ramphis), Dimitri Kavrakos (King). Chor and Orch of Metropolitan Opera, New York/James Levine. Dir: Sonja Frisell; video dir: Brian Large. DG VHS 072 416–3; LD:−1.

3. Maria Chiara (Aida), Ghena Dimitrova (Amneris), Luciano Pavarotti (Radames), Juan Pons (Amonasro), Nicolai Ghiaurov (Ramphis), Paata Burchuladze (King). Chor and Orch of La Scala, Milan/Lorin Maazel. Dir: Luca Ronconi; video dir: Derek Bailey. Virgin VHS VVD 3782.

4. Herva Nelli (Aida), Eva Gustavson (Amneris), Richard Tucker (Radames), Giuseppe Valdengo (Amonasro), Norman Scott (Ramphis), Dennis Harbour (King). Robert Shaw Chorale, NBC Symphony Orch/Arturo Toscanini. RCA VHS 790 346; LD 780 346.

Aida, daughter of the Ethiopian ruler Amonasro, is a slave of the conquering Egyptians. She is in love with Radames, Captain of the Egyptian guard. He is also loved by Amneris, princess-daughter of the Egyptian King and she is wildly jealous of his love for Aida. Once again there is ample opportunity for Verdi to display his gifts for projecting human emotions on a larger canvas, here a war between Egypt and its Ethiopian neighbours. The scene at the end of Act 2 is Verdi at his most grand and extrovert, complete with marches and ballet. Always stirring the senses, it has made the opera a great favourite for both indoor performances and outdoor ones, when large sets and seemingly endless cohorts of soldiers can be deployed. However the heart of Verdi's score lies in the varying and contrasted dialogues among the main characters in which emotional tension is to the fore.

The work takes a deal of conducting and singing. These demands are not consistently met on these video versions, although the performance from the Verona Arena in 1981 comes close to fulfilling all Verdi's requirements. The all-Italian cast naturally enough brings to the singers' declamation an authentic sound not heard throughout the rival sets. Chiara, who appears to greater advantage here than five years later in Milan, looks the part, acts with dignity, sings with sovereign phrasing and fine-limned tone: *piano* effects are almost all ravishing. No wonder the large audience capitulates to her. Cossotto was for some twenty years reigning Amneris here – and indeed elsewhere. Her reading was caught just before her voice started to decline and she projects grand, imperious sound in a grand, imperious reading, a shade shy in matter of quiet singing. She brings down the house – rightly – at the close of the judgment scene.

Martinucci, macho in looks with heroic tenor to match, sings Radames with inspiriting élan, and duets impressively with his Aida and Amneris. Scandola, a great bear of an Amonasro, offers a baritone of truly Verdian weight unusual today. The basses singing Ramphis and the King might with advantage have exchanged roles, as the former, the more important part, is poorly sung. Chorus and orchestra respond willingly to Guadagno's lively and direct conducting, one of the performance's most telling assets.

The production was new the previous season at Verona. Vittorio Rossi, designing his third *Aida* for the huge Arena, creates memorable stage pictures, including a *coup de théâtre* in the triumphal scene that provokes spontaneous applause. Eight bulwarks twenty metres up along the lip of the Arena, two obelisks at stage level and a versatile set of pyramid and wedge shapes centre-stage, subtly lit, provide an imaginative yet, given the venue, surprisingly economical framework for the action – only 150 rather than the customary 600 personnel were apparently employed. The director Sbragia handles principals and chorus skilfully, the choreography is stylish and in character, and Large has done his appreciable best to catch everything on video.

All this makes a startling contrast with the empty glitz and gold on display at the Met in 1989. Piling Pelion on Ossa, Frisell succeeds only in dissipating the work's true nature in conspicuous show for its own sake, although it has to be said that the finale with the Met's two stages used to show the incarcerated Aida and Radames below a temple rite on the upper stage is mightily impressive. The costumes are risible, the ballet uninventive.

The singers seem on the whole to be running through routine interpretations. Millo knows how Aida's music should sound and sings with a deal of Verdian refinement when her vibrato isn't too intrusive. Her acting is from stock, and none too good stock at that. Domingo, obviously in strained voice, is a surprisingly ordinary Radames at least until the last two acts when he evinces more style and feeling. Zajick offers the scale and drive of a true Amneris, but of facial expression there is none. Milnes still looks a fiery, upright Amonasro, but his baritone is now forced and dry. The basses are, if anything, more dire. Levine's conducting is predictably heavy-handed with a bass-loud orchestra to boot.

The 1985 staging at La Scala by Ronconi attempts, none too successfully, a fresh look at the piece. A mobile, flexible Egypt arises from the bowels of the earth as if it had just been brought to light. Interior scenes, such as Amneris's apartments, are a rethinking of the orientalism in the style of Alma-Tadema. The triumph scene suggests a film montage of ruined sphinxes and historical ghosts of the past, rather a mess; the ballet is unconvincing. The Nile scene features a reed boat.

Maazel's conducting is perfunctory and inflexible. Chiara, as already suggested, is not as happy or convincing as at Verona. Dimitrova, an Aida, is miscast as Amneris; Pons is no more than an efficient Amonasro. Which leaves Pavarotti, looking ridiculous in a Pyramid-like dress. His singing is, as ever, ardent, well phrased and committed even if his basically lyric voice is here asked to go beyond its natural capability.

The Toscanini film of a 1949 concert is an invaluable record, in the general sense, of him as a conductor. It is fascinating to watch his mastery over singers and players, and to note his taut command of a work in which he made his debut as a conductor. Indeed his unflagging control of tempi and his masterly shaping of the whole should be followed by his contemporary successors, but seldom is.

None of the singers is exactly ideal and most looked scared, as well they might, of the elderly maestro. The best of them is

Valdengo, whose incisive baritone and innate sense of firm characterisation is an object-lesson in Verdian style under Toscanini's inspired tutelage. Nelli, a favourite with Toscanini in every sense, is a soft-grained Aida but one with surprising reserves of power. As Radames, the young Tucker has the vocal means for the part but is a wooden interpreter. Gustavson at least attempts to act out her role, even if the results are a shade embarrassing. She sings no more than adequately. The Shaw choir contributes strongly. But how wonderful it would have been to have heard and seen Toscanini conduct the work with one of his notable casts at La Scala in the 1920s, an opportunity missed.

The sound is reasonable, the camerawork rudimentary; as a historical document this is still of immense value.

Avoid the 1994 Covent Garden performance, now on video. It is inadequately staged and D'Intino's Amneris apart, indifferently sung.

Otello

1. Kiri Te Kanawa (Desdemona), Claire Powell (Emilia), Placido Domingo (Otello), Robin Leggate (Cassio), Ramon Remedios (Roderigo), Sergei Leiferkus (Iago), Roderick Earle (Montano), Mark Beesley (Lodovico). Chor and Orch of the Royal Opera House, Covent Garden/Georg Solti. Dir: Elijah Moshinsky; video dir: Brian Large. Castle VHS CVI 1718; Pioneer LD: PLMCC 00851. Subtitles.

2. Mirella Freni (Desdemona), Stefania Malagù (Emilia), Jon Vickers (Otello), Aldo Bottion (Cassio), Michel Sénéchal (Roderigo), Peter Glossop (Iago), Mario Macchi (Montano), José Van Dam (Lodovico). Chor of Deutsche Oper, Berlin, Berlin Philharmonic Orch/Herbert von Karajan. A film directed by Karajan. DG VHS 072 401–3; LD:−1.

3. Kiri Te Kanawa (Desdemona), Flora Raffanelli (Emilia), Vladimir Atlantov (Otello), Antonio Bevacqua (Cassio), Adriano Schiavon (Roderigo), Piero Cappuccilli (Iago), Orazio Mori (Montano), Gianfranco Casarini (Lodovico). Chor and Orch of Verona Arena/Zoltan

Pesko. Dir: Gianfranco de Bosio; video dir: Preben Montell. Castle VHS CVI 2025. Subtitles.

Verdi's penultimate opera is the culmination of his lifelong fascination with Shakespeare. Having at last found a librettist (Arrigo Boito, himself a composer, *qv*) to his way of thinking, one who could turn a long play into a taut libretto (3,000 lines reduced to 800), Verdi in his full maturity set it to music with a new-found mastery of free structure. Melody, rhythm and harmony are carefully combined to make one of the most direct, compelling scores ever penned for the stage. Verdi places inordinate demands on his conductor and on his principals, who must be actors with commanding voices.

Of the three available performances, that filmed at Covent Garden in 1992 is far and away the most significant. Timothy O'Brien's scenery is aptly Italianate in flavour with rich yet sombre colourings and impressive columns. Within, Moshinsky directs his principals and chorus alike with impressive naturalism. The crowd scenes look convincing; the relationships between the characters are boldly delineated without ever stepping over into artificality. With Large managing to capture almost everything of importance and keenly focused camerawork, this is an object lesson in how to film a live occasion for the home.

Solti's conducting, in his eighties, may not be as visceral as it ought to be, and he is inclined to extremes of slow and quick tempi, but he is responsive to the changing mood of the drama, draws good playing from the ROH Orchestra, and supports his singers alertly.

The most important reason for acquiring this video is Domingo's comprehensive reading of the title part, possibly his best role, one that he has made very much his own. He encompasses every facet of the Moor's temperament: deep love for Desdemona, incipient, then overpowering jealousy and final tragedy. Facial expression and body language second his tense, confident singing. The lyrical impulse of his singing is compensation enough for any want of heroic ring in his voice, and his long phrasing fulfils Verdi's demands. The sheer honest strength and agonised force of the portrayal are unforgettable.

He forms an ideal partnership with Leiferkus's wholly plausible Iago, a man with an evil mission who disguises it with subtle wiles. His diction is as incisive and meaningful as one could wish; only Italianate warmth of tone is missing in his very Russian baritone. Te Kanawa's Desdemona remains warmly and evenly sung. Some of the lustre in her tone and the spontaneity of her acting ten years earlier (see page 105) has been lost, but all is forgiven in her deeply tender, touching account of her Act 4 Willow Song and Ave Maria. Powell's Emilia, Leggate's Cassio and Remedios's Roderigo are well acted and sung, completing pleasure in a well-prepared and riveting interpretation.

The Karajan film of 1974 derives from the production, also by Karajan, then current at the Salzburg Festival. That was an exciting event, but somewhere along the way to the studio/location, the spontaneity of the performance has been lost. All the acting looks artificial and/or stilted. Old-fashioned costumes and make-up jar with the attempt to open out the action. The lip-synch is crude. Something remains of Vickers's towering Otello, a great man struck down by a fatal flaw, also one who stretches to extremes of tenderness and cruelty not quite touched even by Domingo. He sings in raw, forceful tones that strike to the heart of the matter, not an easily appreciated reading but one with its own validity. Glossop makes a credible Iago, and sings a suave, insinuating account of the part, a fair souvenir of his forgotten art. Freni is a sweet-voiced appealing Desdemona, phrasing with gratefully idiomatic style. The supporting cast is nothing special.

Karajan's interpretation is no match for his earlier sound-only recording, now on Decca CD. The Berlin Philharmonic offers rather a thick sound and the Berlin Chorus aren't very convincing. The sound quality is superior on laserdisc.

The staging at Verona in 1982 is notable for Vittorio Rossi's handsome sets. On the higher steps a Crusader castle is suggested. At stage level, two structures revolve to show towers, great hall, bedroom. Projections complete the illusion. De Bosio's handling of the drama is often unimaginative but he does produce a colourfully impressive tableau for the big ensemble in Act 3 (this has a chunk excised from it, a practice followed by Karajan but not at Covent Garden, thank goodness).

As Otello, Atlantov seems at first to have only one fixed expression at his disposal, but gradually the impression of a noble but rather simple man destroyed by jealousy begins to strike home, and in some ways his is the most credible Otello of all because this Otello is so obviously an honest, upright general. Again his singing begins by being merely effective in a rudimentary way – plenty of stamina, a clarion-like delivery, firm verbal accents – but in the third act, his Otello evinces the torment within. When he throws down his beloved Desdemona before the assembled crowd, it is as a man driven, tragically, to the deed. In Act 4 the contrast between implacable fury and despair, when he realises he has been hoodwinked, is deeply moving. This isn't as intelligent or carefully thought-out an Otello as those of Domingo and Vickers, but in its own way just as formidable.

Te Kanawa also takes time to come into her own. Hampered by a totally unbelievable wig of blonde curls, she looks and sings in a blank way until Act 3. Then as her Otello gains in dramatic stature she does the same. As always, the Willow song and Ave Maria are the fitting climax of her portrayal, but the audience ruin the latter by breaking in with applause during its final phrase. Cappuccilli offers his well-known Iago, a bluff, forcefully sung interpretation, telling in the wide open spaces of Verona. Pesko conducts an under-characterised reading, not helped by an unusually backward recording of the orchestra. In sum perhaps the subtleties of *Otello* are not best encountered at Verona, but enough excitement is engendered to make one overlook some absence of refinement in this performance all round.

The film directed by Zeffirelli, which mauls the score, isn't at present available. In any case Domingo's Moor is more successfully preserved on stage at Covent Garden.

Falstaff
1. Katia Ricciarelli (Alice Ford), Barbara Hendricks (Nannetta), Brenda Boozer (Meg Page), Lucia Valentini-Terrani (Mistress Quickly), Dalmacio Gonzalez (Fenton), John Dobson (Dr Caius), Francis Egerton (Bardolfo), Leo Nucci (Ford), Renato Bruson (Falstaff), William Wilderman (Pistol). Chor and Orch of the Royal

Opera House, Covent Garden/Carlo Maria Giulini. Dir: Ronald Eyre; video dir: Brian Large. Castle VHS CVI 2001. Subtitles.

2. Karan Armstrong (Alice Ford), Jutta Renate Ihloff (Nannetta), Sylvia Lindenstrand (Meg Page), Marta Szirmay (Mistress Quickly), Max-René Cosotti (Fenton), John Lanigan (Dr Caius), Peter Maus (Bardolfo), Richard Stilwell (Ford), Gabriel Bacquier (Falstaff), Ulrik Cold (Pistol). Chor of Deutsche Oper, Berlin, Vienna Philharmonic Orch/Georg Solti. A film by Götz Friedrich. Decca VHS 071 403–3; LD:−1.

3. Kay Griffel (Alice Ford), Elizabeth Gale (Nannetta), Reni Penkova (Meg Page), Nucci Condò (Mistress Quickly), Max-René Cosotti (Fenton), John Fryatt (Dr Caius), Bernard Dickerson (Bardolfo), Benjamin Luxon (Ford), Donald Gramm (Falstaff), Ugo Trama (Pistol). Glyndebourne Chorus, London Philharmonic Orch/ John Pritchard. Dir: Jean-Pierre Ponnelle; video dir: David Heather. Pickwick VHS SLL 7014. Subtitles.

4. Raina Kabaivanska (Alice Ford), Janet Perry (Nannetta), Trudeliese Schmidt (Meg Page), Christa Ludwig (Mistress Quickly), Francisco Araiza (Fenton), Piero De Palma (Dr Caius), Heinz Zednik (Bardolfo), Rolando Panerai (Ford), Giuseppe Taddei (Falstaff), Federico Davià (Pistol). Vienna State Opera Chor, Vienna Philharmonic Orch/Herbert von Karajan. Dir: Karajan; video dir: Ernst Wild. Sony VHS SHV 48422; LD: S2LV48422.

5. Mirella Freni (Alice Ford), Barbara Bonney (Nannetta), Susan Graham (Meg Page), Marilyn Horne (Mistress Quickly), Frank Lopardo (Fenton), Piero De Palma (Dr Caius), Anthony Laciura (Bardolfo), Bruno Pola (Ford), Paul Plishka (Falstaff), James Courtney (Pistol). Chor and Orch of Metropolitan Opera, New York/James Levine. DG VHS 072 434−3; LD:−1.

Verdi, collaborating again with Boito on an adaptation of Shakespeare, once more produced a masterpiece. His last opera, writtten when he was already in his eighties, is a miracle of deftly woven comedy achieved by the most economical of means, using swift-moving action, complex ensembles, the many melodies now woven into a through-composed, seamless texture. It is only right that such a perfect work should be so worthily and generously represented on video.

Pride of place must go to the joint Covent Garden/Los Angeles staging of 1983, conducted by Giulini, which is a profoundly satisfying experience on all sides. Eyre, a notable director of Shakespeare in the theatre, here brought all his skills in that field into the opera house so that for once the work is not treated merely as a comic romp but as warm, very human comedy, matching the inspiration of playwright and composer.

The subtlety of Boito's libretto and Verdi's score is rewarded with a detailed, carefully delineated staging that presents us with a believable Windsor, sets and costumes exactly right, peopled by equally believable characters. None is more intelligently enacted than Bruson's classic Fat Knight. Wholly eschewing the traditional japes attempted by most interpreters, he paints a portrait of an old codger, noble in lineage, who is quite credible as an elderly lover. His is a rueful, even cynical old soldier with perhaps a touch of Quixote about him, remaining dignified even in his most ludicrous moments, sorrowful when he comes a cropper, a real person, not a mere butt for the amusement of others. Nor is there anything in Bruson's singing of the usual nudge or wink, or indeed fudging of the vocal line practised by ageing baritones. Here is an artist in the plenitude of his powers singing with mellow resonance and a naturally delivered, true line.

Ricciarelli, looking a credibly seductive Alice Ford, recovers from a somewhat uncertain, swoopy start, in vocal terms, to fulfil expectation, most of all in her naughty staccato scheming in Acts 3 and 4. Boozer's Meg is an acceptable fellow conspirator. Valentini-Terrani is a vital Quickly, using her eyes to great effect and singing with clear diction. Nucci's voice may be a shade light for Ford, but he presents a nice portrait of a puzzled, then jealous husband. Hendricks is a charming Nannetta but her singing is sometimes on the pinched side especially beside Gonzales's personable, mellifluous Fenton. The minor characters are well done.

Over all presides Giulini as a wise, well-seasoned interpreter, who knows the value of understatement, or rather letting Verdi speak for himself. He unfolds the score surely, carefully as an autumnal comedy with the finest shades of amber in its colouring. The special mood of each act is unerringly delineated, the first rumbustious, the second mercurial, the third mysterious, nocturnal, the fourth fantastic – in the literal sense. Again and again Giulini makes one think of the *originality* and wondrous detail of this score. The sound is faithful to the Covent Garden acoustic and Large catches most of the lived-in feeling of the performance.

Friedrich's film conducted, in typically sprightly fashion, by Solti takes the piece away from the proscenium arch in a way familiar from Ponnelle's many efforts (see *passim*). As such it is highly diverting. The action is almost balletic in its ceaseless movement, and includes scene-setting episodes without music before each act. It would be impossible for singers to perform while acting so furiously as lip-synch is, of course, employed. Not all the effects come off in this rather too frenetic effort but a lively mind is always at work.

Bacquier has some visual counterpart for practically every syllable of his part, and being the notable singing-actor he is, they are all intelligently thought out and done with such conviction as to be on the whole convincing. As this Falstaff's paunch is ridiculously large, Friedrich makes much of his immobility. Bacquier's singing is rich-hued and generously pointed. Stilwell manages his Fontana disguise as well as anyone and conveys all the distress of Ford's big outburst. Armstrong leads the merry wives almost too youthfully with a sensual touch that makes Falstaff's lust the more understandable, as does Lindenstrand's insinuating Meg. Szirmay is a fruity, slightly unidiomatic Quickly, Ihloff a visually and vocally delectable Nannetta and Cosotti a sweet-voiced, Italianate Fenton.

We are back in the theatre for the other three versions, of which the 1977 Glyndebourne staging by Ponnelle (for once caught working in the theatre rather than on film) is easily the most satisfying. It's a typical example of Glyndebourne ensemble at its best, full of exuberant high spirits youthfully employed. Ponnelle's decor and staging teems with fruitful ideas, as might be expected of that inventive director, for the most part serving the drama and music as Boito and Verdi projected it. Only the annoying presence of a facetiously directed boy and the addition of Master Page as a silent character who can never get his word in seem questionable. Admittedly there isn't the depth of characterisation or all the genuine feeling Eyre brings to the work, but the high spirits on all sides, the detailed management of the Act 2 finale and the serious treatment of Ford's monologue are all to Ponnelle's credit. His sets bring us a distant view of Windsor and of idealised green fields while indoors all is cosily correct.

Gramm is a true *cavaliere* of a Falstaff: we can tell that this man is an idealist *manqué* with a natural dignity of manner and singing. Griffel is a tall, merry Alice, Penkova a vivid Meg, Condò a younger than usual Quickly – all the better for it – who fairly bristles with high spirits. Gale is a somewhat thin-voiced Nannetta, Cosotti again a near-ideal Fenton. Their love-making in Act 1 silhouetted behind sheets is a masterstroke. Dickerson and Trama make a rascally pair as Bardolph and Pistol. Pritchard's reputation is well served by his prompt, well-paced account of the score. The mono sound is adequate, the video direction excellent. This is another performance that serves as a historical reminder of the old, intimate theatre, now gone for ever.

The carelessly made Salzburg version is not one of Sony's happier efforts in visual terms, but the aural recording is fine. The decor is dully traditional, Karajan's own stage direction is mildly entertaining but too often wanting in humour that comes from within, while the aged maestro's conducting is slow and over-studied, particularly when compared with his old EMI sound-only set. Taddei is very much the famous baritone giving *his* reading, a jovial one in a generalised way as far as acting is concerned. The interest comes from his authentic, classic account of his vocal part: indeed he acts with his voice rather than his body, which brings its own rewards in terms of subtle nuance. That is further emphasised when he partners Panerai's Ford in the Garter Inn duet: two seasoned Italians baritones making the most of this superbly written encounter.

Kabaivanska sings a likable, full-bodied Alice but misses the naughty humour of the scene with Falstaff. Ludwig is miscast as Quickly, altogether too Viennese. Perry is a pale Nannetta, Araiza a bland Fenton. This set is only worthwhile as a souvenir of Taddei's and Panerai's considerable art.

The latest version, taken from the Met in 1993, has almost nothing to commend it. Little remains of the detail of Zeffirelli's admired 1965 staging except the obvious mugging and pratfalls. Levine conducts heavily. Plishka hasn't the voice for Falstaff. Pola is a coarse, negative Ford. Freni is frankly too old for Alice. Horne plays herself as Quickly. Which leaves Bonney's delightful Nannetta, Lopardo's stylish Fenton and Graham's charming Meg to console us, plus the veteran De Palma singing as if he were half his age, as Dr Caius. Large's thoughtful video direction is wasted on such a paltry, tired staging, as is DG's lovely sound picture.

Richard Wagner (1813–83)

Der fliegende Holländer

1. Lisbeth Balslev (Senta), Anny Schlemm (Mary), Robert Schunk (Erik), Graham Clark (Steersman), Simon Estes (Dutchman), Matti Salminen (Daland). Chor and Orch of Bayreuth Festival/Woldemar Nelsson. Dir: Harry Kupfer; video dir: Brian Large. Philips VHS 070 406–3; LD:−1. Subtitles.

2. Hildegard Behrens (Senta), Anita Välkki (Mary), Raimo Sirkiä (Erik), Jorma Silvasti (Steersman), Franz Grundheber (Dutchman), Matti Salminen (Daland). Chor and Orch of Savonlinna Opera Festival/Leif Segerstam. Dir: Ilkka Bäckman; video dir: Aarno Cronvall. Teldec VHS 9031–71486–3; LD:−6.

3. Julia Varady (Senta), Anny Schlemm (Mary), Peter Seiffert (Erik), Ulrich Ress (Steersman), Robert Hale (Dutchman), Jaakko Ryhänen (Daland). Chor and Orch of Bavarian State Opera/Wolfgang Sawallisch. Dir: Henning von Gierke; video dir: Eckhart Schmidt. EMI VHS 99 1311–3; LD:−1. Subtitles.

Wagner turned to the legend of the tortured Dutchman sailing the seven seas in search of redemption after he had endured a stormy crossing of the North Sea, which can be said to blow through every bar of this revolutionary work, the first in which Wagner's new kind of music-drama took wing. From the superb overture onwards the music is imbued with a force till then unknown in opera. Although a few passages refer back to the conventions of *Singspiel*, they are forgiven in face of the music for the central pair, depicting the obsession of Senta with the legendary figure of the Dutchman she knows only from a portrait, and the desperation of the doomed hero as he seeks redemption through her love. At the same time bluff, greedy Daland and rejected Erik are clearly delineated and the music for the chorus breaks new bounds.

All three videos derive from stage productions, respectively Bayreuth 1985, Savonlinna 1989 and Munich 1992, although the first was made without an audience present. They present strikingly contrasted views of the work. Kupfer's staging for Bayreuth, which survived from 1978 until 1985, is a radical reinterpretation in which Senta, a hypersensitive, hysterical girl, stands at the centre of the drama, on stage from the beginning when she is seen clutching the portrait to her and almost raping it. It is her version of the tormented Dutchman we see, even to the employment of a double during the Act 2 duet to indicate that Senta's ideal is different from the reality. The end, where the enclosed society ignores her death and puts up its collective shutters is an odd gloss on Wagner and smacks of sensationalism. It accords with the use of the original abrupt ending. Elsewhere the Dutchman's red-sailed ship, which splits apart to reveal a black Dutchman chained to a cross, is an astonishing image, but some of Kupfer's ideas are less convincing.

The cast had performed together for thirty-six performances, so there is an all-embracing conviction to the reading, giving the 'heady sensation of total theatre' as the German notewriter avers. Estes delivers the title role with complete commitment, allied to a big, serviceable though not very individual voice. Although the cameras reveal Balslev as a shade mature for her role, and her voice loses focus under pressure, she gives a thrillingly vital account of Senta's part. Salminen boldly enacts Kupfer's view of Daland as a grasping old sailor. Schunk's well-controlled *Heldentenor* manages Erik's awkward, ungrateful music with unusual accuracy and bite. Clark is a perky sailor.

Large manages a number of superimpositions for the Dutchman's ship and so on to further Kupfer's aims. More of the same is to be seen in Cronvall's filming of Bäckmann's traditional production on Savonlinna's open-air stage in front of the ancient, imposing Olavinlinna castle with, for instance, the ghost ship outlined in white dissolving into its stage counterpart. The sets tend to be rudimentary, a platform on which are placed the minimum of props. The Dutchman's ship is represented by a ghostly hulk. Although something of the breadth of the staging has been lost, it is good to see the singers' locks waving in the prevailing breeze conveying the relevant sense of the sea. By and large the pictures aren't as well defined as at Bayreuth.

Segerstam's interpretation isn't as disciplined as Nelsson's at Bayreuth, but it is even more direct and vital. Where Savonlinna scores is in its casting of the main parts. Grundheber has just the right weight of tone for the Dutchman, and uses it to expressive advantage. The words mean so much to him – and to Behrens as his Senta. At first you may be troubled by her mature appearance and by her wobble in Senta's visionary Ballad, but once she gets into her stride, she is a striking exponent of the part, using eyes and body to convey Senta's fatal attraction. The look she gives the Dutchman when she first meets him and his desperate, hungry response convey the essence of the piece more than any stage gimmickry, and in the ensuing duet they translate their feelings in vocal terms closely fashioned to the inward music of this haunting encounter. Here, in the context of a live performance, we are surely in the presence of music-drama as Wagner first conceived it.

Salminen is if possible even more effective as the rough seaman Wagner intended Daland to be than as Kupfer's unsympathetic captain. The local tenors, good to look at, are no more than adequate vocally, although Silvasti's seaman shows a promise he has since fulfilled. On the other hand the local chorus is a match for its Bayreuth counterpart.

On the Munich set, Hale is more than the equal of Grund-heber as the Dutchman, firm in tone and line, the text ideally articulated. Beside him Varady combines the attributes of her rivals on the other versions and has none of their drawbacks in her keenly focused singing, exemplary in both style phrasing and single-minded acting. Focus and projection are here the key to an exemplary portrayal. To add to the vocal advantages here, Seiffert is a superior Erik, one who encompasses the high-lying tessitura and the role's need for fluent singing with apparent ease, and possessing the heroic tone to go with his other attributes. The massive-voiced, Finnish Daland and the youthful seaman need help with their characterisations not provided by the young producer, von Gierke, a designer turned director.

His own decor is a pleasing enough frame for the action, but lacks any strong sense of place or concept, but the seascapes viewed during the overture make their mark and the ocean is also suggested by swaying motion. Within them von Gierke does little more than place the singers strategically and let them fend for themselves, which the three main principals manage admirably, but most of the work's scenic coups, such as the arrival of the Dutchman's ship, his first appearance, the ghost sailors' frightening intervention in Act 3 and the closing apotheosis find him, if you'll forgive the metaphor, at sea.

In spite of these strictures, the performance is carried by Hale, Varady and Seiffert, who play out their own dramas. You won't find here the very personal and dedicated force of Kupfer's riveting production nor the atmospheric feel of the Savonlinna reading, but you will hear the best musical performance, for Munich's ace is Sawallisch, whose command of the score is unrivalled, a conductor who conveys his knowledge of the music to his eager and well-trained players; together they give the tautest of all these three interpretations: in the perfect acoustics of Munich's Nationaltheater, the urge and sway of sea and emotions, the inner workings of the score, are fully encompassed.

Tannhäuser
1. Gwyneth Jones (Elisabeth/Venus), Spas Wenkoff (Tannhäuser), Bernd Weikl (Wolfram), Hans Sotin

(Landgrave). Chor and Orch of Bayreuth Festival/Colin Davis. Dir: Götz Friedrich; video dir: Thomas Olofsson. Philips VHS 070 412–3; LD:—1.

2. Cheryl Studer (Elisabeth), Ruthild Engert-Ely (Venus), Richard Versalle (Tannhäuser), Wolfgang Brendel (Wolfram), Hans Sotin (Landgrave). Chor and Orch of Bayreuth Festival/Giuseppe Sinopoli. Dir: Wolfgang Wagner; video dir: Brian Large. Philips VHS 070 435–3; LD:—1.

To an extent this work, concerning the medieval minstrel-knight of the title torn between the delights of profane love offered by Venus and the pure love of Elisabeth, is a throw-back to more conventional opera. Many of the situations and some of the music are reminiscent of Parisian grand opera of the day, but the third act shows sustained inspiration, sheerly Wagnerian in form, that foretells the works of the composer's maturity. It exists in two forms, the Dresden original, tauter than the longer Paris version which has an ex-panded Venusberg scene.

Both videos stem from the Bayreuth Festival, the first a Friedrich staging of 1978, the second a Wolfgang Wagner pro-duction of 1989. In every way the former is superior to the latter. The stage of duckboards shaped in a triangle obviously refers to Tannhäuser and his two opposed women. At the song contest, the accompanying harp evidently operates itself, perhaps on Autoharp. The video direction concentrates on close-ups, each principal seen expressing his or her in-timate emotions. During the overture we see Tannhäuser full-face, emoting urgently behind his harp's strings.

Friedrich presents Tannhäuser very much as the outsider fighting against one of the most self-satisfied, obviously uni-form and uniformed societies that could be imagined so that the long Act 2 set-pieces simply emphasise his isolation, their smugness. Venusberg, finely choreographed by John Neu-meier, is an overtly erotic place, super-sensual, justifying the Paris version though later this staging reverts to the Dresden alternatives. Alone of the conformists, Elisabeth perceives the knight's torment and suffers with him. Movement of the principals and chorus are ideally at one with Friedrich's concept. True music-drama is thus enacted.

Jones's doubling of Venus and Elisabeth is a convincing tour de force, her seductive, quivering sex-goddess succeeded by her ingenuous, faithful Elisabeth, whose suffering is graphically conveyed in Act 3, particularly as she drags herself offstage, a broken, dying figure. Jones is in untiring voice, though you have to cope with the beat in her tone and her habit of stretching up to a note, faults that have always marred her singing. Wenkoff is an intense, involved Tannhäuser, with the wherewithal, rare today or any day, to do justice to the role by virtue of firm tone, stylish phrasing and deep feeling, carrying out all Friedrich's vision of the part. Weikl sings Wolfram in a warm, easy manner and acts with due concern. Sotin's experienced, upright Landgrave and excellent subsidary knights complete a near-faultless cast.

Davis has always shown a penchant for this work, and he reveals both its internal and external elements, evincing a keen ear for sonority and balance, between voices and instruments and within the orchestra itself, while retaining an overview of the score. The sound recording catches all these advantages reasonably well.

By the side of that performance, the more recent staging is sadly disappointing. Wolfgang Wagner directs a bland, representational, neat but bloodless reading of his grandfather's work that dulls all its revolutionary features into the conventional and ordinary, unbelievably poor ballet included. The characters hardly seem to relate to each other so that interest is focused on generalities. The rostrum set of early postwar Bayreuth vintage here looks pretty pointless. There's pleasure to be had listening to Sinopoli's reading, which is taut and fiery, and the Festival's chorus and orchestra respond eagerly to his highly dramatic approach.

Studer's glorious, rich-hued singing as Elisabeth is the only redeeming feature of an indifferent cast and she projects much if not quite all of the character's inner feelings in her well-groomed singing. Versalle, who has an anonymous stage presence, sings the title role in a tenor ill-equipped for the severe task in hand. Brendel is a very ordinary Wolfram; Sotin has become a stolid Landgrave. Engert-Ely's Venus is another uninteresting portrayal. Even Large's experienced hand as video director can do little with such poor material.

Lohengrin

1. Cheryl Studer (Elsa), Gabriele Schnaut (Ortrud), Paul Frey (Lohengrin), Ekkehard Wlaschiha (Telramund), Eike Wilm Schulte (Herald), Manfred Schunk (King Henry). Chor and Orch of Bayreuth Festival/Peter Schneider. Dir: Werner Herzog; video dir: Brian Large. Philips VHS 070 436–3; LD:−1.

2. Karan Armstrong (Elsa), Elizabeth Connell (Ortrud), Peter Hofmann (Lohengrin), Leif Roar (Telramund), Bernd Weikl (Herald), Siegfried Vogel (King Henry). Chor and Orch of Bayreuth Festival/Woldemar Nelsson. Dir: Götz Friedrich; video dir: Brian Large. Philips 070 411–3; LD:−1.

3. Cheryl Studer (Elsa), Dunja Vejsovic (Ortrud), Placido Domingo (Lohengrin), Hartmut Welker (Telramund), Georg Tichy (Herald), Robert Lloyd (King Henry). Chor and Orch of Vienna State Opera/Claudio Abbado. Virgin VHS VVD 841; Pioneer LD PLMCD 000011.

Liszt conducted the premiere of this work at Weimar on 18 August 1850. Although Wagner had completed it exactly three years before that first night, personal vicissitudes had prevented an earlier performance. The story of the mysterious, anonymous knight of the title who comes to save Elsa from the false accusations of Friedrich von Telramund and his evil, envious wife Ortrud inspired the composer to the most lyrical of his scores, which probably accounts for the fact that it was for years his most popular work in Italy, sung in Italian translation. At the same time it shows further advances in Wagner's methods, especially his innovative probing of his characters' psychology, most notably that of the pure, dedicated but vulnerable Elsa, prey to the suggestive insinuations of Ortrud, who plants in Elsa's mind the seeds of doubt about her upright saviour. How can she marry, Ortrud asks, a man whose name and origins are un-known to her? After her wedding to Lohengrin she demands to know his name – and all is lost.

Film director Herzog's 1987 staging for Bayreuth, the video version dating from the 1991 revival, is an imaginative, thought-provoking recreation of the work's strange world. The snowy landscape for Act 1 is peopled with barbaric henchmen of King Henry and Telramund. Lohengrin arrives, an otherworldly figure breaking the prevailing gloom through an ice pack. Act 2 is set beside the River Scheldt re-presented by real water lapping the shore, which oddly evaporates in mid-act. Act 3 is situated on a bleak meadow with a rampant silver swan as the bridal bedhead. The close, with Elsa and Ortrud left alive, is an unconvincing gloss on the original, and the boy Gottfried wears allover tights and a harness of swan's wings. Lohengrin's sword has a corkscrew bend. But these quirky ideas only serve, paradoxically, to emphasise the illusion of a medieval, slightly menacing romance.

Vocally the performance is uneven. Studer suggests most of Elsa's possessed, visionary character and she sings the role in vibrant, impassioned vein. By her side Frey's Lohengrin sensitively sung, is a bit of a cipher. Wlaschiha's Telramund is a tremendous presence, and the baritone sings the role with all the biting diction and menacing tone it calls for. Schnaut delivers a sock-it-to-'em Ortrud more notable for edgy power than for subtlety of interpretation. Schunk sings boring old Henry's music with strength but not enough pro-file. Schulte is a model of a Herald, delivering his pronouncements in firm, ringing tone. Schneider's reading is thorough and confident but short on conveying the work's interior meaning. Choir and orchestra are superb.

Sound and picture are exemplary in definition, as they are, particularly on laserdisc, on the film of Friedrich's 1982 pro-duction for Bayreuth, another worthwhile view of the piece. Günther Uecker's sets offer a pattern of black squares pierced with silver studs, forming the background to most scenes and Large in his video direction defines them during the Prelude to Act 1. Forestage is a collection of logs behind which charac-ters seek shelter from time to time. The swan is a swirling projection on the scrim, beneath which are seen feeble real-isations of the Scheldt. The couch on which the Act 3 love scene takes place is quite an evocative prop. Within this eco-nomic setting Friedrich moves his principals with the kind of conviction characteristic of his best work in the opera house: the first contact of Elsa with Lohengrin and the tender con-cern of Elsa for Ortrud after her dream are just two examples. He is also masterly in controlling the seemingly interminable assemblies of Act 2.

The performance of Armstrong (Mrs Friedrich) is impres-sive up to a point. She presents a more worried, complex Elsa than is usual, but her intelligent acting is often lamed by laboured singing. Hofmann looks everyone's ideal Lohen-grin, proud and ardent, and here his singing matches his appearance, culminating in an eloquently shaped Narration and Farewell. Disharmony and evil are vividly represented by Connell's vicious, malevolent Ortrud, although she just occasionally goes over the top, and she potently energises the weak soul of Telramund, delivered by Roar in forceful, steady but uningratiating tones. Vogel is a routine Henry, but Weikl a quite out-of-the-ordinary Herald.

The sound recording catches ideally the Bayreuth acoustic, allowing us to hear Nelsson's firm command of the work's structure and his sensitivity to its lyrical aspects. This is an engrossing, stark alternative to Herzog's interpretation, and Large does it full justice in his filming.

Large is again in charge at Vienna in 1992 for staging at the Vienna State Opera. Unfortunately this is a rehash of a seven-teen-year-old production that's dim in every sense of that epithet, and there's not much even Large can do to enlighten or enliven it. The one shaft of light comes with the appear-ance of Domingo in the title role, resplendent in silver costume, come to rescue the unflatteringly robed and coif-fured Studer. Although not a *Heldentenor* in the classic sense of the description, Domingo has the attributes of golden tone, a firm line and a reasonable command of the text, and he tires hardly at all through the long assignment. He doesn't look quite the youthful knight of the libretto's – and Elsa's – im-agining, but there's something to be said for this bearded, dark-hued saviour as a change from convention.

Studer's singing is superior even to that heard from her at Bayreuth, with many exquisite touches leavening the richness of her tone in *forte* passages, and she manages to look elated, tormented and in love as the situation requires. Welker commands the biting, frustrated manner Telramund's role calls for and provides a telling portrait of a weak man fighting back against the odds. He is urged on to nefarious deeds by Vejsovic's forceful, slightly blustery Ortrud. Lloyd is at his appreciable best as a wise rather than tedious King and Tichy's Herald is boldly delivered.

Abbado and his Vienna forces are perhaps the heroes of the performance, unstinting in their grand and direct approach to the score, quite the equal of their Bayreuth counterparts, but the absence of any positive view of the work stagewise lames this worthy effort: it is never as convincing or arresting as the two readings from the Green Hill, although ideally one would want the best features of all three.

Tristan und Isolde

Johanna Meier (Isolde), Hanna Schwarz (Brangäne), René Kollo (Tristan), Robert Schunk (Melot), Hermann Becht (Kurwenal), Matti Salminen (King Mark). Chor and Orch of Bayreuth Festival/Daniel Barenboim. Dir: Jean-Pierre Ponnelle; video dir: Brian Large. Philips VHS 070 409–3; LD:−1.

Wagner himself could hardly explain, years after its composition, how he had managed to write this work in a single span of inspiration, so sustained and unified is its concept. However many times it may have been seen or heard, the fatal love story of Tristan and Isolde, with its many psychological and philosophical undertones, found in Wagner's own libretto, exerts its extraordinary power to sweep the listener into its maelstrom.

The work is meagrely though worthily represented on video by one version, this 1982 revival of Ponnelle's 1981 production. Each act, in his own scenery, is dominated by a single symbol: Act 1 by the huge prow of a ship; Act 2 by a vast, gnarled oak; Act 3 by the splintered shell of a tree set on a bleak promontory. To this impressive decor is added an inspired use of colour and light, most telling in the love duet where Ponnelle conjures up a woodland scene of magical delight, then plunges the loving pair into complete darkness for their moment of supreme bliss. When King Mark breaks in on them, the drab light of dawn manifestly destroys the lovers' illusions.

A few stage props contribute to the consistency of Ponnelle's concept. Isolde is first seen in the Prelude enveloped in a massive silver cloak, presumably hiding her true soul. The potential lovers drink their draught at the end of that act from a copper dish. They swear love in death, in Act 2, beside a pool from which they drink as they begin their rapturous duet. Controversy concerns only the final scenes, in which Tristan does not die where Wagner intends but imagines the final events in a dying delirium. Isolde appears to him as an angelic saviour, all in white, the others remaining as shadowy figures on a backcloth.

As ever Ponnelle direct his principals to good purpose, emphasising their physical contact. Meier's Isolde is a slim, affecting figure well matched to Kollo's dark-hued, intent Tristan, wild and searing in his last-act hallucinations. Meier's voice is compact and appealing, though short on sheer power. Kollo's tenor isn't the most tractable or pleasing of instruments but he uses it intelligently. Schwarz's warm, concerned Brangäne is an undoubted asset; so is Salminen's dignified, moving Mark. Becht is a rough-hewn Kurwenal, inclined to bark.

Barenboim does not always knit together episodes into a coherent whole, but in this early attempt at the work he shows sympathy with its melos, even when the means are questionable. Picture and sound are as favourable as always from this venue.

Die Meistersinger von Nürnberg
Mari Anne Häggander (Eva), Marga Schiml (Magdalene), Siegfried Jerusalem (Walther von Stolzing), Graham Clark (David), Bernd Weikl (Hans Sachs), Hermann Prey (Beckmesser), Jan Vermeersch (Kothner), Manfred Schenk (Pogner). Chor and Orch of Bayreuth

Festival/Horst Stein. Dir: Wolfgang Wagner; video dir: Brian Large. Philips VHS 070 413–3; LD:–1.

In his sole comedy, Wagner lavished his system of interlocking motifs on a piece depicting midsummer madness combined with worldly wisdom in the Nuremberg of Hans Sachs's time. There the cobbler-poet saves not only the master-guild from a silly mistake in rejecting the noble knight von Stolzing but also the lovely Eva, daughter of Pogner, from the clutches of the frustrated, sour town-clerk Beckmesser. Then he fulfils her romantic dreams by making possible her marriage to Stolzing. Here civic pride, however misplaced, the follies of the human heart, the intrigues of the small-minded are depicted in music of a gloriously expansive nature over a long, leisurely evening in the theatre, or on your home screen in Wolfgang Wagner's traditional, 1981 staging at Bayreuth, filmed in 1983.

In Wolfgang's own designs Nuremberg looks bright, spick and span, more like Nuremberg today than what it was like in Sachs's time. They serve his purpose well enough in setting before us his grandfather's timeless comedy in straightforward, unfussy terms, although this approach fines away some of the work's rougher edges and satire, something that the casting only serves to emphasise. Such a personable, youthful Sachs as Weikl might not be a bad match himself for Eva. His singing is warm and well phrased but lacks something in nobility and intensity of utterance. Beckmesser as played and sung by Prey is hardly the bitter, buttoned-up character of its creator's intent but a boring buffoon with little spite in him, and Prey's singing is altogether too mellifluous for the part.

As portrayed by Jerusalem, Walther is a bit of a stick, not quite the fiery, fervent knight of Wagner's imagining. Clark is a lively but slightly metallic-sounding David. Häggander makes a delightfully positive, warm Eva, Schiml, a youthful Magdalene, Schenk a stolid Pogner. Stein conducts a pleasing, unfussy account of the score that ultimately, like the whole, falls short of the ideal. Large is there once more to record it faithfully for posterity.

Der Ring des Nibelungen

1. *Das Rheingold* Julie Kaufman (Woglinde), Nancy Gustafson (Freia), Angela Maria Blasi (Wellgunde), Birgit Calm (Flosshilde), Marjana Lipovšek (Fricka), Hanna Schwarz (Erda), Robert Tear (Loge), Josef Hopferwieser (Froh), Helmut Pampuch (Mime), Robert Hale (Wotan), Florian Cerny (Donner), Ekkehard Wlaschiha (Alberich), Jan-Hendrik Rootering (Fasolt), Kurt Moll (Fafner). Bavarian State Orch/Wolfgang Sawallisch. Dir: Nikolaus Lehnhoff; video dir: Shokichi Amano. EMI VHS MVB 99 1276 3; LD: LDE 99 1276 1 (LD: subtitles).

Die Walküre Julia Varady (Sieglinde), Hildegard Behrens (Brünnhilde), Marjana Lipovšek (Fricka), Robert Schunk (Siegmund), Robert Hale (Wotan), Kurt Moll (Hunding). Bavarian State Orch/Wolfgang Sawallisch. Dir: Nikolaus Lehnhoff; video dir: Shokichi Amano. EMI VHS MVB 99 1279 3; LD: LDE 99 1279 1 (LD: subtitles).

Siegfried Julie Kaufmann (Woodbird), Hildegard Behrens (Brünnhilde), Hanna Schwarz (Erda), René Kollo (Siegfried), Helmut Pampuch (Mime), Robert Hale (Wanderer), Ekkehard Wlaschiha (Alberich), Kurt Moll (Fafner). Bavarian State Orch/Wolfgang Sawallisch. Dir: Nikolaus Lehnhoff; video dir: Shokichi Amano. EMI VHS MVB 99 1283 3; LD: LDE 99 1283 1 (LD: subtitles).

Götterdämmerung Hildegard Behrens (Brünnhilde), Julie Kaufmann (Woglinde), Angela Maria Blasi (Wellgunde), Lisbeth Balslev (Gutrune), Birgit Calm (Flosshilde), Marjana Lipovšek (First Norn), Ingrid Karrasch (Second Norn), Penelope Thorn (Third Norn), Waltraud Meier (Waltraute), René Kollo (Siegfried), Hans Günter Nöcker (Gunther), Ekkehard Wlaschiha (Alberich), Matti Salminen (Hagen). Bavarian State Orch/Wolfgang Sawallisch. Dir: Nikolaus Lehnhoff; video dir: Shokichi Amano. EMI VHS MVB 99 1287 3; LD: LDE 99 1287 1 (LD: subtitles).

2. *Das Rheingold* Hilde Leidland (Woglinde), Eva Johansson (Freia), Annette Küttenbaum (Wellgunde), Jane Turner (Flosshilde), Linda Finnie (Fricka), Birgitta Svendén (Erda), Graham Clark (Loge), Kurt Schreibmayer (Froh), Helmut Pampuch (Mime), John Tomlinson

(Wotan), Bodo Brinkmann (Donner), Günter von Kannen (Alberich), Matthias Hölle (Fasolt), Philip Kang (Fafner). Orch of Bayreuth Festival/Daniel Barenboim. Dir: Harry Kupfer; video dir: Horant H. Hohlfeld. Teldec VHS 4509–91122–3; LD:—6 (LD: subtitles).

Die Walküre Nadine Secunde (Sieglinde), Anne Evans (Brünnhilde), Linda Finnie (Fricka), Poul Elming, (Siegmund), John Tomlinson (Wotan), Matthias Hölle (Hunding). Orch of Bayreuth Festival/Daniel Barenboim. Dir: Harry Kupfer; video dir: Horant H. Hohlfeld. Teldec VHS 4509–91123–3; LD:—6 (LD: subtitles).

Siegfried Hilde Leidland (Woodbird), Anne Evans (Brünnhilde), Birgitta Svendén (Erda), Siegfried Jerusalem (Siegfried), Graham Clark (Mime), John Tomlinson (Wanderer), Günter von Kannen (Alberich), Philip Kang (Fafner). Orch of Bayreuth Festival/Daniel Barenboim. Dir: Harry Kupfer; video dir: Horant H. Hohlfeld. Teldec VHS 4509–94193–3; LD:—6 (LD: subtitles).

Götterdämmerung Anne Evans (Brünnhilde), Hilde Leidland (Woglinde), Eva-Maria Bundschuh (Gutrune), Annette Küttenbaum (Wellgunde), Jane Turner (Flosshilde), Birgitta Svendén (First Norn), Linda Finnie (Second Norn), Uta Priew (Third Norn), Waltraud Meier (Waltraute), Siegfried Jerusalem (Siegfried), Bodo Brinkmann (Gunther), Günter von Kannen (Alberich), Philip Kang (Hagen). Orch of Bayreuth Festival/Daniel Barenboim. Dir: Harry Kupfer; video dir: Horant H. Hohlfeld. Teldec VHS 4509–94194–3; LD:—6 (LD: subtitles).

3. *Das Rheingold* Kaaren Erickson (Woglinde), Mari Anne Häggander (Freia), Diane Kesling (Wellgunde), Meredith Parsons (Flosshilde), Christa Ludwig (Fricka), Birgitta Svendén (Erda), Siegfried Jerusalem (Loge), Mark Baker (Froh), Heinz Zednik (Mime), James Morris (Wotan), Alan Held (Donner), Ekkehard Wlaschiha (Alberich), Jan-Hendrik Rootering (Fasolt), Matti Salminen (Fafner). Orch of Metropolitan Opera, New York/James Levine. Dir: Otto Schenk; video dir: Brian Large. DG VHS 072 418–3; LD:—1.

Die Walküre Jessye Norman (Sieglinde), Hildegard Behrens (Brünnhilde), Christa Ludwig (Fricka), Gary

Lakes (Siegmund), James Morris (Wotan), Kurt Moll (Hunding). Orch of Metropolitan Opera, New York/ James Levine. Dir: Otto Schenk; video dir: Brian Large. DG VHS 072 419–3; LD:−1.

Siegfried Dawn Upshaw (Woodbird), Hildegard Behrens (Brünnhilde), Birgitta Svendén (Erda), Siegfried Jerusalem (Siegfried), Heinz Zednik (Mime), James Morris (Wanderer), Ekkehard Wlaschiha (Alberich), Matti Salminen (Fafner). Orch of Metropolitan Opera, New York/James Levine. Dir: Otto Schenk; video dir: Brian Large. DG VHS 072 420–3; LD:−1.

Götterdämmerung Hildegard Behrens (Brünnhilde), Kaaren Erickson (Woglinde), Hanna Lisowska (Gutrune), Diane Kesling (Wellgunde), Meredith Parsons (Flosshilde), Gweneth Bean (First Norn), Joyce Castle (Second Norn), Andrea Gruber (Third Norn), Christa Ludwig (Waltraute), Siegfried Jerusalem (Siegfried), Anthony Raffell (Gunther), Ekkehard Wlaschiha (Alberich), Matti Salminen (Hagen). Orch of Metropolitan Opera, New York/James Levine. Dir: Otto Schenk; video dir: Brian Large. DG VHS 072 421–3; LD:−1.

4. *Das Rheingold* Norma Sharp (Woglinde), Carmen Reppel (Freia), Ilse Gramatzki (Wellgunde), Marga Schiml (Flosshilde), Hanna Schwarz (Fricka), Ortrun Wenkel (Erda), Heinz Zednik (Loge), Siegfried Jerusalem (Froh), Helmut Pampuch (Mime), Donald McIntyre (Wotan), Martin Egel (Donner), Hermann Becht (Alberich), Matti Salminen (Fasolt), Fritz Hübner (Fafner). Orch of Bayreuth Festival/Pierre Boulez. Dir: Patrice Chéreau; video dir: Brian Large. Philips VHS 070 401–3; LD:−1.

Die Walküre Jeannine Altmeyer (Sieglinde), Gwyneth Jones (Brünnhilde), Hanna Schwarz (Fricka), Peter Hofmann (Siegmund), Donald McIntyre (Wotan), Matti Salminen (Hunding). Orch of Bayreuth Festival/Pierre Boulez. Dir: Patrice Chéreau; video dir: Brian Large. Philips VHS 070 402–3; LD:−1.

Siegfried Norma Sharp (Woodbird), Gwyneth Jones (Brünnhilde), Ortrun Wenkel (Erda), Manfred Jung (Siegfried), Heinz Zednik (Mime), Donald McIntyre (Wanderer), Hermann Becht (Alberich), Fritz Hübner

(Fafner). Orch of Bayreuth Festival/ Pierre Boulez. Dir: Patrice Chéreau; video dir: Brian Large. Philips VHS 070 403–3; LD:—1.

Götterdämmerung Gwyneth Jones (Brünnhilde), Norma Sharp (Woglinde), Jeannine Altmeyer (Gutrune), Ilse Gramatzki (Wellgunde), Marga Schiml (Flosshilde), Ortrun Wenkel (First Norn), Gabriele Schnaut (Second Norn), Katie Clarke (Third Norn), Gwendolyn Killebrew (Waltraute), Manfred Jung (Siegfried), Franz Mazura (Gunther), Hermann Becht (Alberich), Fritz Hübner (Hagen). Orch of Bayreuth Festival/ Pierre Boulez. Dir: Patrice Chéreau; video dir: Brian Large. Philips VHS 070 404–1; LD:—3.

Wagner's vast epic remains one of the linchpins of Western art, more than fourteen hours of music-drama dealing with the eternal matters of love, death and power, personal responsibility and moral behaviour. It can now be viewed as the culmination of more than a hundred years of musical development in the German-speaking world after which nothing could or would be the same again. It is impossible to conceive of a work that is structurally more complex, logical or unified. It calls for an answering inspiration on the part of its interpreters – directors, conductors, singers.

The four performances on video provide, in their differing ways, satisfying attempts at the impossible task of encompassing all aspects of the great work. Although none inevitably tells the whole story, each draws you into the work and holds your interest from start to finish. To watch and listen to all four one after the other would result in *Ring* fatigue: viewed over a period of time, and in three instances lived with for a few years, I can contrast and compare them with some degree of familiarity. Two stem from the Bayreuth Festival: the centenary staging by Chéreau, filmed in 1980, and the Kupfer production, filmed in 1992, both in the last of their four seasons at the Festival, both at performances videoed *in situ* before the start of the Festival. The Bavarian State Opera production, by Lehnhoff, was committed to film at live performances in 1989, the Metropolitan staging by Schenk at live performances in 1990.

The first three are controversially conceptual interpretations (all roundly booed when first seen); the fourth is a modern adaptation of Wagner's stipulated ground-plan with old-fashioned, representational decor by Günther Schneider-Siemssen, sometimes beautiful, more often tedious. In places the first three can seem wrong-headed, but as total visions of the work, each is an astonishingly unified achievement, much more likely to bear repetition than the unadventurous Schenk. One only has to compare Jerusalem's Siegfried, an awkward, uninvolving interpretation at the Met, with his electrifying performance under Kupfer for the point to be made. Whereas both Chéreau and even more Kupfer deploy their gifts at *Personenregie* to masterly effect at Bayreuth, with emphasis on eye and body contact among the principals, Schenk treats them conventionally and often boringly.

At this stretch of time, Chéreau's basically Marxian reading, which took the work away from its given, mythical world and placed it in a nineteenth-century industrial context, can now be seen as a trailblazing event that many have copied without ever quite achieving his technical assurance as regards settings (by Richard Peduzzi) or movement. Its daringly novel interpretation of milieu and characterisation will always remain controversial, but as a whole it works excitingly. Kupfer, sometimes hampered by his designer Hans Schavernoch's gloomy wastes, comes close to Chéreau in persuading his singers to act with total conviction and in some cases surpasses the French director's efforts in that respect. Lehnhoff at Munich, in Erich Wonder's quirky scenery, is somewhat more reticent and economical, less athletic, in his direction, but often comes up with revelatory moments such as the finely proportioned, geometric set for *Walküre* Act 2 and the moment when the back of the stage opens up in Act 3 of *Siegfried* to reveal a vista of the Rhineland.

While Kupfer manages almost entirely to exclude nature, Chéreau magically retains it but shows it in a new light, as in the forest of *Siegfried*, Act 2, seen as a brutally enclosed, post-nuclear holocaust hole by Kupfer, who places the whole piece in a bleak, bombed-out future. Yet Kupfer can conjure up inspired pictures by imaginatively using his basic set, which has been unflatteringly likened to a vast airport runway.

Wotan/Wanderer seems to approach from infinity as he struggles across the wasteland to seek out Erda at the start of _Siegfried_ Act 3, and _Das Rheingold_ begins with a stunning coup: a green laser-beam tunnel to represent the Rhine, continuing with a cinematic Walhalla and a Nibelheim that looks like a sci-fi laboratory. The gods and goddesses here are a set of groupies and gangsters, taking a step forward to Chéreau's view of them as a bunch of factory disputants. The close of the Kupfer is an unaccountable misjudgment: the bored upper class of a futuristic society watch the downfall of the gods on their TV sets with the people cowed behind and two children kitschily holding hands in front. What a letdown.

Both Chéreau and Kupfer strongly suggest the physicality of the cycle's key relationships. Kupfer's Wotan is a man whose body language is palpable. His boiler-suited Siegfried is a rough, callous youth only growing up once he has met Brünnhilde. In both stagings, but particularly in Kupfer's, characters appear without licence from the stage instruction, sometimes puzzlingly so. Lehnhoff's move more circumspectly, act more conventionally.

All three have been astutely directed for video. The concentration, in the case of the Bayreuth versions, on the principals obviates any reservations one may have about the scenery. Again and again, a look or a movement tells us volumes about a character's inner feelings. The many hours of rehearsals and number of performances that had taken place before each staging was committed to posterity is clear from the conviction shown by every member of both casts, a marvellous interlocking of action and music, evident also, though to a lesser extent, at Munich. The bright, clear lighting in the Chéreau performance helps to delineate the action. The predominantly darker Kupfer isn't quite so easily accommodated, but the light on faces helps to overcome that drawback. The Lehnhoff comes somewhere in between. By contrast the Schenk, for all its realistic detail, looks paradoxically unreal, locked in a time warp and over-decorated. It triumphs in one respect with the most dangerous dragon in any version, one that really presents a visible threat, horrid claws and all, to Siegfried. By its side Chéreau's wooden beast dragged on by extras on a trolley is one of his few failures. Schenk (and Large) also score with the magical journey through the fire.

The balance between singers and orchestra is, as in the theatre itself, near ideal in both Bayreuth versions, with the more recent version having the advantage of a clear, sometimes almost too clear, digital recording. The Munich, though keenly balanced, is sometimes too recessed as a whole. At the Met, as usual, the orchestra is given undue prominence in keeping with Levine, favouring saturation of sound at the expense of translucency. A certain emphasis on the conductor is underlined when he is the only man in the pit actually to be filmed, a fatal mistake in the Prelude to Act 3 of *Siegfried*, especially when this is so well handled in the other versions. Curtain calls at the Met are another miscalculation.

Boulez's interpretation is direct, dynamic, exhilarating, having grown in confidence through familiarity over four years working with the Bayreuth orchestra and by cleansing the scores of traditional accretions. There remain times, such as Wotan's farewell, where one would like more relaxation but by and large his reading marches ideally with what is going on above: a thrilling unity and unanimity are achieved in this hard-edged, clear-eyed reading.

Sawallisch at Munich had conducted several cycles before this one was recorded. His is a basically lyrical, unhurried interpretation with an emphasis on legato, finely honed speeds and an indefinable but palpable sense of forward movement. The playing of the Bavarian State Opera Orchestra is almost on a par with that of its Bayreuth counterparts. What Boulez and Sawallisch miss in terms of the metaphysical, inward side of the cycle is found in Barenboim's grander, more impulsive reading, at times too fast or too slow but in most respects, especially in the latter two works, thrillingly incandescent and probably the best played of all, the Met not excepted.

An ideal cast might be achieved by some sort of conflation of singers. Where Brünnhilde is concerned one would actually like a blend of the three sopranos concerned: Jones's refulgence, Behrens's warmth and thrilling top register, Evans's consistency and understanding. As it is Evans's tone is at times evidently too lightweight for her part and slightly too grainy in tone. Behrens, particularly at Munich, has trouble with her lower register (which is worn). Jones – in the earlier operas (she is superb in the finale) – can be squally. All three overcome deficiencies to give deeply considered, convincing, carefully shaded interpretations, the minutiae of their parts nicely observed as they portray challenging Valkyrie, ardent lovemate, dramatic heroine. Behrens is occasionally too much the tragedy queen, especially at the Met, a mistake not made by Jones, in spite of her all-in acting, or by Evans, in some ways the most moving yet paradoxically the most realistic and tough of all Brünnhildes, thanks partly to Kupfer's insightful direction.

None of the Siegfrieds is satisfying in every way. None has a really beautiful voice. Jerusalem, too much of a booby at the Met where he is also out of voice, is at his best for Kupfer at Bayreuth, where he conveys the uncouthness of the youthful Siegfried and sings with refined variety of phrase and timbre. Kollo looks too podgy not to say mature and we are not always consoled for his hard, over-vibrant tone by his intelligence of phrase. Jung, surely inspired by Chéreau, alternates between being a chunky bully and a chubby charmer. His delivery can be jerky, but all the notes are hit solidly and in the middle, and he fails none of Wagner's severe tests on his serviceable tenor. He is probably, all round, the most acceptable of the three, but Jerusalem for Kupfer is a very positive, enthusiastic anti-hero.

All the Wotans are English-speaking. Tomlinson's ruffian of a Wotan, a very physical portrayal, is sung with all that bass's total commitment. For the most part he is in secure voice even if the tone isn't as ingratiating as one might wish. Whenever he is on stage, the tension is palpable, not least in his *Walküre* despair and eloquence. McIntyre, with a lighter but securer voice than Tomlinson, is tireless and involving, a thoroughly schooled reading of an unsympathetic interpretation (by Chéreau) of the part. Hale pours his whole soul and body into the role, compensating by his intensity for a bass-baritone less powerful than those of his rivals. His world-weary Wanderer, in comparison with Tomlinson's athletic portrayal, follows on his vigorous Wotan in *Rheingold*, his anguished god in *Walküre*, comparable with the great Hotter in his monologue and farewell, he and Behrens drawing the best from each other. Morris sings with strength and authority, but conveys little of the role's heart. As Wotan's alter ego, Alberich, von Kannen and Becht (both Bayreuth) are by a hair's breadth more vital and biting than Wlaschiha on the other two versions, all presenting the gnome's frustrations and anger arrestingly.

Altmeyer and Hofmann are a believably ecstatic Sieglinde and Siegmund for Chéreau, which is more than can be said for Norman and Lakes for Schenk. Varady and Schunk have their moments but are a shade overparted (Moll's overbearing Hunding commands Act 1 of *Walkyre*). Not so Secunde as a highly charged Sieglinde and Elmoung as a virile, piratical Siegmund, perhaps the most personable of all the Volsungs, and vocally deeply satisfying for Kupfer.

There are few weaknesses among the other roles. In *Rheingold* Zednik's scheming entrepreneur of a Loge for Chéreau vies for attention with Tear's foppish assumption for Lehnhoff, Clark's alert, witty entertainer for Kupfer, and Jerusalem's dull dog for Schenk. Lipovšek's harridan of a Fricka (Lehnhoff), is less attractive than Schwarz's concerned reading (Chéreau), a Fricka who attempts to win back her erring husband (she is also a moving Erda for Lehnhoff). Ludwig, Schenk's Fricka, is simply past her best. Svendén is, twice, a grave, mystical Erda, just right, although Wenkel for Chéreau has the more appropriately dark, imposing alto voice. Meier's urgent, comely Waltraute graces both the Lehnhoff and Kupfer cycles; neither Killebrew nor Ludwig (for all her authority caught too late in her career) are Meier's equal. Among the basses, Salminen is a towering Fasolt and Hunding for Chéreau and manages as easily Lehnhoff's cocktail-king Hagen as Schenk's more conventional reading, his voice voluminous and headily evil. Kang's gangster Hagen for Kupfer is less impressively sung, Hubner's overweening factory manager for Chéreau somewhere in between. All Gunthers are a shade elderly.

Zednik's comic-tragic Mime (Chéreau) is much to be preferred to his older self (Schenk) and to the dullish Pampuch (Lehnhoff), but not to Clark's cheeky, over-confident reading, the best sung of the three (Kupfer). Woodbirds are all good, but Leidland (Kupfer), also a fine Woglinde, is possibly the most pure-voiced of all. Chéreau's *belle-époque* Rhine-maidens are particularly comely and probably best directed.

By and large Chéreau's view remains the most consistent and the most consistently carried out vision. Kupfer is more unevenly inspired but at his best he offers remarkable *aperçus*, as when Evans-Brünnhilde gives Gutrune a killing look in Act 2 of *Götterdämmerung* or Hagen stalks Brünnhilde in his frustration at not regaining the ring during the Immolation. But then one recalls Chéreau having Erda unwind from a shroud in the first scene of *Siegfried* Act 3 and realises that he can be just as perceptive. The sets for the Kupfer, especially the giant, deserted boiler for the first act of *Siegfried*, are often impenetrable or perverse. Both interpretations will shock the unwary or the complacent cocooned or schooled in more conventional readings. Lehnhoff has individual moments and individual readings of overwhelming conviction, but it doesn't wear as well as its rivals – I don't care for the superimposition of close-ups in many of the orchestral transformations – nor is Sawallisch as viscerally exciting as Boulez and Barenboim. Schenk is only for those who want something more conventional.

Subtitles for those with teletext are available on the Teldec and EMI laserdisc versions. The Bayreuth sets have booklets for each opera including interviews with the respective directors. The Munich/EMI version has a single booklet in its large back box with an article by Lehnhoff. On the whole, the Kupfer/Barenboim is by a small margin the recommended choice, but it would be advisable to sample something of each cycle before making a final decision.

Parsifal

1. Waltraud Meier (Kundry), Siegfried Jerusalem (Parsifal), Bernd Weikl (Amfortas), Franz Mazura (Klingsor), Kurt Moll (Gurnemanz), Jan Hendrik Rootering (Titurel). Chor and Orch of Metropolitan Opera, New York/James Levine. Dir: Otto Schenk; video dir: Brian Large. DG VHS 072 435–3; LD:–1. Subtitles.

2. Eva Randová (Kundry), Siegfried Jerusalem (Parsifal), Bernd Weikl (Amfortas), Leif Roar (Klingsor), Hans Sotin (Gurnemanz), Matti Salminen (Titurel). Chor and

Orch of Bayreuth Festival/Horst Stein. Dir: Wolfgang Wagner; video dir: Brian Large. Philips VHS 070 413–3; LD:—1.

3. Yvonne Minton (Kundry, acted by Edith Clever), Reiner Goldberg (Parsifal, acted by Michael Kutter and Karin Krick), Wolfgang Schöne (Amfortas, acted by Armin Jordan), Aage Haugland (Klingsor), Robert Lloyd (Gurnemanz), Hans Tschammer (Titurel). Prague Philharmonic Chor, Monte Carlo Philharmonic Orch/ Armin Jordan. A film by Hans Jürgen Syberberg. Artificial Eye VHS Op 1.

Wagner's last opera shows his motif-inspired method of composing at its most impressive as he tells the mythical tale of the knight Parsifal. As an uncouth youth he kills a sacred swan in the land of the grail-keepers, led by the revered Gurnemanz, inciting their disdain. In Act 2 Parsifal is found under the spell of the equivocal Kundry, slave to the evil, self-castrated Klingsor, himself a mortal enemy of the Knights of the Grail. Eventually rejecting Kundry's wiles and destroying Klingsor's magic power, he returns to Monsalvat, home of the knights, as a transformed, Christ-like figure who heals the wound of the stricken king Amfortas (who was a victim of Klingsor's viciousness), and renews the Grail's power.

Both the stage versions, the first from 1993 Metropolitan, the second from 1981 Bayreuth, are basically traditional productions. Syberberg's 1982 film is an eccentric view of the piece, stimulating though perverse. The safest recommendation is the most recent set, not least because it houses one of the most thrilling performances on all videos, Meier's electrifying Kundry. She is the glamorous, seductive temptress of Act 2 and at the same time the tortured soul of the outer acts, having thought herself voice, body and soul into all aspects of the part. Hers is a wholly remarkable achievement, and the stuff of which legends are made, on a par with, say, Callas's Tosca.

Nobody else in this performance could hope to match Meier's assumption of her role, but the cast, a tired-sounding Klingsor apart, is as good as you are likely to encounter today. Moll is a worldly-wise Gurnemanz singing gravely, beautifully, but not always achieving the spiritual element of the noblest of his predecessors. Similarly Weikl's Amfortas is well routined but not exceptional in tone or accent. Jerusalem, though his voice no longer has its former bloom, sings reliably, and enacts the petulant youth and the redeeming saviour with a deal of conviction.

Within Günther Schneider-Siemssen's outmoded style of decor, Schenk's direction is sensible if conventional, quite realistic in its effects with topless Flowermaidens and a deal of erotic action allowed in Act 2. Levine's predominantly slow tempi often make Wagner seem portentous, but according to its own lights it is a well-executed reading superbly played. Large has filmed the performance with all his customary acuity. He was also responsible for the video of the Bayreuth version, Wolfgang's adequate inscenation, reverential before Grandfather's masterpiece but also dulled in effect, the decor, by Wolfgang and Reinhard Heinrich, impressionistic, nebulous. Klingsor's Garden is, perhaps appropriately, tacky. The transitions have none of the mystery and majesty of Wieland Wagner's legendary, long-lasting production, sadly unrecorded in visual terms.

Stein's musical direction is equally unexceptional, and Kapellmeister-ish. Jerusalem is here a more youthful, ebullient Parsifal than in New York, Weikl a fresher Amfortas. Randová offers a powerful Kundry, but has none of the variety or subtlety of Meier. Sotin is an anonymous Gurnemanz, Roar a superbly malevolent Klingsor. There remain the wonderful singing and playing of the Bayreuth forces to give this performance true distinction: there's none so dedicated as those on the Green Hill.

The Syberberg film offers a different, non-representational experience, the story unfolded in a surreal background based on a vast, craggy landscape. The transitions lead through an unpopulated country overlooked by Germanic emblems ending, of course, with the obligatory Nazi flag. The homoerotic transformation of handsome Michael Kutter as Parsifal into nubile Karin Krick when kissed by Kundry is as misplaced as it is hilarious. Nor do either have much relation to Goldberg's heroic tenor. Lloyd playing himself as Gurnemanz only shows up the inadequacies of the others' miming. Edith Clever as Kundry is perhaps the best of the actors, but her efforts at mouthing to Minton's singing are laughable. Jordan, the conductor, also plays a forceful Amfortas. He should have remained in the pit where he gives a refreshingly brisk account of the score, but his Monte Carlo force aren't comparable in technique with their counterparts.

Charles Gounod (1818–93)

Roméo et Juliette

Leontina Vaduva (Juliette), Anna Maria Panzarella (Stephano), Sarah Walker (Gertrude), Roberto Alagna (Roméo), François Le Roux (Mercutio), Peter Sidhom (Capulet), Robert Lloyd (Frère Laurent). Chor and Orch of Royal Opera House, Covent Garden/Charles Mackerras. Dir: Nicolas Joël; video dir: Brian Large. Covent Garden Pioneer/Castle VHS CVI 1771. Subtitles.

Gounod's romantic work, reasonably faithful to Shakespeare, has been justly termed one long, interrupted love duet. It certainly depends for its success on the performances of its principals. In the 1993 Covent Garden staging that essential was abundantly provided; indeed it served to propel Alagna into stardom, not necessarily for his own good. His heady tenor and fine-grained phrasing fill Roméo's music with just the right kind of glamour, though there is a tendency to harden at the very top of his register under pressure. Physically he is ideal for the romantic lover: although small of stature his boyish good looks win all hearts and he acts with a deal of genuine feeling, particularly when in consort with his Juliette.

Vaduva is an ideal Juliette. In the theatre, on the staging's first night, she seemed a shade overparted and out of voice. At this later performance she sings with a freshness and élan that perfectly suit Gounod's grateful writing for his soprano. Even more impressive is the way in which Vaduva suggests Juliette's girlish nature burgeoning into palpitating love as she responds eagerly to Roméo. In the role's closing stages

she is infinitely touching and vulnerable. The supporting
roles are equally well taken. Le Roux is a mercurial Mercutio,
Sidhom a dignified Capulet, Lloyd a paternal friar, Walker a
characterful Gertrude (she is shamefully uncredited in the accompanying material), Panzarella a perky Stephano, an
entirely superfluous part with a single, attractive solo.

Mackerras conducts a loving account of the score (given
almost complete), sometimes lavishing almost too much care
on it at the expense of forward movement. The staging is
dully traditional, but it at least has the virtue of forming an
unobtrusive background to the principals upon whom Large
very rightly concentrates his cameras. The sound picture is
excellent.

Jules Offenbach (1819–80)

Les Contes d'Hoffmann

1. Luciana Serra (Olympia), Ileana Cotrubas (Antonia),
Agnes Baltsa (Giulietta), Claire Powell (Nicklausse),
Placido Domingo (Hoffman), Geraint Evans (Coppé-
lius), Nicola Ghiuselev (Dr Miracle), Siegmund
Nimsgern (Dapertutto), Robert Lloyd (Lindorf),
Gwynne Howell (Crespel). Chor and Orch of Royal
Opera House, Covent Garden/Georges Prêtre. Dir: John
Schlesinger; video dir: Brian Large. Castle VHS CVI
2045. Subtitles.

2. Natalie Dessay (Olympia), Barbara Hendricks (An-
tonia), Isabelle Vernet (Giulietta), Brigitte Balleys
(Nicklausse), Daniel Galvez-Vallejo (Hoffmann), José
Van Dam (Coppélius, Dr Miracle, Dapertutto, Lindorf),
Gabriel Bacquier (Spalanzani, Crespel, Schlemil). Chor
and Orch of the Lyon Opera/Kent Nagano. Dir: Louis
Erlo; video dir: Pierre Cavassilas. Pioneer LD PLMCB
00931.

Offenbach's work is based on the picaresque figure of the
lawyer/poet Hoffmann and his adventures with three
women. Jules Barbier's libretto created a psychological and
allegorical story of the writer himself whose loves become

facets of the same woman. His four malign adversaries personify an evil influence and are usually sung by the same bass-baritone. Nicklausse is Hoffmann's *alter ego* and his artistic muse. The problems in performing the piece are mainly textual. The composer died before completing it and nobody knows precisely what form it might have taken had he lived a little longer. We can be sure that the traditional version, current until recent research changed matters, is in many ways corrupt including music not intended for this work, such as Dapertutto's 'Scintille diamant' and the septet, both in the Giulietta act, although they are admittedly effective additions.

For the 1981 Covent Garden staging, Prêtre played safe, substantially adhering to the old edition, which has always worked well on stage. Schlesinger's production neatly blends the real with the surreal and is set in William Dudley's atmospheric sets. But it isn't a very authentic account, musically speaking, leaning towards 'internationalists' rather than a truly French style with no Francophone singer in the cast. Domingo has dominated the title part for many years. He acts the muddled and often distraught lover to the life and sings with his customary éclat and burnished tone, but his style is too unsubtle for the requirements of Offenbach's writing for his tenor.

The evil figures are unfortunately divided among four singers and as none, bar Lloyd's Lindorf, has good French, nothing is gained by the division. Serra is a finely articulate, accurate Olympia, Cotrubas – most sympathetic of Hoffmann's loves – a moving Antonia, Baltsa a properly alluring, brassy Giulietta. Powell is in her element as a cynical yet concerned Nicklausse. The smaller parts are well taken. Prêtre's conducting is a shade unstable and overblown, but always prompt in support.

The Lyon staging – renamed '. . . des Contes d'Hoffmann' – couldn't be more different. Set within the bare walls of a madhouse, Erlo creates a Marat/Sade sense of disorientation and runs the three tales into one. The chorus is offstage; inmates watch and mime reactions to the strange doings of the principals. Olympia is a paraplegic, Giulietta I know not what. It makes a puzzling and by the end tiresome rethink, somewhat tedious to watch.

The version is based on Michael Kaye's newish, supposedly definitive edition of the score, but then *that* has been further – and questionably – refashioned by Dominique Riffaud. At least the original dialogue, or some of it adapted by Riffaud, replaces the corrupt recitative (used at Covent Garden) and the whole is kept down to an Offenbachian scale. Much more important, it is sung by experienced and excellent Francophone singers who go to prove how wrong is the blown-up vocalisation we so often hear these days in this and other French works.

Most pleasing of all is the mellifluous, unforced singing of Galvez-Vallejo, a real find, as Hoffmann, singing his three solos in an idiomatic, truly Gallic manner. Dessay sings Olympia's aria with refined tone, but the added high notes in verse two are unpleasing and unnecessary. Hendricks is a pure-toned but rather cool Antonia remaining somewhere outside the crazy staging, as she well might. Vernet is a deliberately blowzy Giulietta, singing in the vein of Crespin, her teacher, an excellent model. Van Dam adapts his familiar portraits of the baddies to the new circumstance and sings with wit and point in his seemingly ageless voice. As Nicklausse, Balleys has a sprightly mezzo to match her engaging presence.

Essential subtitles are excluded by Pioneer, but the video direction is expert, letting us gauge Erlo's eccentricities. Castle, which has skeletal captions, is by and large the safe recommendation, but there is still room for an imaginative treatment of this intractable but ever-fascinating work.

Johann Strauss (1825–99)

Die Fledermaus
1. Pamela Coburn (Rosalinde), Janet Perry (Adele), Brigitte Fassbaender (Orlofsky), Josef Hopferweiser (Alfred), Eberhard Waechter (Eisenstein), Wolfgang Brendel (Falke), Benno Kusche (Frank), Fraz Muxeneder (Frosch). Chor and Orch of Bavarian State Opera/Carlos Kleiber. Dir: Otto Schenk; video dir: Brian Large. DG VHS 072 400–3; LD:−1.
2. Nancy Gustafson (Rosalinde); Judith Howarth

(Adele), Jochen Kowalski (Orlofsky), Bonaventura Bottone (Alfred), Louis Otey (Eisenstein), Anthony Michaels-Moore (Falke), Eric Garrett (Frank), John Sessions (Frosch). Chor and Orch of the Royal Opera House, Covent Garden/Richard Bonynge. Dir: John Cox; video dir: Humphrey Burton. Pioneer Virgin VHS VVD 952; Pioneer LD PLMCD 00721.

3. Kiri Te Kanawa (Rosalinde), Hildegard Heichele (Adele), Doris Soffel (Orlofsky), Dennis O'Neill (Alfred), Hermann Prey (Eisenstein), Benjamin Luxon (Falke), Michael Langdon (Frank), Josef Meinrad (Frosch). Chor and Orch of Royal Opera House, Covent Garden/ Placido Domingo. Dir: Leopold Lindtberg; video dir: Humphrey Burton. Castle VHS CVI 2023.

4. Joan Sutherland (Rosalinde), Monique Brynnel (Adele), Heather Begg (Orlofsky), Anson Austin (Alfred), Robert Gard (Eisenstein), Michael Lewis (Falke), Gregory Yurisich (Frank), Graeme Ewer (Frosch). Chor of Australian Opera, Elizabethan Sydney Orch/Richard Bonynge. Dir: Anthony Besch. Virgin VHS VVD 781.

Towering above Strauss's other operettas and most of its successors, this ebullient work has delighted generations of audiences since its Viennese premiere in 1874. At once a celebration of the Viennese waltz and a sharp satire of the Viennese society of the composer's day (*cf* Schnitzler), the cynicism saves the story and music from the taint of sentimentality. It needs to be done with understanding of the traditional style, however much some of the dialogue may be updated. Unfortunately all the three Anglophone performances have directors, conductors and principals who prefer to turn the work into an often tedious romp. So out of style is the Australian performance that it isn't worth closer examination.

Where the conducting is concerned you only have to listen to a few bars of the overture from Kleiber's hand, in the 1985 Munich staging, to realise that he has the secret of the work's rhythms and manner denied to Domingo and Bonynge.

There's champagne in Kleiber's beat where those of his rivals seem more like flat beer. Then the Munich players have the music in their bones while their London and Antipodean counterparts do not. Indeed Kleiber is undoubtedly the most cogent reason for preferring the DG version.

Schenk has lived with the piece all his professional life, either portraying the speaking role of the gaoler Frosch or directing it. He knows the secret of keeping speech and music on the boil: the production at Munich has pace and holds attention throughout where the others often descend into boredom and banality, with the evenings further drawn out by seemingly endless star turns in the party scene. The sets at Munich are _gemütlich Biedermeyer_ and look lived in. Here Covent Garden does provide a valid alternative in Julia Trevelyan Oman's exquisitely observed decor. The 1983 Covent Garden production is a polyglot affair, with a mixed cast performing in a mélange of languages in an attempt to make the piece more palatable to an audience most of whose members would be ignorant of the original. The result is a flurry of musical and visual gags foreign to Strauss's original. In 1990 the house had another go using the same scenery, but inviting John Mortimer to do an English translation which, hovering between wit and facetiousness, is far too modern-orientated given that the staging remains set in period.

If one takes the members of the casts side by side, Munich doesn't have such an advantage. Coburn is an attractive enough Rosalinde but she lacks the charisma of the lively Te Kanawa, here portrayed as a British wife of her Austrian husband, or the insouciance of the utterly delectable Gustafson, who acts and sings her part more glowingly than either of the other sopranos. Heichele and Perry are both entrancing Adeles. Howarth's portrayal is pert but very English.

In all cases Eisenstein is given to baritones of a certain age when it was originally written for a tenor. Prey is the most engaging by virtue of his well-groomed singing, understanding of Eisenstein's sly, raffish character and general bonhomie, though he does tend to overdo the last. Waechter is simply too old and too vocally raddled: he compensates by going into histrionic overdrive at every opportunity. Otey, more like a matinee idol than a Viennese _rentier_, acts in quite the wrong style. Both the British tenors turn Alfred into a lud-icrous caricature of an Italian tenor, with far too much licence allowed in singing snatches of arias, not at all what the authors intended. Hopferweiser is all the more amusing for not stepping out of character. All the Falkes are pleasing, but Brendel inevitably has the advantage of singing in the original. The three veteran basses who take Frank make much of little, but the English singers again tend to guy their part, whereas Kusche plays it straighter.

Fassbaender is outright winner in the trousers role of Orlof-sky, catching the bored and slightly sinister sides of the character to perfection, and singing his/her couplets, 'Chacun à son gout', as to the manner born. In 1983 at the Royal Opera Soffel looks uncomfortable with a bald head, and fussy busi-ness and dialogue. In 1990 the house fetched up with the wheeze of giving the role to a counter-tenor: a moment's thought would have revealed the anachronism of having a low speaking voice and a high singing one. The Royal Opera performances stretch the jokes hereabouts, at the start of Act 2, to excess. In the party scene Covent Garden I has Prey, Hinge and Bracket (where are they now?) and Charles Azna-vour as guests prolonging an already extended act. In Covent Garden II there is more justification for the appearance of party guests, Sutherland, Horne and Pavarotti singing an aria each and duetting together as homage to Sutherland on her retirement: the farewell is rather touching, most of all the diva's own frail but eloquent 'Home, sweet home' after which the house gives her a standing ovation. None of the versions uses Strauss's intended ballet music for the party, replacing it with other pieces by him. The choreography at Covent Gar-den is by Frederick Ashton, and as graceful as you would expect from that source.

Frosch always presents a problem. The Munich-inclined jokes of Muxeneder will be lost on a British audience, amus-ing though he is, particularly as DG offers no subtitles, a bad omission. In Covent Garden's multilingual show, Meinrad hovers uneasily between Viennese and English jokes, and fails to raise more than a few titters. Sessions offers a comic turn, funny but already dated.

The winner generally speaking has to be Munich, most of

all because of the fizz Kleiber applies to the score and the ability of Schenk to stay just, but only just, the right side of farce. Of course those wanting the star turns will go for the 1990 Covent Garden version. The Australian account is really beyond the pale for all except those who must have Sutherland, way past her prime, attempting Rosalinde and having a whale of a time according to her own, endearing lights.

Video direction and sound are good on all the three main versions, except that the Munich video has the voices too backward in relation to the orchestra. That version also, quite rightly, lets us see a deal of Kleiber's vivacious conducting. On the accompanying material for the Pioneer laserdisc of the 1990 Royal Opera performance nowhere is there any indication that this is a New Year's Eve Gala at which Sutherland was making her farewell, an extraordinary oversight.

Alexander Borodin (1833–87)

Prince Igor
Anna Tomowa-Sintow (Yaroslavna), Elena Zaremba (Konchakovna), Alexei Steblianko (Vladimir), Sergei Leiferkus (Igor), Nicola Ghiuselev (Galitsky), Paata Burchuladze (Khan Konchak). Chor and Orch of the Royal Opera House, Covent Garden/Bernard Haitink. Dir: Andrei Serban; video dir: Humphrey Burton. Decca VHS 071 421–3; LD:−1. Subtitles.

Borodin's sprawling epic was left uncompleted at his death after eighteen years' labour on it. Various hands helped to complete the orchestration, among them Rimsky-Korsakov and Glazunov, and no critical edition has yet appeared. Since Act 3 was the most sketchily composed, it has often been omitted in performance, but its inclusion is essential to an understanding of this musical pageant of medieval Russia. Even when it is included many loose ends are left untied. Yet, for all its inconsistencies and an episodic nature typical of Russian opera, Borodin's score is the only one, other than Tchaikovsky's best-known pieces in the medium, and Mussorgsky's *Boris Godunov*, to have stood the test of time as a regular part of the repertory. The plot tells of the conflict between Russia and the Polovtsians. The music for the former is folk-inspired; for the latter Borodin invented an exotic idiom very much his own as exemplified most of all in the famed Polovtsian Dances, often played as a concert item.

In Andrei Serban's panoramic yet economic staging for Covent Garden in 1990, many of the problems attendant on staging this lengthy, somewhat sprawling work virtually disappear. In turn he unerringly depicts the suffering of Mother Russia, the pagan joys and lusts of Konchak's entourage and in between Galitsky's roistering. Liviu Ciulei's pinewood, unit set and Deirdre Clancy's colour-coded costumes are all of a piece with the ethos of this gratifyingly unified production. There is perhaps too much emphasis on drunkenness, ungovernable desire and brutal killing, or maybe they are not quite convincingly enough enacted by an army of extras, but the conviction of the whole overcomes reservations about detail.

Haitink's conducting is cogently limned, distinguishing between different moods and milieux, and brings out the epic nature of the writing. It wants only something of raw Russian vitality. Both the Royal Opera House chorus and orchestra acquit themselves well. The figure of Igor, the patriot and Yarsoslavna's faithful husband, who is captured by the Polovtsian ruler Konchak, is sung in proud, determined fashion by Leiferkus in those firm, incisive tones of his, words very much to the fore. His account of Igor's song of homesickness, one of the most eloquent arias in all Russian opera, is most movingly done. Tomowa-Sintow's Yaroslavna stands out for the soprano's all-embracing characterisation of that sad, dignified, vulnerable heroine. Although the close-ups unflatteringly reveal a motherly figure and features, Tomowa-Sintow overcomes those disadvantages by the commitment of her singing and acting, the former long-breathed, lustrous, eloquently accented, all its qualities fused into a deeply moving account of her Act 4 solo. Yaroslavna's rule, in Igor's absence, is challenged by Prince Galitsky, her debauched brother. That part is taken gleefully by Ghiuselev who, encouraged by Serban, spares us nothing of Galitsky's wilful cruelty and insistent lechery.

As Igor's son Vladimir, tenor Steblianko looks older than his father and his acting is stock, but his singing is as sturdy as the part requires. As Konchakovna, Konchak's nubile daughter with whom Vladimir is infatuated, Zaremba is ideally cast, her mezzo dark-hued and sultry, her specific timbre catching Konchakovna's sensual utterance to perfection. Burchuladze revels in the contrast of Konchak's character, catching both his rough-hewn earthiness and generous soul, which shows unexpected compassion towards his prisoner Igor. This is a highly spiced, sumptuously sung portrayal. Francis Egerton and Eric Garrett overdo the roles of the itinerant musicians Eroshka and Skula, unconvincing as Russians, more like British music-hall comics. Robin Leggate is suitably devious as the equivocal Ovlur. As the Polovtsian Maiden, Gillian Webster takes her one chance eagerly.

Burton's video direction is exemplary and the sound is of a high standard.

Amilcare Ponchielli (1834–86)

La Gioconda

Eva Marton (Gioconda), Ludmila Semchuk (Laura), Margarita Lilowa (La Cieca), Placido Domingo (Enzo), Matteo Manuguerra (Barnaba), Kurt Rydl (Alvise). Chor and Orch of the Vienna State Opera/Adam Fischer. Dir: Filippo Sanjust; video dir: Hugo Käch. Virgin VHS VVD 726; Pioneer LD: PLMC 00611.

Ponchielli's one outright success is a strong, consistently melodious score with a succession of effective situations. The libretto is by 'Tobia Gorro', Arrigo Boito, Verdi's librettist and a composer in his own right (*qv*), in anagrammatical disguise. It is brought to life by a taut text and by the composer's ability to write arias and ensembles that really stir the listener's emotions, provided the singers can meet their stringent demands.

Ponchielli is particularly successful at suggesting the feelings of his heroine, the eponymous ballad singer ironically named Gioconda, an unhappy girl whose love for the sea-faring Genoese nobleman Enzo Grimaldi in seventeenth-century Venice is not returned as he loves Laura, wife of Alvise, an agent of the Inquisition. The evil spy Barnaba loves Gioconda and ruthlessly manipulates her feelings to achieve his ends but, rather than submit to him, she commits suicide but not before she has arranged for him and Laura to escape the clutches of Alvise.

This video was taken at the Vienna State Opera in 1986, a new production, staged and designed by Filippo Sanjust. His decor is lavishly conceived to create the milieu of the four acts: the courtyard of the Doge's palace, Enzo's brigantine by the Grand Canal, the interior of the Ca' d'Oro Palace, and the ruin of Gioconda's palace on the island of Giudecca. Each, appropriately coloured, is lavishly conjured before our eyes. Unfortunately Sanjust has never been as good at activating his principals as he is at making sets, and this effort is no exception. Practically everything comes from stock, leaving the singers to fall back on their own devices.

Marton is a strong, effective and, in Act 4, moving Gioconda, but her thick, gritty tones are seldom shaded into anything more subtle. Semchuk's mezzo, in the part of Laura, is a more attractive voice, but she also sings in a single colour and with too little legato and not enough Italianate brio. As Enzo, Domingo is as ever strong and purposeful, but not perhaps in easiest voice in a role that stretches even the best of tenors. As Barnaba, the veteran baritone Manuguerra revels in playing the villain and always creates life when he is on stage, but his tone often lacks resonance. Rydl is too Germanic as ruthless, cruel Alvise and lacks the needed presence. Fischer draws efficient playing from the State Opera Orchestra, but his sense of rhythm is often erratic. All in all, this interpretation misses the presence of more Italian-trained singers.

Laserdisc has a decided edge here over the video version, both in terms of sound and picture.

Camille Saint-Saëns (1835–1921)

Samson et Dalila

1. Shirley Verrett (Dalila), Jon Vickers (Samson), Jonathan Summers (High Priest), John Tomlinson (Abimelech), Gwynne Howell (Old Hebrew). Chor and Orch of Royal Opera House, Covent Garden/Colin Davis. Dir: Elijah Moshinsky; video dir: John Vernon. Castle VHS CVI 2026. Subtitles.
2. Shirley Verrett (Dalila), Placido Domingo (Samson), Wolfgang Brendel (High Priest), Arnold Voketatis (Abimelech), Kevin Langan (Old Hebrew). Chor and Orch of the San Francisco Opera/Julius Rudel. Dir: Nicolas Joel; video dir: Kirk Browning. Virgin VHS VVD 393.

Saint-Saëns was one of the longest lived composers of his day, but he never repeated the huge success enjoyed by this work, which still sustains its place in the repertory. Surviving the shafts of Bernard Shaw, bans by the Lord Chamberlain and cries of 'oratorio' from American pundits, it continues to hold the attention of audiences whenever it is performed, not least for its combination of the pagan and the exotic. The composer learnt from many of his predecessors but forged his own style in creating a piece in which authority, compassion, sensuality and tragedy all play their part.

The 1981 Covent Garden version serves Saint-Saëns well. Moshinsky's acutely observed production is set within the evocative sets of the Australian painter Sydney Nolan, whose dun colours are enlightened by Maria Björnson's brightly coloured dresses and David Bintley's erotic choreography for the famous Bacchanale, which suggests at once an orgy and a fertility rite.

Davis's conducting is highly sympathetic to Saint-Saëns's subtle orchestration and harmony. He nicely balances energy with sensuousness, and shows marked sympathy with Samson's remorse in Act 3, when blinded and enfeebled he turns the mill-wheel and expresses his agony of heart. But then Davis and Vickers always worked at white heat together. Although no longer in pristine voice, Vickers creates an arresting portrait of a dignified man brought down by a single temptation, singing with stentorian, heroic voice and acting with his customary authority. He is seduced by the sinuous, sultry presence and singing of Verrett, and the chemistry between her and Vickers is palpable. Summers is a forcefully hieratical High Priest, Tomlinson a leering Abimelech, Howell a sympathetic Old Hebrew. Sound and picture are no more than average.

The 1981 San Francisco version is not recommended except for Domingo's committed Samson. Verrett is not as involved or as involving as at Covent Garden in the same year. The production is quasi-Hollywood and right over the top, good for a laugh, not much more, and sound quality is indifferent.

Georges Bizet (1838–75)

Carmen

1. Maria Ewing (Carmen), Leontina Vaduva (Micaëla), Luis Lima (Don José), Gino Quilico (Escamillo). Chor and Orch of Royal Opera House, Covent Garden/Zubin Mehta. Dir: Nuria Espert; video dir: Barrie Gavin. Virgin VHS VVD 950; Pioneer LD PLMCD 0091. Subtitles.
2. Maria Ewing (Carmen), Marie McLaughlin (Micaëla), Barry McCauley (Don José), David Holloway (Escamillo). Glyndebourne Festival Chor, London Philharmonic Orch/Bernard Haitink. Dir and video dir: Peter Hall. Castle VHS CVI 2018. Subtitles.
3. Agnes Baltsa (Carmen), Leona Mitchell (Micaëla), José Carreras (Don José), Samuel Ramey (Escamillo). Chor and Orch of Metropolitan Opera, New York/James Levine. Dir: Paul Mills (after Peter Hall); video dir: Brian Large. DG VHS 071 409–3; LD:—1. Subtitles (LD only).
4. Julia Migenes (Carmen), Faith Esham (Micaëla), Placido Domingo (Don José), Ruggero Raimondi (Escamillo). Chor of Radio France, Orchestre Nationale de France/Lorin Maazel. A film by Francesco Rosi. Columbia Tristar CVR 20530. Subtitles.

Questions of edition plague *Carmen*, as they do so many French operas. Originally performed with dialogue, for years it was given with the recitatives by Ernest Guiraud written after the composer's death. In recent times the dialogue has been restored (as is the case in these three performances), but that presents its own problems for non-French singers, many of those in smaller parts (and not only smaller ones) speaking in execrable French. Then Fritz Oeser's well-meaning but wrong-headed restoration of music sensibly cut for dramaturgical reasons by Bizet before the premiere has given opera houses headaches about what exactly to include.

In the most amenable of these versions, Mehta unfortunately includes more of Oeser than would seem wise, weakening the structure of the piece and he conducts it too waywardly. In other respects the performance has much to commend it. The sets may be conventional, but Espert's direction (1991), much derided at the time of the first performances, works splendidly on video, emphasising the fraught, tempestuous nature of the relationship between Carmen and José, based on her erotic charge which simply overwhelms him, driving him to compulsive infatuation, the core of Bizet's opera based on Prosper Mérimée's novel.

Ewing's Carmen, more finely honed and vocally idiomatic than at Glyndebourne in 1985 (see page 148), is a riveting presence, at once fatalistic, sensual, free-spirited and vulnerable. Her body language combined with those huge, staring saucer eyes of hers ensnares José, who becomes putty in her hands – as does her audience. Ewing's mastery of French helps; she delivers lines such as 'Je suis amoureuse' (in the tavern quintet) and 'la mort' (in the card scene) with idiomatic flair. Her singing is throughout intelligently weighted and pointedly phrased, nowhere more so than in the Seguedille. Lima's José is a fit partner for this Carmen.

The opera could as well have been named 'Don José' as it is his, not Carmen's, character that develops and changes during the course of the work, and Lima conveys ideally the way the soldier moves from shy, mother-dominated youth to possessed, then fatally jealous lover. He sings the role with equal intelligence, his line, tone and breath control well tailored to Bizet's often awkward writing for his tenor. Vaduva is near-perfect as Micaëla, catching the girl's winsome charm without cloying. She acts appealingly and sings her aria with clear, affecting tone. Quilico is a trifle lightweight for Escamillo, but sings and acts with proper insouciance in excellent French. Smaller parts are taken more or less adequately by Covent Garden regulars among whom the Mercédès of Jean Rigby, a Carmen herself, stands out.

The Laserdisc sound and picture are superb, the VHS less so. Gavin's video direction is too inclined to focus on Carmen and no one else, understandable when she is Ewing but unfair to others, particularly José.

Ewing also appears in the Glyndebourne/Hall staging of 1985, more wilful, athletic and self-indulgent than at Covent Garden: a 'lissome *jolie laide*' as she was described by one perceptive writer at the time of the production's first night. When she reached the Royal Opera six years later, most of the contrivance had been ironed away without losing a whit of magnetism. By the same token the interpretation at Glyndebourne is more spontaneous, witty and youthfully daring. Some of her singing here may be more reminiscent of a *chansonnière* than an opera singer, but whenever Ewing's Carmen is on stage the results are riveting.

Ewing is not so well supported as at Covent Garden except by Haitink, most idiomatic of the four conductors in bringing out the sensuousness of Bizet's writing and cleansing the score of excessive fat and sentimentality, but sometimes he is inclined to lethargic tempi. McCauley's tenor is too wiry for the good of Bizet's music, but he is quite convincing as the mother-loving boy fascinated and then obsessed by Carmen, and comes into his own in an impassioned finale. McLaughlin's Micaëla, suitably demure, is soundly sung. The Escamillo is weak. Jean Rigby is once more an alluring Mercédès.

This version has the inestimable advantage of presenting a complete version of the dialogue, which helps explain José's actions by filling in his background. Xavier Depraz, as Zuniga, speaks such fluent French that he shows up the heavy accents of the rest (Ewing had not yet quite mastered the language). This is very much a play with music, which was probably Bizet's real intention, and accords with the original concept in being performed in an intimate theatre. Hall directs the dialogue, indeed the whole reading, with his customary eye for pertinent detail in John Bury's traditional sets, recreating a true French tradition of performance. The tavern, a shadowy, gypsy hideaway, is particularly evocative. The movement is at all times natural. The picture and sound quality are no more than average.

Hall's traditional staging was expanded a great deal to fit on to the Met's stage, although he is not credited on the video and much of the perceptive detail has been lost in the move across the Atlantic. Here the title role is taken by Baltsa, who reigned in the part until Ewing assumed it. In 1987 she remains a lithe, athletic Carmen who stalks and then captures her prey through sheer willpower. Sung in that tangy, almost harsh mezzo of hers, with head and chest register no longer seamlessly united, her gypsy still exudes rampant sexuality and bestrides the stage and José with equal aplomb. Carreras, her regular stage partner in this work through the 1980s, gives his all-in, ardent portrayal of a shy boy turned mad by Carmen's wiles, but though the spirit is willing, the voice has already lost its ease and sheen, but he does manage an exquisite high B flat at the close of the Flower Song. Levine conducts a big-scale, unsubtle performance.

Mitchell is a simple, forthright Micaëla, though her tone is a trifle thick for Bizet's needs. Ramey is a stock, uninteresting, but vocally strong Escamillo. Small parts are inadequately sung and accented. Bury's decor and costumes, looking expensive, are highly coloured and pleasing on the eye, and Large gives us a good impression of the often-crowded, busy action. Picture and sound are high class.

The Rosi film is something else, perhaps the most successful film of an opera ever done on location, this one in Andalucia. All Rosi's skills and imagination in conjuring up milieux and atmosphere allied to his marvellous gifts at providing the right texture, angle and range for his shots make this a wonder for the eye, one that almost reconciles the irreconcilable of marrying the naturalistic demands of the cinema with the more artificial and enclosed requirements of opera. The sun-baked Andalucian countryside and the authentic feel of its people form the vivid foreground for the genre scenes and an apt background to the tragedy of its two principals who have been directed by Rosi with the utmost acuity and sensitivity. Migenes is to the life the freedom-loving, sensual, street-wise, defiant girl of Mérimée's and Bizet's imagining, and her light, lyric voice proves almost ideal for purveying all the carefree insouciance of the role in the early scenes yet able to adopt the darker colourings called for by the last two acts.

She is worthily matched by Domingo's José, turning from stiff, stolid, home-loving soldier to possessed, obsessed lover with deep, staring eyes that become quite frightening in Acts 3 and 4 as he begins desperately to challenge and then menace Carmen. This detailed portrayal surpasses anything the tenor has done in the part in the opera house, and his well-varied, tense, impassioned singing perfectly seconds his acting performance. This Carmen and José combine with Rosi to make the finale truly tragic as Rosi counterpoints conflict and death in the bullring with that outside it in an empty forecourt. Raimondi surpasses his usual, somewhat lacka-daisical form with a portrait of a confident, almost feline toreador, and his singing is fluently French in style. Esham sings warmly as Micaëla but gives a somewhat pallid account of herself on screen. The small parts are well taken.

Maazel conducts a keen, fast-moving account of the score that is all the better for this approach. Controversially he uses the Oeser additions and emendments to the Choudens score, but makes them work quite effectively. The sound is better than ordinary, the picture magnificent. At the current asking price of under £9 this is an outright bargain.

As an interesting, historical pendant to the mainstream issues is a VAI issue (69209) of 'Scenes from Bizet's *Carmen*' recorded in 1959 at the Bolshoi when Mario Del Monaco caused something of a sensation with his Don José, largely because the Soviet Union (as Russia then was) had been long starved of anything but local talent. He looks a stiff and/or melodramatic actor and his stentorian tone, while viscerally exciting, proves inappropriate to the role. He sings in Italian (except when he switches briefly to French in the Act 2 ex-cerpts) while the rest of the cast sings in Russian. No, the main interest here is in the thirty-four-year-old Irina Arkipho-va's gloriously sung Carmen, heard in the Habanera Seguedille, Act 2 duet and finale, such suave, well-modu-lated singing, such a sense of both the character's dignity and magnetism. The legendary Russian baritone Pavel Lisitsian makes a fleeting appearance as the toreador in the final scene, looking a trifle mature for the role but singing like a god. Alexander Melik-Pashayev is the vital conductor.

Modest Mussorgsky (1839–81)

Boris Godunov
Larissa Diadkova (Fyodor), Olga Borodina (Marina), Alexei Steblianko (Grigory), Yevgeny Boitsov (Shuisky), Sergei Leiferkus (Rangoni), Robert Lloyd (Boris Godunov), Alexandr Morosov (Pimen), Vladimir Ognovenko (Varlaam). Chor and Orch of the Kirov/Valery Gergiev. Dir: Andrei Tarkovsky/Stephen Lawless; video dir: Humphrey Burton. Decca VHS 071 409–3; LD:−1. Subtitles.

Mussorgsky portrays the Russian people in a series of great choruses and crowd scenes unequalled in opera. Set against this vivid and realistic background is the personal tragedy of the tormented and conscience-stricken Tsar who has attained the throne through the murder of the true heir Dimitri. Mussorgsky gives him a profile worthy of Shakespeare. His powers of characterisation extend to the romantic, self-deluding false pretender Grigory, masquerading as the murdered Tsarevich; Boris's shifty adviser Prince Shuisky, leader of the Boyars; the scheming Polish prelate Rangoni; and the ambitious Polish Princess Marina; not forgetting the earthy Varlaam and the plaintive Simpleton. Each is given specific and pointed music.

The vicissitudes of the work's genesis is a story in itself. It was first written in only seven taut scenes in 1868–9, enlarged and refashioned in 1871–2, performed and published in a reduced version in 1874. Then, after Mussorgsky's death, Rimsky-Korsakov 'improved' the orchestration in a version that was for long standard. Today most conductors prefer to give Mussorgsky's original, largely faithful to 1871–2. That is the edition played by Gergiev in this superb performance from the Marynsky Theatre in St Petersburg.

151

It is based on film director Tarkovsky's tradition-breaking production for Covent Garden in 1983. After his untimely death, it was transferred to the Kirov in 1990 whence it was filmed. It has a distinct advantage over its Covent Garden predecessor in its predominantly Russian cast, chorus and orchestra. There before our eyes process a whole gallery of boyars, princes, miscreants, downtrodden peasants, each face almost out of a painting. Then Nicholas Dvigoubsky's decor well contrasts the squalor of the public scenes with the grandeur and glitter of the private palaces.

Frontstage, as it were, are some of the best of the current generation of Russian singers, not a dud among them. If one scene deserves to be singled out, that must be the one between Marina and Rangoni in the Polish (third) act where Borodina's sensual, wilful, wheedling Princess and Leiferkus's repressed, scheming priest spar with each other. Both are portrayals hard to conceive being bettered. This encounter is an object-lesson in what operatic singing and acting should be about.

Almost as rewarding are the virile, heroic Grigory of Steblianko, Morozov's grave, haunting – though too youthful – Pimen (the monk who puts ideas of claiming the throne into Grigory's head), Diadkova's attractive Fyodor (the Tsar's son), Ognovenko's rip-roaring Varlaam, and Boitsov's inveigling Shuisky. All are caught on the wing, giving spontaneous, dedicated performances as part of a well-integrated ensemble, subtly directed by Lawless.

At their head is the sole survivor of the 1983 cast, Robert Lloyd as Boris. He presents a figure agonising over his misdeeds, troubled within while never upsetting the verities of secure tone and even line. Everything he does is thought through and outwardly convincing, yet he cannot hide his British figure and features, which look misplaced in the part, the more so on video. Nor does his tone have the richness and depth of his most notable predecessors from Slav countries.

Gergiev is another of the performance's heroes. Seldom if ever, not even when Abbado conducted the production at Covent Garden, has the score sounded so arresting, so married to this panorama of Russian life in the seventeenth century. His own orchestra responds to his well-defined beat with playing of point and precision. The chorus sound confident and idiomatic, seconding their looks under his firmly controlled direction.

Humphrey Burton's video direction is impeccable. So is the picture and sound. Subtitles are provided. What more could one want?

Khovanshchina

1. Joanna Borowska (Emma), Ludmila Semtschuk (Marfa), Vladimir Atlantov (Andrei Khovansky), Yuri Marusin (Golitsin), Heinz Zednik (Scribe), Nicolai Ghiaurov (Ivan Khovansky), Anatoly Kocherga (Shaklovity), Paata Burchuladze (Dosifey). Chor and Orch of the Vienna State Opera/Claudio Abbado. Dir: Alfred Kirchner; video dir: Brian Large. Pioneer LD PLMCC 00631.

2. Tatiana Kravtsova (Emma), Olga Borodina (Marfa), Yuri Marusin (Andrei Khovansky), Constantin Pluzhnikov (Golitsin/Scribe), Bulat Minjelkiev (Ivan Khovansky), Viacheslav Trofimov (Shaklovity), Nikolai Okhtnikov (Dosifey), Chor and Orch of the Kirov, St Petersburg/Valery Gergiev. Dir: Fyodor Lopukhov; video dir: Brian Large. Philips VHS 070 433—3; LD:—1. Subtitles.

This work has a peculiarly modern relevance as it depicts internecine squabbles and intrigues among various groups in Russian society, here in the seventeenth century at the time of the modernising Peter the Great's accession, although censorship forbade him to be represented on stage. Conjured before us in their different guises are the Old Believers led by the prelate Dosifey, two princely factions led by Khovansky, father and son, and the individual figures of Prince Golitsin, representing the Tsar's viewpoint and the wily, freebooting Shaklovity. All are placed within a panoramic portrait of downtrodden Russia in all its glory and degradation. Mussorgsky observes his country's predicament with his customary empathy – and with bleak realism.

The composer left the score unfinished. Once more his successors came to his rescue. In his vivid interpretation Abbado employs Shostakovich's faithful completion with the choral ending devised by Stravinsky. He shows a welcome rapport with Kirchner's staging transferred to the screen by Brian Large, who manages to give an impression of the breadth of the production and of Erich Wonder's vivid sets while also emphasising the personal conflicts of the principals.

As the older Khovansky veteran Ghiaurov cuts an impressive figure although his tone sometimes sounds dry under pressure. Kocherga is a properly implacable Shaklovity, Burchuladze an imposing Dosifey, though his vibrato is intrusive. Atlantov makes a forceful Andrei Khovansky; Marusin's highly individual tenor and style of acting are well suited to the reforming, sophisticated Golitsin. Best of all is the dark mezzo of Semtschuk, who gives a riveting portrayal of the intense, fanatical Marfa. The most important heroes are the chorus and orchestra; both cover themselves in glory.

The only disappointment concerns the presentation. Pioneer provides poor back-up, containers and booklet being inadequate in content and style. Nor are subtitles, so essential here, provided.

The version recorded at the Marynsky in 1992, a fit partner for its *Boris*, is even more compelling, chiefly because it preserves, in the best sense, a tradition of performing the work only possible to see and hear in Russia. As you watch this authentic staging in realistic sets, one has to wonder if modern 'concepts' of this or any work can really improve on creating, in the country of origin, a production that conforms to the given libretto and score. This magnificently lit and designed (Fyodor Fedorovsky) staging holds the attention from first to last – and that through 3 hours and 25 minutes of music, for Gergiev plays the score absolutely complete, including the scene between Golitsin and the Lutheran pastor in Act 2, almost always excluded.

His is a splendid reading, energetic or ruminative as the work demands, and making the very most of Shostakovich's orchestration. His players dig deep into the wells of their collective knowledge of Mussorgsky's particular idiom and psyche. The Kirov Chorus is no less admirable, a multitude of interesting faces making up a convincing whole, and of course properly Russian in timbre – as is the sound of every soloist.

Right from the start we catch the note of authenticity in Pluzhnikov's Scribe, a portrait of special significance, a wily, frightened, scheming eccentric with an unforgettable face. Can this be the same tenor who presents Golitsin with equal aplomb, a eupeptic, wilful yet forward-looking aristocrat? Both parts are sung in that peculiarly incisive timbre only Russian tenors possess. Marusin, who here transfers from Golitsin, his role with Abbado, to the selfish, libidinous Andrei Khovansky, is another in the same mould. As his commanding father, Ivan Khovansky, Minjelkiev is a formidable figure, his sense of power projected on a strong, if not very appealing, bass.

Trofimov makes the most of Shaklivity's aria sorrowing over the fate of Russia. Okhtnikov, a noted Boris, is here a resolute and imposing Dosifey who uses his resonant bass and piercing eyes to convey the man's religious conviction, though you can well imagine this man as a formidable boyar in his previous incarnation in life.

But the performance of the set is Borodina's overwhelming Marfa. For once you believe that this beautiful, sad-looking woman is yearning to be restored to Andrei Khovansky's arms, her earthly, womanly passions vying with her religious faith. Borodina sings her two solos with glorious tone and lovely phrasing, for which she is noted: her scene in Act 3 with Dosifey is infinitely moving.

The direction – Large yet again – is exemplary, giving us the piece's true flavour, and the sound is good to excellent. Subtitles here are a great help in sorting out the various strands of plot and argument in this panoramic masterpiece.

Peter Ilyich Tchaikovsky (1840–93)

Eugene Onegin
1. Teresa Kubiak (Tatyana, acted by Magdaléna Vašaryová), Julia Hamari (Olga, Kamila Magálová), Anna Reynolds (Mme Larina, Antonie Hegerliková), Enid Hartle (Filipyevna, Vlasta Fabiánová), Stuart Burrows (Lensky, Emil Horváth), Michel Sénéchal (Monsieur Triquet, František Filipovsky), Bernd Weikl (Onegin, Michal Dočolomnansky), Nicolai Ghiaurov (Gremin,

Premyl Koˆi). John Alldis Chor, Orch of the Royal Opera House, Covent Garden/Georg Solti. A film by Petr Weigl. Decca VHS 071 124–3; LD:−1.
2. Mirella Freni (Tatyana), Sandra Walker (Olga), Jean Craft (Mme Larina), Gweneth Bean (Filipyevna), Peter Dvorsky (Lensky), John Fryatt (Monsieur Triquet), Wolfgang Brendel (Onegin), Nicolai Ghiaurov (Gremin). Chor and Orch of Chicago Lyric Opera/Bruno Bartoletti. Dir: Pier Luigi Samaritani; video dir: Kirk Browning. Castle VHS CVI 2037.

Few operas are so immediately attractive and haunting as Tchaikovsky's elegiac work based on Pushkin's poem of the same name, in which the bored, seemingly heartless Onegin rejects the affections of the ingenuous Tatyana after she has addressed him in an impassioned missive (the famous letter scene) only to regret his decision a few years later when he meets her again at a ball as a married woman. Although she still loves him, she refuses to break her marriage vows. Olga, Tatyana's younger sister, adores the poet Lensky (who introduces Onegin to Tatyana at the latter's home). At a local party Onegin flirts with Olga to the despair of the sensitive Lensky, who is killed by Onegin in the subsequent duel. Tchaikovsky empathises with all his principals in turn and characterises them unforgettably.

Unlike Tchaikovsky's later opera, *The Queen of Spades* (see page 159), this one is poorly represented on video (though as we go to press the wonderful Glyndebourne staging of 1994 has just been released by Decca.—VHS 079 202–3. Weigl's 1988 film is not as successful as his version of Delius's *A Village Romeo and Juliet (qv)*, although it has some of the same attributes. Filmed, like the Delius, on location in what was Czechoslavakia, using local actors, its settings are apt to the story and intelligently applied to the score, not least in the loving detail of Tatyana's bedroom. The actors mime perfectly to the 1974 Decca recording and look their parts, a rather too mature Lensky apart. The most apt and appealing is the Tatyana, who changes unerringly from the innocent romantic of Act 1 to the dignified woman of Act 3. She conveys all the eagerness of the letter scene, all the heartbreak of its outcome, with one marvellous shot showing her as a lonely, deserted figure in a beautiful landscape. There is poetry here and a keen eye for matching movement to music.

Unfortunately Weigl spoils things by ruthlessly cutting the score by some forty minutes to suit his own cinematic ends. The musical performance is competent rather than inspired. Solti conducts promptly but without sufficient involvement or idiomatic impulse. Everything is correct, little more. Kubiak sounds slightly mature for Tatyana – and for her film counterpart – but sings with firmness, feeling and an authentic Slav timbre. Weikl has the right weight and tone for Onegin, but his interpretation isn't quite as keenly profiled as it should be. Burrows's Lensky has the right plangent sound and he shapes his music with feeling. Hamari is a lively Olga, and all the smaller parts are well cast.

Still, this carefully thought-out film is more worth seeing and hearing than the dull, conventional Chicago Lyric Opera staging of 1985, unhelped on video by the dim lighting of the decor: nothing strikes home with much immediacy. Freni, singing her first Tatyana at the age of fifty, inevitably looks too mature for the part. Weakly directed, she emotes in only the conventionally operatic way, evincing little of the sensitive Tatyana's inner feelings. She sings the part with her usual attention to the vocal verities, but the portrayal remains earthbound and unconvincing. Brendel suggests too little of Onegin's *bon ton* or, later, desperate passions, singing warmly but in too generalised a fashion.

Dvorsky's Lensky is as uninteresting as a character as a singer though his voice is always adequate to the demands placed on it. Ghiaurov is an authoritative but rusty Gremin. The smaller roles want point and conviction. Under Bartoletti's run-of-the-mill conducting this is an interpretation that measures up to Tchaikovsky's endearing work only in the most basic terms of unfussy, impersonal efficiency. The sound is rather muted, the video direction unimaginative.

The just-released Glyndebourne Set features Graham Vick's unforgettably moving production and Elena Prokina's equally memorable Tatyana.

The Maid of Orleans

Nina Rautio (Joan of Arc), Maria Gavrilova (Agnès Sorel), Oleg Kulko (Charles VII), Vladimir Redkin

(Lionel), Mikhail Krutikov (Dunois). Chor and Orch of the Bolshoi/Alexander Lazarev. Dir: Boris Pokrovsky; video dir: Brian Large. Teldec VHS 4509–94191–3.

Tchaikovsky's Joan of Arc opera is based on Schiller's drama, heavily adapted by the composer in his own libretto. Too often in this intermittently inspired work, he seems to be working at well below his best, deliberately writing a piece with the French market in mind and thereby sacrificing his own plaintive urgency of utterance. The only character really demanding attention is Joan herself because for her Tchaikovsky went to the heart of the matter, carrying over identification with his given heroine from his recently completed *Onegin*, and it is her music, in particular her famous farewell at the end of Act 1, her narration in Act 2 and the second (of two) duets with her beloved but fated Lionel, that makes the piece viable. So it is hardly surprising to find those two roles the most convincing in this 1993 Bolshoi performance (recorded in the theatre without an audience present). The rest, as the Tchaikovsky scholar Gerald Abraham once suggested, are merely characters in fancy dress.

The video is worth seeing and, more importantly, hearing for Rautio's superb reading of the title role, for which her rounded, firm tone, honestly moulded phrasing and simple, slightly naïve style of acting perfectly fit her. Whenever she is on stage there is something worthwhile to see and hear. Redkin as Lionel, though he has much less to do, reveals a strong, pleasing baritone and upright presence, near-ideal for the English renegade who falls for Joan. Credit is also due to Krutikov as a fiery, bold Dunois: his typically Russian bass invests his subsidiary role with rewarding character. The remainder of the singers exhibit the worst characteristics of Russian singing, unsteady and/or clumsy, technically all too fallible.

The staging, new in 1990, reached Glasgow that year, the Metropolitan in 1991 with other singers, but with Lazarev as the constant. His conducting is vital rather than penetrating, not always making the most of an admittedly awkward, episodic score. Pokrovsky's staging is unbelievably old-fashioned in its stand-and-sing, oratorio-like view of the work within a central stage area designed in realistic style by Valery Leventhal. The double parade of winged white angels, some in person, other in huge cut-outs, at the end of Scene 1 is frankly risible. The uneasy costuming, part medieval, part modern evening-dress, is unconvincing. Joan's final ascension, borne to heaven over flames from below, has a certain conviction. Pokrovsky seems to have given his charges little guidance in their acting, which is rudimentary to a fault. Only Rautio, by her sincerity, overcomes that drawback.

Large is left to make the best of it, by concentrating on essentials, but even he can't make such a paltry affair truly credible. The sound is adequate, no more. Still it is well worth investigating this performance for the sake of Rautio, who triumphs wonderfully over adverse circumstances. She is in many ways the most admirable of the new roster of Russian sopranos. Teldec hardly helps its case by failing to provide subtitles.

The Queen of Spades
1. Nancy Gustafson (Lisa), Felicity Palmer (Countess), Marie-Ange Todorovich (Pauline), Yuri Marusin (Herman), Sergei Leiferkus (Tomsky), Dimitri Kharitonov (Yeletsky). Glyndebourne Festival Chor, London Philharmonic Orch/Andrew Davis. Dir: Graham Vick; video dir: Peter Maniura. Pioneer LD PLMCC 008412.
2. Maria Gulegina (Lisa), Ludmila Filatova (Countess), Olga Borodina (Pauline), Gegam Grigorian (Herman), Sergei Leiferkus (Tomsky), Alexander Gergalov (Yeletsky). Chor and Orch of Kirov Opera/Valery Gergiev. Dir: Yuri Temirkanov; video dir: Brian Large. Philips VHS 070 434–3; LD:—1. Subtitles.

For this, his second most popular opera, Tchaikovsky again turned to Pushkin, but here the libretto by Modest Tchaikovsky, the composer's brother, alters the emphasis of the story. Pushkin's succinct tale has a cold-blooded officer seeking the secret of the three cards from the old Countess and uninterested in Lisa except insofar as she can gain him access to the old lady, who possesses the required information. In the

opera, Herman becomes an almost Byronic hero torn between genuine love for Lisa and his obsession with gambling.
Whatever the arguments about these changes, the libretto
ideally suited Tchaikovsky's penchant for creating the moods
and passions of unhappy romances and delineating them
against a public background. He also created a unique character in the eccentric, selfish, haunted old Countess.

Both the videos, in their contrasted ways, are worthy of the
composer's extraordinary score, one that probes into the
depths of the principals' characters. Vick at Glyndebourne in
1992 exactly reflects the highly charged emotions and brood-
ing sense of menace that pervade the music, creating a
psychodrama that compels eye and ear. Richard Hudson's
decor admirably melds semi-abstract modern with the more
realistic and picturesque elements essential to the piece. The
set is basically a white box slanted from left to right, its walls
splashed, Gerald Scarfe-like, with black paint and sometimes
placed at a disorientating angle to mirror Herman's incipient
madness. Vick takes every chance to maximise its imaginative
possibilities and directs his principals with an unerring sense
of private torment within public ceremonial; the ball scene,
and its pastoral divertissement, set to pastiche Mozart, is wittily contrived.

Davis's conducting catches most but not all of the score's
romantic sweep and inner, dislocating turbulence. Much of
the music is lovingly and sensuously turned, but the psychological undercurrents, and impassioned outbursts are better
adumbrated by Gergiev in the St Petersburg performance.

Marusin, a formidable presence on stage, is the crazed Herman incarnate as he heads towards madness. His singing is
something else. His 'fixed' tenor is used unsparingly and
with a certain heroic ferocity, but a consistent tendency to
approach notes from the flat side seriously compromises his
reading. As his Lisa, Gustafson offers a portrayal of an
anxious, faithful, impressionable girl driven to distraction
and suicide by the unhinged behaviour of her beloved. These
portrayals are all the more compelling on video where every
expression is caught in close-up. That is even truer of
Palmer's electrifying Countess, the ruins of a strong-willed

woman recalling her eventful past and then murmuring her Grétry air with mesmerising delicacy. Leiferkus is elegant and commanding as the free-living Tomsky. Kharitonov sings Yeletsky's expressive aria with warm tone and a firm legato. Todorovich is an attractive Pauline.

The sound recording, which has plenty of aural range, could with advantage have given greater prominence to the voices. Maniura's video direction catches almost every nuance of his stage counterpart's discerning work. Large is no less successful at catching the breadth of the more traditional St Petersburg production, caught in the same year, 1992, as the Glyndebourne, but, as in the rival set, the voices are a shade too reticently recorded.

The direction may be old-fashioned in the manner of performances in the Soviet era, but the grand, realistic settings (costumes in period) are always apt to the piece, and in one scene, the appearances of the Countess's ghost in Herman's barracks, St Petersburg surpasses Glyndebourne in frightening effects – but then it has the advantage of a large theatre's technical apparatus. Temirkanov allows the Countess, controversially, to rise from her chair rather than staying transfixed in it. In that role Filatova is demonstrably too youthful for her role, given so many close-ups, but hers is a riveting portrait and she makes more of the text than Palmer at Glyndebourne. Leiferkus is again magnificent in his airy definition of Tomsky's equivocal character. Gergalov is a handsome Yeletsky, who sings his grateful piece in appealingly soft-grained tones, Borodina an enchanting Pauline.

Grigorian begins as little more than a conventional tenor singing with all-purpose fervour. Gradually he builds into his performance a sense of Herman's unhinged mind in his tone, eyes and body language, and he is certainly securer in voice than Marusin. At the heart of the performance on this occasion is Maria Gulegina's intense, vibrant Lisa. Her acting suggests all Lisa's unjustified faith in Herman and her growing desperation at each new disillusionment. Her interpretation is as good as any reason for sampling this version, quite different from but just as convincing as the Glyndebourne.

Antonin Dvořák (1841–1904)

Rusalka

Eilene Hannan (Rusalka), Cathryn Pope, Eileen Hulse, Linda McLeod (Wood Nymphs), Ann Howard (Ježibaba), Phyllis Cannan (Foreign Princess), Fiona Kimm (Kitchen Boy), John Treleaven (Prince), Edward Byles (Gamekeeper), Rodney McCann (Water Spirit). Chor and Orch of English National Opera/Mark Elder. Dir: David Pountney; video dir: Derek Bailey. Virgin VHS VVD 392. In English.

Of Dvořák's ten operas, *Rusalka* is undoubtedly his masterpiece. A fairytale fantasy involving the love of the wood nymph Rusalka for a human Prince (unnamed) and her tortured relationships with her grandfather the Water Spirit and the Witch Ježibaba, who throws a spell on Rusalka, striking her dumb before her lover. Eventually, when she is able to speak, another spell will cause the Prince to die should he kiss Rusalka. The psychological implications of the score are multifarious. In his post-Freudian staging for ENO (first staged in 1985, videoed the following year), David Pountney interprets the work as a girl's realisation of her sexuality and depicts the consequences of her rejection by her first love, the Prince.

Rusalka is here an adolescent girl in a Victorian nursery, Ježibaba her evil governess, the Water Spirit her elderly relation helpless in a wheelchair, the other nymphs her younger sisters. Rusalka's legs are bound by bandages as symbol of her virginity (or is this merely to indicate she's a mermaid?) until Ježibaba cuts and unwinds them, sending her off in a whirl to meet her Prince. In his castle (Act 2) she is isolated in a glass cage, unable to communicate with the real world and taunted by the sophisticated Foreign Princess, rival for the Prince's hand. She flees back to the nursery, now a sad, abandoned place. She seeks Ježibaba's aid, but Ježibaba merely wreaks her revenge on mankind by throwing her new spell on Rusalka. When the Prince comes to seek her out and then willingly accepts his fate Rusalka, still haunted by his initial rejection, wanders off into the woods.

For once a modern production marches with the original intention of the story. Within Stefanos Lazaridis's evocative yet simple setting, the plot unfolds convincingly, and enhances a wonderful score that combines Czech-inspired motifs and a lyrical line for the voices with Wagnerian harmony into a richly rewarding pattern of sound tinged throughout with tragic force but leavened by the lighter scenes for Rusalka's sisters and the characters of the Gamekeeper and the Kitchen Boy.

Elder in the pit conducts with passionate intensity and a firm command of the work's structure. He and Pountney persuade Hannan to give the performance of her career as a frightened, disturbed, infinitely sad Rusalka. Howard sings and plays Ježibaba as a close cousin (which she is) to the Witch in *Hänsel und Gretel* (*qv*). Treleaven's Prince is ardent, though a shade eupeptic-looking for a young lover. McCann's Water Spirit is moving as a troubled but helpless onlooker. Kimm and Byles are amusingly hyperactive as Kitchen Boy and Gamekeeper, portrayed by Pountney as floppy dolls. The nubile trio of Wood Nymphs are, suitably, close cousins of the Rhine Maidens. Picture and sound are excellent in catching the character and presence of a riveting production. Rodney Blumer's translation is exemplary.

Arrigo Boito (1842–1918)

Mefistofele
Gabriele Benacková (Margharita, Elena), Dennis O'Neill (Faust), Samuel Ramey (Mefistofele). Chor and Orch of the San Francisco Opera/Maurizio Arena. Dir: Robert Carsen; video dir: Brian Large. Pioneer LD PLMCC 00691.

Boito is best known as librettist of Verdi's later masterpieces, *Otello* and *Falstaff*, but he was a composer in his own right though remembered today only by this work. It had a troubled gestation and premiere (1868), because of its unworkable length and layout (Boito had strong reforming ideas about what an opera should be). Eventually the composer substantially revised it, and in its new, four-act form it proved a success, and has remained in the repertory, particularly in Italy, not least because the title role is a gift for a dramatic bass. Toscanini conducted it at La Scala with Shalyapin in 1901. Its most recent interpreter has been Samuel Ramey and the performance under review starred him at Geneva, Chicago and San Francisco, from where this video was made in 1992. Musically the work is distinctly uneven, alternating between moments of lyrical beauty and extended note-spinning. As a whole the work bears only a loose connection with its inspiration, Goethe's philosophical masterpiece.

Ramey is the most cogent reason for this issue, for his portrayal of Mephisto is masterly both in its projection of the devil's strong will and blatant cynicism, and in its vocal command right from the moment when he steps up on stage from the pit (slightly spoilt by stagehands seen holding his ladder!) to accept the Almighty's challenge over Faust's soul. A lithe, commanding figure, he never falters vocally or dramatically, dominating the stage throughout. His 'Ecco il mondo' in the witches' Sabbath scene is chilling indeed. Boito wanted Margharita and Helen of Troy (Elena) to be doubled by the same soprano, thereby stressing the concept of the 'Ewigweibliche'. Benacková easily encompasses the roles of innocent Margharita and regal Helen, singing both with vocal allure and a deal of sensitive phrasing, if not always truly Italianate tone. The disappointment here is O'Neill's vocally stretched, dramatically uncommunicative Faust.

Arena conducts with some flair, and the important choral sections are strongly delivered. Carsen's production is pure American kitsch, awful to behold, with ghastly plaster angels, candlelit boxes, prancing, masked dancers, a nude vision of Margharita in the Kermesse scene, and a pretty-pretty garden at Margharita's home. Large's video direction is faultless.

Arthur Sullivan (1842–1900)

The Mikado
Lesley Garrett (Yum-Yum), Susan Bullock (Peep-Bo), Ethna Robinson (Pitti-Sing), Felicity Palmer (Katisha),

Bonaventura Bottone (Nanki-Poo), Mark Richardson (Pish-Tush), Eric Idle (Ko-Ko), Richard Van Allan (Pooh-Bah), Richard Angas (Mikado). Chor and Orch of English National Opera/Peter Robinson. Dir: Jonathan Miller; video dir: John Michael Phillips. Thames VHS TV8122.

The most popular work in the G&S canon is given here in the ENO's now-famous staging by Miller, which takes the piece, delightfully and quite inconsequentially, into a Grand Hotel in 1920s England. That's a cue for dancing maids and bell-hops, Charlestons from the Three Little Maids, a northern lounge-lizard of a Pish-Tush in plus fours, a sneering aristocrat of a Pooh-Bah with palm always at the ready for greasing (Richard Van Allan sardonically amusing), a Katisha who's just leapt out of her aeroplane still sporting her goggles. These and many other inventions adorn a staging that miraculously maintains a unified style from start to finish in Stefanos Lazaridis's all-white hotel lounge. Decorating it are the inevitable piano, a huge wind-up gramophone and an enlarged cocktail glass. Ko-Ko enters as a masher, then turns up in striped blazer and boater. His list is amusingly updated and, cleverly, the references in this video version still ring true. Some of Gilbert's other dialogue is discreetly or not so discreetly amended.

Ko-Ko is played (hardly sung) by Eric Idle whose perplexed, sometimes crazed look and acting are consistently amusing even when he seems to be stepping outside the production to address the audience directly. Katisha, in a gloriously over-the-top performance from Felicity Palmer, is turned into a virago of an aviator, symbol of wronged womanhood. Richard Angas's outsize, swaying Mikado is a gangland boss of paradoxically sinister yet ridiculous character. Garrett, catching the flapper poses to perfection, does a treat of a Charleston, which is not to forget her sensuous, poised account of 'The sun whose rays'. She's partnered by Bottone's chipper Nanki-Poo, with the faint air of seedy co-respondent about him. The staging, like the piece itself, goes slightly off the boil at the start of Act 2. Peter Robinson conducts a trim account of the eternally fresh score.

The picture is slightly fuzzy (at least on my copy) and the sound a shade over-bright, but by and large this is a discerningly directed record (with highlighting of the principals on insets during ensembles) of a gladsome night at the operetta.

Nikolay Rimsky-Korsakov (1844–1908)

Sadko

Valentina Tsidipova (Volkhova), Larissa Diadkova (Nezhata), Marianna Tarassova (Lyubava), Vladimir Galusin (Sadko), Gegam Grigorian (Indian Guest), Alexander Gergelev (Venetian Guest), Bulat Minzelkiev (Viking Guest), Sergei Alexashkin (Sea King). Chor, Ballet and Orch of the Kirov/Valery Gergiev. Dir: Alexei Stepaniuk; video dir: Brian Large. Philips VHS 070 439–3; LD:−1. Subtitles.

Rimsky's fourth opera, completed in 1898 and a special favourite of the fastidious composer, is typical of his work in the genre in its combination of the real world with the fantastic. His own libretto, consisting of seven tableaux, each with its own distinct character, depicts the adventures of the eponymous twelfth-century minstrel, and juxtaposes scenes set in ancient Novogrod, the composer's native district, with others on the enchanted lake and in the kingdom of the Sea King, whose daughter Volkhova enchants Sadko and seduces him away from reality and from his adoring wife Lyubava. The piece is generally and rightly considered Rimsky's best, subtly varying his harmonic language: tonal for the real world, chromatic for that of the Sea King.

Gergiev, director of the Kirov, performing at the famous Marinsky Theatre in St Petersburg, determined to revive the work in facsimiles of the 1920 sets of the painter Konstantin Korovin. The results, as can be gleaned from this video made at a live performance in 1994, are vivid and evocative of a past age's glory as regards the decor: folk-inspired at Novogrod, stars, swans and mists for the enchanted lake; mysterious greens for the Sea Kingdom. But some of the positioning and acting look old-fashioned in the wrong way, static and occasionally unconvincing, most gestures taken from operatic stock.

That hardly matters when the performance is so musically vital and benefits notably from the participation of the Kirov ballet in the big set scenes both in Novogrod and in the Sea King's domain. Gergiev performs the opera in uncut form, thus preserving its well-conceived dimensions, and conducts it with a nice command of its structure. Some of the score doesn't stretch beyond the illustrative and/or descriptive, but in the scenes for the principals, Rimsky writes in an expansive, quasi-Italianate yet highly individual vein with plentiful examples of his gift for haunting melody. And, as ever, his subtlety of orchestral colouring is much in evidence.

The Kirov field a strong cast. Galusin convincingly conveys Sadko's free spirit, and his bright tenor happily blends the lyric with the heroic, even if his tone is inclined to harden under pressure. Tsidipova is an alluring Volkhova with a refulgent, big-scale voice that she deploys with a deal of artistry, especially in her tender lullaby of farewell to the sleeping Sadko (often in the past recorded separately), which she sings before turning herself into a river. Her spell broken, the itinerant hero can return to his faithful wife, Lyubava, after a twelve-year absence. That role is taken by Tarassova, a mezzo with a voice of supple warmth married to Russian strength, surely a star in the making. Her poignant characterisation draws sympathy for this hard-done-by woman. In the other mezzo part, that of the psalter player Nezhata, Diadkova sings with almost as much beauty as her colleague.

Before Sadko sets off on his travels he hears the tales of the Viking, Indian and Venetian merchants (respectively, bass, tenor and baritone), all of whom have songs suitable to their countries. Minzelkiev is imposing as the Viking, Gergelev forthright as the Venetian, but Grigorian, one of the house's leading tenors (see Tchaikovsky's *Queen of Spades*), is curiously clumsy as the Indian. Alexashkin is a properly fiery Sea King, neatly warming his tone as his suspicions of Sadko are overcome.

As a whole this is an issue to treasure. Large's video direction is as faultless as ever. The sound is a model of excellence.

And as the work is one seldom produced in the West – there has been none from a major company in Britain since the war – it's all the more welcome.

Engelbert Humperdinck (1854–1921)

Hänsel und Gretel
Edita Gruberová (Gretel), Norma Burrowes (Sandman), Elfriede Höbarth (Dew Fairy), Helga Dernesch (Mother), Brigitte Fassbaender (Hänsel), Sena Jurinac (Witch), Hermann Prey (Father). Vienna Boys' Chor, Vienna Philharmonic Orch/Georg Solti. A film by August Everding. Decca VHS 071 102–3; LD:–1.

Humperdinck's fairy tale is a delight for children of all ages. Here Wagnerian methods are at the service of a pleasing fantasy. The composer deftly combines simple, folk-like melody, voices light enough to suggest the children who get lost in a wood seeking strawberries and are inveigled into the Witch's snares, and a Wagnerian orchestration apt for portraying an elaborate dream sequence and the Witch's Ride. The piece, which has held its popularity now for almost a hundred years, rightly shows no sign of losing its ability to captivate an audience.

This film quite cleverly melds stage, studio, location and animation in conjuring up Humperdinck's fantasy world, although the use of children watching in the baroque theatre at Linderhof, Ludwig II's imitation of Versailles on a small scale, is a questionable conceit: they sit in the stalls looking – at what? A performance on stage, this film or a combination of both? It's never made clear.

Everding touches realism in showing the poverty of the family's hovel, where the desperate mother has to scrimp and scrape to make ends meet and sends the children off into the forest when they break a treasured jug. Once into the woods, they enter an enchanted world tinged with menace, which is subtly suggested in the evocation of trees, Sandman, Dew Fairy. The Dream Pantomime is well handled, suggesting sentiment without sentimentality. The Witch's house is first seen as an imaginary, painted building, but she, her brew and her oven are filmed inside an ancient barn, while her Ride is truly chilling.

Jurinac changes arrestingly from seeming mother-figure into lurid, cackling hate-figure. Instead of the usual exaggerations, she actually sings the witch's music with accuracy, and full tone, a great improvement. Gruberová and Fassbaender make a fairly credible pair of children, the latter a particularly convincing Hänsel. As the Mother, Dernesch makes much of little, but as the Father, Prey overdoes the drunken mugging. Solti conducts a straight, unsentimental account of the score, beautifully played by the Vienna Philharmonic, caught truly by the sound recording. Lip-synch is, by and large, well managed; the sound recording excellent.

Leos Janáček (1854–1928)

Jenufa
Roberta Alexander (Jenufa), Lynne Davies (Jano), Anja Silja (Kostelnicka), Alison Hagley (Karolka), Linda Ormiston (Mayor's Wife), Menai Davies (Grandmother Buryja), Philip Langridge (Laca), Mark Baker (Steva), Robert Poulton (Foreman), Gordon Sandison (Mayor). Glyndebourne Festival Chor, London Philharmonic Orch/Andrew Davis. Dir: Nikolaus Lehnhoff; video dir: Derek Bailey. Virgin VHS VVD 928. Subtitles.

It was the Prague production of this opera in 1916 that brought fame to Janáček. Very soon the highly original work was given all over Europe, but it was not until the 1950s when Rafael Kubelik and Charles Mackerras began to introduce his operas that the composer became known in Britain and the USA. Since then all his works for the stage have gained currency. *Jenufa* displays at once all his most important traits: his expansive humanity, his love of the sounds of nature, his use of motifs to build his musical structures, the intensity and surpassing beauty of his music. There is a poignancy, lyrical grace and spontaneity in his writing that is unique. He felt that landscapes and people revealed their souls in the 'tracks of sounds that pass our way'.

Jenufa tells of the love of the eponymous heroine for the weak, drunken Steva, by whom she has a child during the course of the opera. Eventually she realises that his half-brother Laca, who adores Jenufa, is worthy of her love. However the plot is driven by Kostelnicka, the Sextoness, grandmother of both Steva and Laca. She murders the baby (and thereby becomes guilt-ridden) in order to make it possible for Laca to marry Jenufa, but the discovery of her deed almost but not quite breaks the bond between the three.

The 1989 Glyndebourne staging, rightly acclaimed at the time, is here preserved in pristine form, sensitively directed for video. Although it is a superb ensemble performance, Silja's Kostelnicka is its outstanding constituent. As ever with this great singing-actress, theatrical excitement is created by her very presence and by the way she thinks herself into the character she is portraying. As there are few more compelling roles in the repertory than Kostelnicka, the rewards are abundant. From her first entry one notices the stiff back, penetrating eyes, sharp features and, of course, uniquely honest voice, one that is used unflinchingly. Behind the seemingly unbending profile, there hides a woman with an intense love for her foster-daughter and an overriding wish to do the best for her, an almost fanatical love that leads her to the fatal deed. All that is expressed in Act 2 with a broad brush of melodramatic gesture that might, in lesser hands, seem to go too far, but in Silja's is soul-searing. Then in Act 3, her sense of guilt and remorse leads her to become frightened by her own shadow, another gesture that could misfire, but is here timed to perfection so as to produce a shudder of horror.

It is just one stroke of many in Lehnhoff's staging that shows his understanding of character. The sets of Tobias Hoheisel are simply effective. Act 1 shows a grassy bank with a mountainous outline behind it, the wall of a red barn, a rotating mill, all designed to confine the action, create a sense of stress. The perspectives of Act 2 are exactly right, the stiff formality of dining table and cupboard in Act 3 almost too severe, and the intrusion of villagers vandalising the furniture in fury at Kostelnicka's act of murder, a *coup de théâtre* that is happily contradicted by the final reconciliation of Jenufa and Laca.

The emotional temperature is often reflected in Wolfgang Göbbel's abrupt changes of lighting, emphasising the rawness of nerve-ends on all sides. Lehnoff persuades all the principals to act and sing with true passion. On video, Alexander may look too old for the title role, but she sings and acts with inner strength, softer colours tempering her often highly charged tone. Langridge conveys ideally Laca's pent-up emotions by means of his plangent tenor and crumpled posture. Baker is a suitably callous Steva, singing the part with a proper touch of carefree force. The supporting cast is strong all round. The accenting of the Czech original is variable.

Andrew Davis conducts the *Urtext* (many supposed 'improvements' were made to the score after the premiere), lovingly aware of both the stark and sympathetic sides of the writing, ably seconding the soul searches taking place onstage.

Katya Kabanova

Nancy Gustafson (Katya), Louise Winter (Varvara), Felicity Palmer (Kabanicha), Barry McCauley (Boris), Ryland Davies (Tichon), John Graham-Hall (Kudryas), Donald Adams (Dikoy). Glyndebourne Festival Chor, London Philharmonic Orch/Andrew Davis. Dir: Nikolaus Lehnhoff; video dir: Derek Bailey. Virgin VHS VVD 929. Subtitles.

The first of Janáček's works to be given in Britain (in the early 1950s), it has since been staged all over the country. It had its premiere at Brno, where Janáček lived, in 1921. The libretto is based on Ostrovsky's *The Storm*. It is the tale of beautiful, impulsive Katya, married to the weak merchant Tichon, but in love with Boris, a cultivated, handsome youth from Moscow. In the end, left alone by Boris and tormented by guilt, Katya throws herself into the Volga. As in *Jenufa* there is a dominating older woman, here the cold, respectable Kabanicha, Tichon's mother. Janáček catches perfectly the claustrophobic atmosphere in which Katya's illicit passion develops.

The same team that staged *Jenufa* (see page 169) at Glyndebourne in 1989 had staged this work a year earlier. Tobias Hoheisel's sets are derived from Russian art during the period of the tale's genesis. They provide primary colours, brightly lit, no shadows. A feverish yellow sky silhouettes moving figures, the interiors a fierce carmine. They are a suitable setting for Lehnhoff's stark, expressionist direction, but, in the final act (of three), when, in the teeth of a storm, Katya reveals her adultery, Lehnhoff fails to create the sense of stifling claustrophobia so essential at that point.

Lehnoff gets his cast to act with astonishing force in delineating their inner feelings and finds an especially ready response from Gustafson as Katya. From her first entry she portrays an emotionally overwrought, super-sensitive and highly impressionable girl, frustrated beyond endurance by the casual attentions of Tichon and longing for the erotic charge of lover Boris. She evinces suppression and fear before the hypocritical Kabanicha who, in private, practises S and M with old Dikoy (at least in this production, a questionable gloss). When Katya finally capitulates to Boris she mirrors the sense of relief tinged with guilt shown in the music. Her terror in the scene before her suicide is equally riveting. Her singing is firm, vibrant, soaring, everything one could want from a Janáček heroine.

Palmer offers a buttoned-up dominating Kabanicha. Her command over Katya and Tichon, in their different ways, is terrifying to behold. No wonder she has Dikoy literally at her feet. Davies suggests Tichon's want of backbone. McCauley's Boris conveys the man's ability to infatuate the repressed Katya. His keen tenor, gleaming enough, is sometimes strained at the top. Winter is a nicely flirtatious Varvara, Graham-Hall a carefree Kudryas. Davis brings out the vivid textures and colourings in the score, but the results are a shade too soft-centred for Janáček. Something tougher is called for. Picture and sound are excellent.

From the House of the Dead
Elzbieta Szmytka (Alyeva), Philip Langridge (Skuratov), Barry McCauley (Filka Morosov), Heinz Zednik (Shapkin), Monte Pederson (Shishkov), Harry Peeters

(Commandant), Nicolai Ghiaurov (A.P. Goryanchikov). Chor of Vienna State Opera, Vienna Philharmonic Orch/ Claudio Abbado. Dir: Klaus Michael Grüber; video dir: Brian Large. DG VHS 072 139–3; LD:—1.

For what proved his final opera, composed when he was seventy-three, Janáček chose Dostoyevsky's novel of the same name, based on the author's experience in prison. Set in a Siberian camp, it is a series of tableaux depicting – in three succinct acts – the inmates and how they are affected by their stark reminiscences of their crimes, but the message is much more universal, touching on the lottery of life and the cruelty of man to man. It is possibly the composer's greatest opera, certainly his most extraordinary. As John Tyrrell, the Janáček scholar, has pointed out, it is a 'collective' opera in which soloists emerge from the background, take centre-stage for a few moments, then recede again. In spite of, or perhaps because of, its theme, it is a deeply compassionate creation.

This Salzburg production of 1992, taken from the large Festival opera house, although at times insufficiently focused, does in the end convey the unremitting harshness of the milieu, the uselessness of life in prison, and the individuality and feeling that can arise even in such circumstances. Eduardo Arroyo's decor was castigated as being a 'designer-gulag' by one hostile critic, but its clean lines and evocation of mood do have the advantage of filling the vast stage effectively and forming a suitable setting for several riveting performances. It is wondrously seconded by Abbado's forceful yet subtle reading of the score, which is played by the Vienna Philharmonic with incisiveness allied to an inner warmth, thus reflecting exactly the feeling of the music. Pain and compassion are held in fine balance.

Giacomo Puccini (1858–1924)

Manon Lescaut
Kiri Te Kanawa (Manon Lescaut), Placido Domingo (Des Grieux), Thomas Allen (Lescaut), Forbes Robinson (Géronte). Chor and Orch of the Royal Opera House,

Covent Garden/Giuseppe Sinopoli. Dir: Götz Friedrich; video dir: Humphrey Burton. Castle CVI 2028. Subtitles.

Puccini's first success, though not among his most cogent works, is wonderfully spontaneous and immediate in its appeal. In his melodically profuse score, the composer captures the ardent, sensual love between Manon and the infatuated Des Grieux in an entirely different way from Massenet in his *Manon*, alighting on different episodes from Abbé Prévost's racy novel. Puccini wrote to his publisher: 'Manon is a heroine I believe in – she cannot fail to win the hearts of the public.' And so it has proved.

The 1983 Covent Garden performance conveys the youthful, romantic ardour of the principals. Te Kanawa nicely contrasts the shy, inquisitive girl heading for a convent and her burgeoning love for Des Grieux in Act 1 with the spoilt, flirtatious hedonist of Act 2, and the desperate, fallen idol of Acts 3 and 4, catching most of the tragic import of the finale in the desert of Louisiana. She may not have quite the ping, the *Italianità*, of traditional interpreters of the part, but her rich-hued, warm tone has its own validity.

Domingo is an ideal Des Grieux. He gives himself completely to the role, remains in character throughout the performance, sings the part with that welcome combination of the lyric and heroic that makes him such a convincing Puccinian, and he matches his tone sensitively to his soprano's. Allen is a suitably raffish Lescaut, singing and acting with wit and point. Robinson is too boorish, not epicene enough as the old roué Géronte who seduces Manon away from Des Grieux with his promise of luxury.

Sinopoli's conducting brings out all the brilliance and colour of Puccini's writing but is inclined to exaggerations of tempi. Günther Schneider-Siemssen's traditional decor is an uncontroversial background to Friedrich's well-observed production, borrowed from the Hamburg Opera. Picture and sound are good. Puccini's early success is well represented by this sole entry in the video catalogue.

La Bohème

1. Ileana Cotrubas (Mimi), Marilyn Zschau (Musetta), Neil Shicoff (Rodolfo), Thomas Allen (Marcello), John

Rawnsley (Schaunard), Gwynne Howell (Colline). Chor and Orch of the Royal Opera House, Covent Garden/ Lamberto Gardelli. Dir: John Copley; video dir: Brian Large. Castle VHS CVI 2014. Subtitles.
2. Mirella Freni (Mimi), Adriana Martino (Musetta), Gianni Raimondi (Rodolfo), Rolando Panerai (Marcello), Gianni Maffeo (Schaunard), Ivo Vinco (Colline). Chor and Orch of La Scala, Milan/Herbert von Karajan. A film by Franco Zeffirelli. DG VHS 072 105–3; LD:—3.
3. Mirella Freni (Mimi), Sandra Pacetti (Musetta), Luciano Pavarotti (Rodolfo), Gino Quilico (Marcello), Stephen Dickson (Schaunard), Nicolai Ghiaurov (Colline). Chor and Orch of San Francisco Opera/Tiziano Severini. Dir: Francesca Zambello; video dir: Brian Large. Virgin VHS VVD 663; Pioneer LD: PLMCB 00281. Subtitles.
4. Cheryl Barker (Mimi), Christine Douglas (Musetta), David Hobson (Rodolfo), Roger Lemke (Marcello), David Lemke (Schaunard), Gary Rowley (Colline). Chor and Orch of Australian Opera/Julian Smith. Dir: Baz Luhrmann; video dir: Geoffrey Nottage. Decca VHS 071 076–3.

Puccini's first masterpiece is notable for its taut, keenly fashioned structure, its economy of characterisation, its abundance of melody. Overriding all is its direct appeal to the emotions that has won it friends ever since its premiere in 1900 and kept it in the standard repertory ever since. The heart and ear warm to Mimi's genuine love for her Rodolfo rudely cut short by her death from tuberculosis and to the youthful exuberance of the four Parisian Bohemians, not to overlook flighty Musetta.

The 1982 revival of John Copley's long-lasting production for Covent Garden is an enjoyable, lived-in experience, distinguished by Cotrubas's affecting and vulnerable Mimi, carefully worked out yet apparently spontaneous as an interpretation, and sung in those peculiarly warm and individual tones of hers. It is a worthy souvenir of her art, in both visual and vocal terms. As her Rodolfo, Shicoff makes a fresh, unroutined impression, singing fervently and with firm incisive tone, but he never quite achieves the true Italianate touch of his rivals here in the part (see below). Zschau's showy Musetta, reasonably well sung, and Allen's youthful Marcello give unexceptional support. The other Bohemians, very much looking their parts, complete a sound ensemble, under the experienced, watchful eye of Gardelli, who gives the most idiomatic reading of the four conductors under review here.

Copley's neatly tailored staging in Julia Trevelyan Oman's highly evocative and appropriate decor is as fresh as at the production's first appearance back in 1974. The voices sound well but the orchestra is rather too far in the background. The video direction captures the essence of a very good evening at the Royal Opera House.

The Zeffirelli/La Scala production is very different. Although it derives from a famous staging at the theatre from as far back as 1963, this film was made expressly for cinema and TV showing in 1967 with the singers acting to their own recording. The lip-synch is a bit hit or miss, which sometimes destroys suspension of disbelief, but the performance has much to commend it, most importantly an Italian-speaking cast with voices to match. Here is the Italian style of singing Puccini at its very best. Freni, a charming, tender, simple Mimi, sings with wonderful warmth and feeling, none better in this role even if she is the least happy miming to her own voice and never looks truly consumptive. She is partnered by one of the most underrated tenors of modern times, Gianni Raimondi, who sings a dream of a Rodolfo as regards both tone and phrasing and – though not in the first flush of youth – creates a convincing portrait of a young, ardent, slightly shy poet.

Panerai's genial yet temperamental Marcello is sung in a vibrant, attractive baritone. Maffeo is the best of all Schaunards, a full-toned voice, a delightful actor. Vinco's Colline is well in the picture. Martino is a brazenly seductive Musetta with voice to match: her Waltz Song is really luscious. Carlo Badioli, doubling as Benoit and Alcindoro, never makes the mistake of guying these interesting cameos of old roués. Karajan draws luxurious sounds from the orchestra of La Scala in a glorious if slightly self-indulgent reading. The orchestra, of course, receives its full due here. Zeffirelli provides colour and fluent movement in his sets and direction. This is a historic performance to cherish.

Zambello's 1989 San Francisco staging is, like the other two, traditional in the best sense. Pavarotti sings an amiable, relaxed, ardent Rodolfo, almost believable as the young poet. Freni's Mimi isn't a match for her earlier assumption: the voice has hardened, the interpretation become fixed though there are still appealing moments in her portrayal. Quilico is a lively Marcello. Ghiaurov still makes something of Colline's Coat Song. The Musetta is no more than adequate. The ancient Italo Tajo turns up in the two cameo roles, almost voiceless but endearing. Severini conducts with great sensitivity for the score's detail and pacing. Sound balance and camerawork are reasonably good. But, for all bar Pavarotti enthusiasts, this must take third place to the first two conventional offerings.

The latest version, from Decca, is a 1993 revival of Luhrmann's highly regarded, updated production for Australian Opera. Since its first appearance in 1990, Luhrmann has become something of a cult figure. This staging takes place in an odd, sometimes puzzling combination of recent decades. The clothing looks *dernier cri*; the Café Momus seems to have slipped in from a 1930s Renoir film. Act 3 at the Customs House, in an unattractive scaffolded setting (a fashion that should soon come to an end), looks bare, and unconnected with the rest, which has, paradoxically, the look of a 1940s comic-strip come to life. However that may be, Catherine Martin's decor certainly seems to have caught the eye of opera-goers who have made the production a smash hit in Sydney, perhaps because it has more affinity with the musical than with Italian opera. As such, it would have been better to perform it in a modern translation than in the original.

Within the eccentric decor, Luhrmann gives new life to old routines, the personal dramas projected sincerely by youthful principals, obviously in love with life and each other. By far the best of them is Hobson's Rodolfo, a tousle-haired gangling youth with film-star looks, a gift of natural, uninhibited, very individual acting and a bright, keen-edged tenor capable of fulfilling all Puccini's demands. Barker is an appealing Mimi in the modern vein, more knowing than vulnerable, at least until the death scene, but as with so many recent interpreters the top of her voice is often strained and unfocused, never filling out Puccini's grateful line with warm tone (*cf* the young Freni). Douglas is an all-too-obviously blowzy, brazen Musetta with voice to match. Her Marcello is the burly, down-to-earth Roger Lemke, who has a pleasingly rounded baritone.

Smith conducts a slightly heavy account of the score but supports his singers sympathetically. Video direction is mainly satisfactory with perhaps a shade too much emphasis on close-ups at the expense of the larger view. The sound recording is well balanced. This is an attractively fresh view of the work, but the singing is hardly good enough to bear much repetition.

Tosca

1. Raina Kabaivanska (Tosca), Placido Domingo (Cavaradossi), Sherrill Milnes (Scarpia). Ambrosian Singers, New Philharmonic Orch/Bruno Bartoletti. A film directed by Gianfranco de Bosio. Decca VHS 071 402–3; LD:–1.

2. Catherine Malfitano (Tosca), Placido Domingo (Cavaradossi), Ruggero Raimondi (Scarpia). Chor and Orch of Rome Radio/Zubin Mehta. Dir: Vittorio Storaro; video dir: Brian Large. Teldec VHS 4509–92698–3; LD: 45409–90212–6.

3. Raina Kabaivanska (Tosca), Luciano Pavarotti (Cavaradossi), Ingvar Wixell (Scarpia). Chor and Orch of the Rome Opera/Daniel Oren. Dir: Mauro Bolognini; video dir: Pepi Romagnoli. RCA VHS 029026–61806–3; LD:–6.

4. Hildegard Behrens (Tosca), Placido Domingo (Cavaradossi), Cornell MacNeil (Scarpia). Chor and Orch of the Metropolitan Opera, New York/Giuseppe Sinopoli. Dir: Franco Zeffirelli; video dir: Kirk Browning. DG VHS 072 426–3; LD:–1.

5. Renata Tebaldi (Tosca), Eugene Tobin (Cavaradossi), George London (Scarpia). Chor and Orch of Stuttgart Opera/Franco Patanè. VAI VHS 69216.

'Shabby little shocker' was one musicologist's notorious verdict on Puccini's melodrama based on Sardou, but that hasn't interrupted the long march of the opera's success with the public. A work so unerringly crafted to capture an audience's emotions is not to be despised: even in an indifferent performance it usually makes its effect.

None of these widely diverse videos is completely successful but each has something to commend it. The 1976 film, made on the locations in Rome where the opera is placed, is just about the most compelling. It is intelligently directed by de Bosio to make the most of the evocative setting yet manages at the same time to concentrate on the personal and specific confrontations of the principals. Angelotti is caught running towards the church before the music begins, Tosca is seen leaving the Palazzo Farnese at the end of Act 2 and a shepherd boy (actually Domingo's son!) is glimpsed at the start of Act 3, but by and large the dramatic verities are preserved, though in fairly conventional form.

The singers cope convincingly with the post-synchronisation of their voices, and they form the only cast in all five sets to look roughly the age of the characters they are enacting, and all have voices of the right weight for their roles. Kabaivanska has been a reigning Tosca for many years; here she is at the peak of her form, catching all Tosca's sensuous, vulnerable and courageous facets. Her reading is finely phrased, keenly sung with unforced, clear tone, bold in line and attack. Domingo, in his absolute prime in 1976, sings an impassioned painter Cavaradossi and shows a deal of finesse in the part's quieter moments. Milnes makes a young Scarpia, credible as a forceful dictator and feared man of action, albeit a somewhat conventionally scowling villain. Alfredo Mariotti offers a blessedly unexaggerated Sacristan, a role usually given to superannuated basses. Bartoletti's conducting may not be as tense and resplendent as some, but he is never less than vital.

The 1992 recording, also done on site, was made under very different circumstances. In a blaze of publicity it was filmed live for television with all the complications arising from singers being in a different place from conductor and orchestra. Although the results have been 'tidied up' for video (no cameras or tea trolleys now in view), it still has an air of improvisation about it. The advantages are a sense of a live occasion, and of courage and daring not felt on the Decca set, and a generous sweep of direction that makes the most of the superb settings: church, palazzo and castle are used with an unerring eye for detail by Andrea Andermann, who conceived the venture. Storaro's cameras manage to follow the principals with astonishing fluidity while placing them in context: the sense of claustrophobia in Act 2 is most striking, and emotions are caught unflinchingly in close-up.

The snag is the casting. Malfitano certainly exudes Tosca's sensuality and nervousness, perhaps to excess. This is a psychological assumption in the modern vein, eyes afire with passion and fear, hands clawing at both lover and intended seducer (this Tosca is obviously horribly fascinated by Scarpia), but the voice loses colour under pressure, a lyric soprano sent to do a dramatic job. Domingo looks old as compared with his earlier portrayals of Cavaradossi and his singing, understandably under the circumstances, hasn't quite its usual freedom. Raimondi's Scarpia, eyes fixed on his prey, suggests a formidable figure of power and lust, but his voice is ill adjusted to the role, too soft-grained, without malice in the tone. Mehta offers a blatant, unsubtle reading. The sound balance between voice and orchestra is good. It's all very exciting, but is it quite Puccini's *Tosca*?

Zeffirelli's 1985 production at the Metropolitan is certainly that, recreating – as he had done at Covent Garden for Maria Callas (*qv*) some twenty years earlier – his gloss on the Roman interiors and exteriors in the theatre using his own designs and costumes (wonderful). He also employs the two stages of the Met to arresting effect in Act 3: the opening outdoor scene being transformed into Cavaradossi's dungeon and then back again for the final tragedy. Sinopoli conducts an equally rich-hued reading of the score, but one that moves at a snail's pace for too much of the time. Behrens is a superb Wagner and Strauss soprano. Moving over to Puccini, she comes a cropper, out of her element visually and vocally, though offering moments of sensitive phrasing as a small consolation for much that is uneven and/or squally. Domingo in the middle of his three interpretations of Cavaradossi on video, sounds out of voice in the first two acts, but sings magnificently in the third and, as ever, he commits himself unstintingly to the character in hand. MacNeil, at sixty-three, a veteran of many *Tosca*s, gives an object-lesson in making the most of reduced resources. He deploys a seductive half voice and his old gift for legato to suggest Scarpia's lascivious intentions and his evil wiles, an elderly satyr to be watched in every sense. Browning's video direction is exemplary.

The Rome Opera House performance, taken in 1990 in the presence of European heads of state (prominently featured at the start and finish: Mitterrand rising to his feet to applaud) is fatally lamed on account of the Stygian gloom of Bolognini's production, in which it is hard to distinguish even the singers' features let alone the quality of the decor. They are more or less left to their own devices. All three principals are simply too old for their roles. Tosca and Cavaradossi are both in their mid-fifties and it shows in visual terms. Kabiavanska, though still a diva to be reckoned with, has hardened her vocal interpretation, no match for her younger self *chez* Decca. Pavarotti is forgiven his plump presence for his liquid, seductive, singing, 'E le lucevan le stelle' given a justifiable encore. Wixell, at almost sixty, remains a formidably articulate and dominating Scarpia, but his voice is diminished in size and colour. Oren is another conductor to take the score too self-indulgently.

Even worse is the veteran Patanè's dreary musical direction of the Stuttgart performance in 1961. This historic offering, in black and white and rather faint picture, is a record of Tebaldi's debut in Germany, more importantly, an invaluable visual souvenir of one of her most famous roles. She gives a fully controlled, carefully studied performance, but seldom gets carried away by a genuine impulse. One longs for more sense of the drama to second the undoubtedly incandescent sounds she is making. The vocal interpretation is rewardingly secure: this is the true Tosca voice, always used musically and intelligently. A pity the reading is so dramatically frigid. Tobin is a safe Cavaradossi, London an imposing, no-nonsense Scarpia, one of the best. Be sure to avoid another VAI Tebaldi *Tosca*: the reproduction there is terrible. Here it is always true to the voices.

Madama Butterfly

1. Yasuko Hayashi (Cio-Cio-San), Hak-Nam Kim (Suzuki), Peter Dvorsky (Pinkerton), Giorgio Zancanaro (Sharpless). Chor and Orch of La Scala, Milan/Lorin Maazel. Dir: Keita Asari; video dir: Derek Bailey. Virgin VHS VVD 341; Pioneer LD: PLMC 00261.

2. Raina Kabaivanska (Cio-Cio-San), Eleonora Jankovic (Suzuki), Nazzareno Antinori (Pinkerton), Lorenzo Saccomani (Sharpless). Chor and Orch of Verona Arena/Maurizio Arena. Dir: Giorgio Chazaletes; video dir: Brian Large. Castle VHS CVI 2007. Subtitles.

3. Mirella Freni (Cio-Cio-San), Christa Ludwig (Suzuki), Placido Domingo (Pinkerton), Robert Kerns (Sharpless). Chor of Vienna State Opera, Vienna Philharmonic Orch/ Herbert von Karajan. A film by Jean-Pierre Ponnelle. Decca VHS 071 404–3; LD:−1.

Puccini's masterly, through-composed music-drama delineating the love, self-delusion and final tragedy of its fifteen-year-old heroine justifiably remains one of the most popular operas ever composed. In it Puccini had perfected and refined both his style of composition and his dramaturgy but he achieved success only after a disappointing premiere had forced him to make drastic revisions. Although the original has been revived in recent times, it has only proved how much more succinct and effective are Puccini's final intentions.

The production at La Scala in 1986 was entrusted to a Japanese team which brought Kabuki traditions to bear on the work with startlingly truthful results. The refined semi-abstract decor purged the work of all the false orientalism often imposed on it, allowing the pure imagination of the score to be revealed without resort to facile exoticism, climaxing in the stunning effect of a red fan simulating the blood flowing from Cio-Cio-San after her suicide and opening out into a large lake of blood with mute witnesses of Kabuki tradition holding up white linen cloths all round. Within this refinement of visual style, the clumsy gait of the European singers is glaringly obvious, but that only serves to contrast the worlds (apart) of Pinkerton and Butterfly.

Hayashi made the title part very much her own during the 1980s and here one can discern why. Her simple, artless, wholly sympathetic acting looks and feels right. Without over-emphasis of gesture, she simply *is* the Japanese girl who places faith in a faithless man and suffers the consequences of her own fatal delusion. Vocally she is almost as impressive, her strong, serviceable voice shaping the familiar phrases with unerring skill and rising wonderfully well to 'Un bel di', 'Che tua madre' and Butterfly's death. She is suitably partnered by Kim's sensitive Suzuki. Dvorsky is a blank stick of a Pinkerton, singing powerfully but without any special sense of Puccinian style. By contrast Zancanaro offers a model of such things as a full-toned and fatherly Sharpless.

Maazel has always shown a special affinity with this piece, examining anew its refined sensibility and offering its distilled essence. He doesn't overwhelm us with its extrovert passion but reminds us how much can be achieved by simply revealing the inner textures and advanced harmonies of the score. Bailey's video direction is faultless, allowing us to judge the rich imagination of the visual interpretation. Picture and sound are particularly excellent on laserdisc.

The 1983 Verona performance is much more traditional. Ulysses Santicchi's naturalistic set is full of well-observed detail but it looks cluttered and even false after the spare, sincere effect of the Milan production. Within it Chazaletes directs his principals as well as the vast spaces of the arena allow in depicting what is in essence an intimate drama, but we have the advantage, as so often on video, of seeing the expressions of the singers at close quarters. In the case of Kabaivanska that is all gain. Her Cio-Cio-San doesn't attempt to be the vulnerable Japanese teenage girl; rather she represents all wronged, deserted women. Not entirely credible as a fifteen-year-old, she compensates with a wide palette of colour and verbal accents that often pierce the heart, especially at 'Triste madre, triste madre' in the finale. Antinori, a little-known tenor, proves a suitably extrovert Pinkerton. His clear tenor rings out freely into the Arena. Saccomani is an uninteresting Sharpless, Jankovic a sympathetic Suzuki.

As ever, Arena plays the music in hand with unassuming authority and a welcome desire to keep the score on the move, never allowing it to descend into sentimentality. As ever, Large handles the problems of filming in the arena with quick-witted acuteness. The sound is more than adequate.

Either of these performances is preferable to the over-blown, dubbed Ponnelle/Karajan film in which everything is portrayed as larger than life. Slow-motion effects, illustration of orchestral passages, flashbacks, an excess of petals in the Flower Duet, a tendency to have the cameras focused on the 'wrong' character or incident only serve here to destroy the fundamental simplicity of the tale, which does not need opening out into wider spaces. Karajan's interpretation, once so unerring (in his sound recording with Callas), has here become sadly self-indulgent, but he does extract the most sensuous, warm playing from the Vienna Philharmonic. Freni has pathos and dignity as Cio-Cio-San, but doesn't penetrate far into the character. Her singing is finely con-toured but in a single dimension. Domingo's handsome, pleasing, gloriously sung Pinkerton makes the character's be-haviour that much more heinous.

La fanciulla del west

1. Carol Neblett (Minnie), Placido Domingo (Dick John-son), Silvano Carroli (Jack Rance). Chor and Orch of the Royal Opera House, Covent Garden/Nello Santi. Dir: Piero Faggioni; video dir: John Vernon. Castle VHS CVI 2020. Subtitles.

2. Barbara Daniels (Minnie), Placido Domingo (Dick Johnson), Sherrill Milnes (Jack Rance). Chor and Orch of the Metropolitan Opera, New York/Leonard Slatkin. Dir: Giancarlo Del Monaco; video dir: Brian Large. DG VHS 072 433–3; LD:−1. Subtitles.

Minnie, the saloon-bar owner, plays mother and confidante to a whole community of gold-diggers in the Far West. She is loved by the bandit Ramerrez, calling himself Dick Johnson, and by Sheriff Rance, who is after Ramerrez's blood. Minnie loves only Johnson and saves him from the Sheriff's clutches in a melodramatic poker-game. The 1910 score, though full of atmospheric touches and as seamlessly composed as its pre-decessors, lacks their immediacy of appeal.

Both the 1982 Convent Garden performance and that at the Met ten years later boast American sopranos in the lead, both giving likeable and convincing portrayals of the tough girl with a heart of gold. Although they sing with a deal of panache, they lack the ultimate decibels that this role for a dramatic soprano really requires, though Neblett probably comes closer to its needs. Domingo very much looks the part of Johnson, and sings with his customary élan in both performances, though the earlier reading inevitably sounds the fresher. Carroli's louring, black-browed Rance is just right in every respect, more acceptable than Milnes's one-dimensional portrayal, sung in tired tones.

Santi and Slatkin both have the measure of the piece, and keep its somewhat sprawling structure under close control. Faggioni's subtly detailed production and Ken Adam's atmospheric sets are superior in every way to their Met counterparts, and Covent Garden scores over the Met in strong characterisation of the smaller roles in which the likes of Gwynne Howell (Jake Wallace), Robert Lloyd (Ashby) and John Rawnsley (Sonora) are outstanding. Infuriatingly the sound here is decidedly inferior to that on the Met version. Even so the Covent Garden is the one to have.

Il trittico: (i) Tabarro; (ii) Suor Angelica; (iii) Gianni Schicchi

(i) Sylvia Sass (Giorgetta), Nicola Martinucci (Luigi), Piero Cappuccilli (Michele), (ii) Rosalind Plowright (Suor Angelica), Dunja Vejzovic (Zia Pricipessa) (iii) Cecilia Gasdia (Lauretta), Yuri Marusin (Rinuccio), Juan Pons (Schicchi). Chor and Orch of La Scala, Milan/Gianandrea Gavazzeni. Dir: Sylvano Bussotti; video dir: Brian Large. Castle CVI 2057. Subtitles.

Il trittico comprises three one-act operas: a lurid melodrama in Paris on the banks of the Seine, a sentimental tragedy in a convent, and a cynical comedy set in fourteenth-century Florence, based on Dante. They demonstrate the advance in Puccini's skills as a composer achieved by 1918, in terms of harmony and structure, while the style of each is appropriate to the subject in hand. At virtually an hour each, they make for a long evening in the theatre and are often presented separately, but they easily fit on to a single video.

These performances derive from a traditional production at La Scala in 1983 by Bussotti, employing a different designer for each piece yet maintaining a unity of style. As a work, *Tabarro* is dark and evocative, compact but rich in atmosphere relating the weary, fruitless lives of the barge-people on the river where they live, love and toil. That is admirably seconded here by the decor and by the conducting of the veteran Gavazzeni. Although her semaphore gestures look old-fashioned, the Hungarian soprano Sass (who has never quite fulfilled her promise) is eloquent as Giorgetta, torn between affection for her husband Michele and desire for the handsome, younger Luigi, here sung in suitably virile tones by the dramatic tenor Martinucci. Cappuccilli suggests all sullen husband Michele's love for his wife and fury when he discovers her infidelity and murders Luigi under the cloak of the title. This is all-round a convincing account of a well-wrought piece.

Angelica, much lower-pitched in terms of dramatic tension, pictures the sad, guilty Angelica (she has mothered an illegitimate son) who has spent seven years in a convent without news of her offspring until her elderly aunt brings news of his death. She commits suicide by taking poison but her appeals for forgiveness to the Virgin are granted and she sees a vision of the child as she dies – curtain. Plowright, despite indistinct Italian, conveys most of Angelica's unhappiness and remorse and makes the dénouement a thing of intense, almost orgasmic passion as Angelica desperately seeks redemption. Vejzovic's Italian is also indifferent: she conveys some but not all of the Princess's implacable, resolute nature in a somewhat dull reading of what can be a gift of a role. The supporting cast is adequate.

Juan Pons rightly takes Schicchi's roguish machinations seriously, not guying them which is the custom, as he impersonates the dead Buoso and deprives the corpse's grasping relatives of their inheritance. As his innocent daughter Lauretta, Gasdia is ideal, but her lover Rinuccio is sung in hard, un-Italianate tones by the then-young Russian tenor Marusin. The staging is singularly routine and unimaginative. Gavazzeni is again a dependable conductor. The video direction and sound quality are both excellent.

Turandot
1. Ghena Dimitrova (Turandot), Cecilia Gasdia (Liù), Nicola Martinucci (Calaf), Ivo Vincò (Timur). Chor and Orch of the Verona Arena/Maurizio Arena. Dir: Giuliano Montaldo; video dir: Brian Large. Castle VHS 2004. Subtitles.
2. Eva Marton (Turandot), Leona Mitchell (Liù), Placido Domingo (Calaf), Paul Plishka (Timur). Chor and Orch of the Metropolitan Opera, New York/James Levine. Dir: Franco Zeffirelli; video dir: Kirk Browning. DG VHS 071 410–3; LD:−1.

Puccini's last and uncompleted opera tells the fairy-tale story, set in ancient Peking, of the cruel, chaste Princess of the title who chops off the heads of all the pretenders to her hand who can't solve her three riddles. At last the Unknown Prince, Calaf, son of the exiled King of Tartary, answers her questions correctly, but he magnanimously agrees to die if Turandot should discover his name by dawn. In desperation Turandot has Liù, the slave girl, who is in love with Calaf, tortured to make her reveal his name. She refuses, then stabs herself. At that point Puccini laid down his pen in a passage of ineffable sadness, and his friend Alfano completed the opera, writing the happy but anti-climatic end, which perhaps Puccini subconsciously shied away from. There the ice Princess finally capitulates to Calaf's ardent suit.

The scoring is highly spiced, bitonal in Puccini's late style, overlaid with Eastern motifs. The plot lends itself to lavish stagings. Of these two, Zeffirelli's, for the Metropolitan in 1987, is the *ne plus ultra* of supershows, way over the top in its fussy effects and excessive choreographing of the action. In the end these are counter-productive, often undermining the singers. Indeed a New York headline of the time said it all: 'Exit, humming, the sets'. Levine's glutinous conducting is a fit partner to this staging, heavy and insistent, stodgy in tempi, and robbing the score of its natural pace, its glow and romance.

All that contrasts starkly with Verona, 1983 vintage, a new staging that year by Montaldo. Here the production, though lavish enough, avoids the Met kitsch and never hinders the progress of the music or the characterisation. Luciano Ricceri's decor makes arresting use of the location showing the roof, balconies and huge staircases (actually those of the venue itself), all blue and white, of the imperial palace and peopling them with credible extras. Arena's straightforward, lucid, quick-moving interpretation accords with the needs of the score, and restores faith in its inspiration after Levine's laborious effort. Besides, Arena opts for the shorter version of the closing duet whereas Levine includes the weak 'Del primo pianto' section which holds up the dénouement to no very good purpose.

Verona also scores over New York in its choice of singers. Whereas Marton's voice sounds hard and untutored in the title role and the cameras betray her age, Dimitrova sings magnificently, looks every inch the haughty princess and throws herself unstintingly into the part's exigent demands. 'In questa reggia' is boldly projected into the wide-open spaces, the riddles delivered in steely tones. She looks regal and, though her acting may be economical to a fault, her commanding presence and body language compensate for want of expressive detail. Full and fervent as Domingo's singing at the Met may be, it is an undoubted pleasure to hear a different timbre and personality for once on video in a heroic role: Martinucci's dark-hued, smouldering looks and voice make him a near-ideal Calaf, though he runs ahead of the beat in 'Nessun dorma' (where Domingo is notably successful, using his long experience to phrase with tenderness and strength of purpose).

Mitchell at the Met is an affecting Liù but her voice has perhaps too many complex overtones for the simple slave-girl's music. The youthful Gasdia at Verona is devastatingly vulnerable and affecting in the part and shades her tone with notable artistry for a soprano so inexperienced at the time, in Liù's three important solos. Liù leads the blind Timur, father of Calaf, and constantly at her side. Vincò and Plishka are both touching in a part that demands more in acting than in vocal terms from its bass exponents. Verona has much the better trio of courtiers, Ping, Pang and Pong: being Italians they can place words on tone with much greater ease than their Met counterparts. The Met performance saw the debut of Hugues Cuenod, at eighty-five, precise and vivid as the old Emperor Altoum, only too keen to get his implacable daughter off his hands.

In his video direction at Verona, Large captures the essence of a night under the stars at the huge arena, making you feel part of that huge audience and suggests the vast spaces of the stage there. As one might expect in a video involving Levine, the orchestra takes undue prominence in the Met show on DG; at Verona, the balance is more natural and the overall sound and picture quite as focused as at the Met. Here then there is a clear and welcome choice.

Claude Debussy (1862–1918)

Pelléas et Mélisande
Alison Hagley (Mélisande), Penelope Walker (Geneviève), Samuel Burkey (Yniold), Neill Archer (Pelléas), Donald Maxwell (Golaud), Kenneth Cox (Arkel), Peter Massocchi (Shepherd, Doctor). Chor and Orch of Welsh National Opera/Pierre Boulez. Dir and video dir: Peter Stein. DG VHS 072 431–31; LD:−1. Subtitles.

This is a model of what a video should be, an ideal realisation in theatrical and musical terms of Debussy's sole masterpiece in the genre that transfers to the smaller medium without losing any of its penetrative power. The composer set the text, an expressionist play by the Belgian dramatist Maeterlinck, as it stands, finding the perfect equivalent in music for its strange, other-worldly story of love, jealousy and betrayal in the mysterious, imaginary kingdom of Allemonde, where time seems to have stood still and everything occurs in a half light.

The distinguished German director Peter Stein staged the work for Welsh National Opera in 1992 to unanimous and justified acclaim. Within Karl-Ernst Hermann's austere, wholly appropriate sets, finely lit by Jean Kalman, Stein catches the very essence of the singular piece. Each of the opera's fifteen scenes is given its own distinctive decor in which the action is played out on several levels, high for the tower scenes, low for the eerie subterranean grottoes. A masterstroke is their subtle evolution from one into another in full view of the audience, offering a visual counterpoint to the interludes. On video we also see the appropriate section of the score at the beginning of each scene.

Debussy's instructions are scrupulously observed. The love scenes have the ethereal, trance-like feeling intended. The violent scenes are brutally enacted. Real sheep appear for Yniold's puzzling encounter with the shepherd and doves for the opening scene of Act 3 where Mélisande lets down her hair. In sum, Stein and his collaborators reflect the ebb and flow of crude realism and fragile dream-life that permeate the work and that Boulez has identified as lying at the heart of Debussy's unique score. As the conductor worked closely with Stein on the preparation of the production, Boulez's interpretation is, of course, perfectly in accord with it, his direction at once direct and luminous, timbres finely balance one with another.

The six-week rehearsal period granted this production obviously paid dividends, not least where the singers are concerned. The paradox of Mélisande's character, a candour married to seeming duplicity, is keenly conveyed in Hagley's properly enigmatic portrayal, sung with an acute ear for French syllables. The headily erotic vibes that pass between her and Pelléas are unerringly conveyed by her and Archer's poetic Pelléas, youthfully ardent in tone and style.

Maxwell's Golaud rightly stands at the centre of the performance, conveying all the character's guilt, jealousy and self-torture in tellingly intense tones and convincingly projected acting. Cox's grave, nobly sung, world-weary Arkel, the elderly father of Golaud and mediator in the incestuous milieu around him, is a deeply moving portrayal. Walker's Geneviève is properly dignified and compassionate. As Yniold, the treble Burkey is remarkably assured. All move with a natural ease and confidence that can only come from lengthy acquaintance with their roles. Conductor and director have ensured that diction is clear throughout.

Stein's own video direction has the cameras always in the right place at the right time. The picture is clear and the sound uniformly excellent. Subtitles are sensibly provided.

Frederick Delius (1862–1934)

A Village Romeo and Juliet
Helen Field (Vreli, acted by Dana Mořavkova), Arthur Davies (Sali, acted by Michal Dlouhy), Thomas Hampson (Dark Fiddler). Arnold Schönberg Chor, Austrian Radio Symphony Orch/Charles Mackerras. A film by Petr Weigl. Decca VHS 071 134–3; LD:—1.

Delius's most successful opera is based on a novel by Gottfried Keller, itself inspired by a report in a Swiss newspaper telling how a youth of nineteen and a girl of seventeen had fallen in love but failed to win their parents' consent because of mutual antagonism. The young couple danced all night in a local inn, then committed suicide. That story forms the core of the libretto, Delius's own, for his opera, a tale that suited Delius's anti-establishment, amoralistic ideas and his pantheistic love of nature. He set it to some of his most glorious music, heavily inspired by the Wagner of *Tristan* and *Parsifal*. The mood of the piece is predominantly ruminative and dreamy, and includes 'The Walk to the Paradise Garden', well known as a concert piece on its own account. What the work lacks in dramatic incident, it gains in its richly saturated texture and subtle use of leading motifs, gleaned from Wagner's idiom yet transmuted into Delius's own, utterly individual style.

Weigl's imaginative film matches the beauty and otherworldly quality of the score. It was made in Czechoslovakia, as it then was (in 1989), and exploits the unspoilt nature of the countryside to second the idyllic nature of the story. More controversially it uses, with one exception, actors to mime the Decca recording conducted by Mackerras. The somewhat mature voices of Field and Davies hardly march with the youthfulness of Mořavkova and Dlouhy, whose lovely bodies and features, and expressive faces, suit Delius's concept to perfection. Hampson acts to his own singing, and paradoxically looks rather too young for the mysterious figure of the Dark Fiddler! Weigl's actual direction is faultless in depicting the pure, doomed love of Vreli and Sali. Delius's score cries out for the open air, so that the views of the countryside during the long orchestral passages and wordless sections mirror the lyrical fluidity of the music. Delius is done proud.

Mackerras realises all the richness and subtlety of Delius's music. Although a shade strenuous, Field and Davies sing with fluency and ardour.

Pietro Mascagni (1863–1945) and Ruggero Leoncavallo (1858–1919)

(i) Cavalleria rusticana (Mascagni); (ii) Pagliacci (Leoncavallo)

1. (i) Elena Obraztsova (Santuzza), Fedora Barbieri (Mamma Lucia), Axelle Gall (Lola), Placido Domingo (Turiddu), Renato Bruson (Alfio). Chor and Orch of La Scala, Milan/Georges Prêtre. Film directed by Franco Zeffirelli. Philips VHS 070 103–3; LD:−1. (ii) Teresa Stratas (Nedda), Placido Domingo (Canio), Florindo Andreolli (Peppe), Alberto Rinaldi (Silvio), Juan Pons (Tonio). Chor and Orch of La Scala, Milan/Georges Prêtre. Film directed by Franco Zeffirelli. Philips VHS 070 104–3; LD:−1.

2. (i) Shirley Verrett (Santuzza), Ambra Vespasiani (Mamma Lucia), Rosy Orani (Lola), Kristian Johannson (Turiddu), Ettore Nova (Alfio). Chigi Academy Chor, Philharmonic Orch of Russe/Baldo Podic. Dir: Mario Monicelli; video dir: Peter Goldfarb. VAI VHS 69065.

3. (ii) Eva Likova (Nedda), Jon Vickers (Canio), Pierre Boutet (Peppe), Louis Quilico (Silvio), Robert Savoie (Tonio). Chor and Orch of Radio-Canada, Montreal/ Otto-Werner Mueller. VAI VHS 69203. Subtitles.

4. (ii) Onella Fineschi (Nedda, acted by Gina Lollabrigida), Galliano Masini (Canio, acted by Afro Poli), Gino Sinimberghi (Peppe), Tito Gobbi (Silvio, Tonio). Chor

and Orch of the Rome Opera/Giuseppe Morelli. A film
directed by Mario Costa. Pickwick VHS SL 1058.

Cav and *Pag*, as they have become affectionately known, have
virtually been inseparable partners almost since their
creation. Both epitomise what became known as *verismo*, that
is operas relating to everyday events in the lives of ordinary
people. These pieces are obvious companions in that they
both deal with passion, jealousy and murderous revenge in
close-knit Italian communities: the first set in a Sicilian village, the second in a Calabrian town. In *Cav* Turiddu,
Santuzza's man, has deserted her for his former love Lola,
now wife of the teamster Alfio. When Alfio discovers her infidelity from Santuzza, he demands a duel with Turiddu (the
Rustic Chivalry of the title) during which he slays his rival.
Pag concerns a travelling *commedia dell'arte* troupe, headed by
Canio, married to a younger wife, Nedda. When he discovers
Nedda's affair with the handsome youth Silvio, he murders
her during a performance, then attacks and kills Silvio.
Nedda has been betrayed by the hunchback Tonio, who has
revealed to Canio Nedda's adultery in revenge for her re-
jection of his advances.

Zeffirelli's two films were made cheek by jowl in 1982. The
action of *Cav* is opened out into the Sicilian landscape with
richly coloured results merging imperceptibly on to a set of La
Scala for certain of the intimate colloquys. Zeffirelli also takes
the opportunity given by film to make motives explicit. In the
prelude we see Turiddu leaving Lola's house at dawn espied
by Santuzza, thus setting up the plot. Turiddu sings his
opening serenade while riding off happily into the countryside having just left Lola. Stopping to turn his horse he
catches sight of the returning Alfio. During the famous Intermezzo Santuzza wanders round the fields filled with
remorse. We see an aerial view of the combat in which Alfio
knifes Turiddu, which usually takes place offstage. With his
eye for detail Zeffirelli shows us shots of the beautiful Sicilian
countryside, peasants toiling in the fields with their livestock
beside them, and we glimpse the baroque church, built of
grey lava stone, that dominates everything. All rural Sicily is
here.

Does this setting dwarf the principals? Happily no. Domingo sings a suitably insouciant yet paradoxically intense Turiddu, Obraztsova may not have the most pleasing of timbres, but her Santuzza is a portrayal of a woman driven to extremes by Turiddu's infidelity, a black-clothed figure of wronged womanhood, even if this sometimes shades over into harshness and misses some of the role's pathos. Bruson's Alfio, lean and eagle-eyed, is sung in biting tones. Veteran Barbieri makes a significant contribution as Turiddu's mother, Mamma Lucia, conveying all her fear of the inevitable outcome. The only downside is Prêtre's unstable conducting.

Pag was shot on a large studio set in Milan, although Zeffirelli cleverly suggests an outdoor milieu. He moves the action forward credibly to the inter-war years and his nicely flowing direction always leads the eye to the appropriate spot or face. When that concerns Stratas's vulnerable Nedda, torn between young lover and older husband, the results are illuminating, moving, because Stratas is such an eloquent singing actress even if her singing as such leaves something to be desired. The look of sheer misery as she makes up for the play during the Intermezzo is unforgettable. Domingo gives one of the most notable performances of all his many on video, a match for his Otello and Chénier (*qqv*), conveying all the pathos of a big-hearted man struck down by jealousy and inner torment. Pons is a properly gross, mean Tonio, Rinaldi a sensuous Silvio.

These two performances, although on sale separately, make a thoroughly enjoyable pair and show how the genre of video can excel itself away from the opera house when an inspired hand is in charge. Dubbing is convincingly managed. The sound and picture are first-rate.

The other account of *Cav* derives from a performance at the Theatre of the Chigi Music Academy in Siena given to mark Mascagni's centenary in 1990. The star attraction is Verrett undertaking her first Santuzza. Although in her sixtieth year at the time, she remains a great performer. Sometimes her tone sounds frayed, but that can be overlooked in the context of a reading that reveals all Santuzza's pain of the heart. This Santuzza may move about the stage in a somewhat stately fashion, but her body language speaks volumes. Johannson has a strong but rather inflexible tenor and his acting abilities on this evidence are negligible. The rest isn't more than provincial Italian, the conducting and playing no more than adequate, but it's worth a look for Verrett, who introduces the video with enthusiasm and charm from the Piazza del Campo in Siena. Sound and picture are of high quality.

The two extra performances of *Pag*, both in black and white, are each of historical interest. The first, a live recording on Radio Canada in 1955, enshrines the Canio of the twenty-eight-year-old Vickers looking far too youthful for his role but already singing with that raw, heroic individuality of tone and phrase that was to make him an international star within five years. Everything else about the performance looks homespun and unconvincing, though it is also interesting to see and hear baritones Quilico and Savoie, both of whom were to join Vickers at Covent Garden a year or so later.

The Rome film of 1946 is a far more important document. It catches the thirty-three-year-old Gobbi doubling as a way-over-the-top Tonio (eyeing the camera as though he were in Grand Guignol and singing in a deliberately eccentric way) and as a handsome, credible Silvio. As that character he woos on screen the luscious Nedda of Gina Lollabrigida in the woods (this was an on-location film before Zeffirelli had been invented). She mimes to the voice of the vibrant Fineschi, a ranking Italian soprano of the day who reminds us how the part should sound. Gobbi's performance of Silvio's seductive music is a model of fine-grained and mellifluous singing.

Canio is acted by Afro Poli (a baritone of the day) but sung by Masini, who gives an object-lesson in how to read the role. His account of the famous 'Vesti la giubba' is impassioned, long-breathed, plaintively accented.

The sound and picture, camerawork imaginative for its day, are tolerable.

Richard Strauss (1864–1949)

Salome
1. Teresa Stratas (Salome), Astrid Varnay (Herodias), Hanna Schwarz (Page), Hans Beirer (Herod), Wieslaw

Ochman (Narraboth), Bernd Weikl (Jochanaan). Vienna Philharmonic Orch/Karl Böhm. A film by Götz Friedrich. DG VHS 072 109–3; LD:−1.

2. Maria Ewing (Salome), Gillian Knight (Herodias), Fiona Kimm (Page), Kenneth Riegel (Herod), Robin Leggate (Narraboth), Michael Devlin (Jochanaan). Orch of Royal Opera House, Covent Garden/Edward Downes. Dir: Peter Hall; video dir: Derek Bailey. Pioneer LD PLMCB 00791. Subtitles.

3. Catherine Malfitano (Salome), Leonie Rysanek (Herodias), Camille Capasso (Page), Horst Hiestermann (Herod), Clemens Bieber (Narraboth), Simon Estes (Jochanaan). Orch of Deutsche Oper, Berlin/Giuseppe Sinopoli. Dir: Petr Weigl; video dir: Brian Large. Teldec VHS 9031-73827–3; LD: −6.

Strauss's setting of a German translation of Oscar Wilde's play was his first major success in the opera house. The resulting score in colour, harmony and texture that were bold, original and erotically explicit caused the predictable sensation. Even today they have lost little of their power to stimulate controversy as to whether they are thrillingly vivid or merely vulgar and off-putting. A satisfying performance, while exposing the wonderful immediacy of Strauss's writing, should not become merely blatant.

These video versions find three American sopranos outdoing each other in portraying the spoilt, depraved, sixteen-year-old Princess of Judaea, Ewing and Malfitano in live performances, the first at Covent Garden in 1992, the second at Berlin two years earlier (Malfitano has since triumphed at Covent Garden in another production). Stratas, who has never sung the part on stage, learnt it specifically for the Friedrich/Böhm film made in 1974, yet it is Stratas, even more than her rivals, who *is* Salome while they, for all their striving, never quite achieve Stratas's instinctive understanding of the role.

In the first place Stratas looks the part, in terms of age and appearance. Her slim, elfin figure, her at once frail, vulnerable and lascivious appearance and her almost teenage-like voice surely encapsulate exactly what Strauss was looking for in his Salome. When he asked Elisabeth Schumann, like Stratas by vocal nature a Susanna rather than a Salome, to learn the role (she refused) he must have had this kind of sound in his mind – crystalline, pure yet inwardly erotic. Then under Friedrich's subtle, detailed direction, she uses her body and face to utterly riveting effect. Constantly tactile in her longing for Jochanaan's mouth and embrace she – and Friedrich – use her hands to create the sense of physical desire while at 'Mich hast du nicht gesehen' you sense Salome's desperate, unhinging longing and later in the final scene a necrophiliac ecstasy that is at once horrible and unmissable. Through much of this scene Salome is shown in close proximity with the severed head. Earlier Stratas-Salome seems to be having an orgasm after Jochanaan has been led back to his dungeon and her frustration at his rejection of her advances overwhelms her. It is altogether an extraordinary reading seconded by singing often of the utmost refinement and ease with phrasing that is instinctively right. But then she has in support that nonpareil among Strauss interpreters – Karl Böhm – who not only gives Stratas sympathetic support but conducts the whole score with an intensity and refulgence (aided by the Vienna Philharmonic at its best) that the other conductors cannot match.

As Jochanaan, Weikl, given hair-encrusted features and a furry costume, has a weird, possessed look that seems not unresponsive to Salome's beseechings. He sings trenchantly. Beirer's galumphing, weird Herod seems to house a quite sharp mind. Varnay is a crazed, twitching hag of a Herodias. Ochman is a sturdy Narraboth, the young Hanna Schwarz a watchfully tense Page. The support is all exemplary. They all appear in Friedrich's magnificently decadent production, a court of depraved, staring, preening inhabitants, at once realistic and expressionist and very much at one with the Wilde/Strauss concept. The work is directed with a keen eye for the outrageous, just as is Friedrich's *Elektra* (see p. 199).

Hall's 1988 staging for his then wife Maria Ewing was revived at Covent Garden in 1992 when this video was made. It plays the work straight in John Bury's Klimt-like, *Jugendstil* decor. Ewing is a wilful, single-minded Salome, a spoilt child with probing, dark, gleeful eyes. This Salome is self-absorbed, acting out her fantasies, as in the Dance, almost to herself, seemingly mentally unhinged from the start. That Dance, ending up in nudity, is a tour de force of erotic suggestiveness. Ewing's singing is a law unto itself. She resorts to sometimes grotesque effects, notably unwanted *Sprechstimme* to overcome the limitations of a voice not quite at one with Strauss's demands on it, yet ultimately effective in its own, highly nuanced, bizarre way.

Devlin is a harsh-voiced Jochanaan without the charisma vocally or dramatically for the part though he delivers it with honest conviction. Riegel is one of those strident, Mime-like Herods, but he too justifies his means by the ends he achieves. Knight is a traditionally raddled Herodias, Leggate a lyrical Narraboth, but some roles are undercast with worn voices. Downes conducts a convincing but not always sensual enough account of the score. Hall avoids excessive effects, and by the same token misses some of the piece's decadence. Bailey's video direction is as good as it can be given the gloom of the production's lighting. The subtitles will be welcome for newcomers to the work.

If the cameras reveal Ewing as being somewhat too old for the title role, that is even more the case with Malfitano, but by force of her personality and intelligence she almost overcomes that drawback. Hers is a magnetic, dominating, slightly repulsive Salome. Malfitano acts her concept with acrobatic dexterity and single-minded devotion. She manages to convey, as well as any, the girl's sexual awakening before Jochanaan's imposing body and her growing obsession. She comes closer than her rivals to having the true voice for Salome in theatrical terms and sings the part with steady, controlled and flexible tone, hardening only occasionally under extreme pressure. We see the effort being expended by Malfitano's athletic portrayal through the perspiration frequently on her brow.

Estes, a somewhat stolid, statuesque Jochanaan, declaims with intensity. Hiestermann is a neurotic, superstitious Herod, unsteadily sung. As Herodias veteran Rysanek turns in a magnificent portrait of epicene decline and depravity. Sinopoli conducts the score with a fair blend of sensuousness and dramatic bite, avoiding exaggeration.

Weigl's Berlin staging, economic almost to a fault, is successful at making the most of key events, such as the way in which Salome gradually comes into contact with the Prophet's body. Josef Svoboda's set, inevitably with this designer, is dominated by staircases: it happily marries the real with the abstract in conveying Herod's abnormal court practice. The darkness of the staging leaves little leeway for Large to show contrasts. Picture and sound, especially on laserdisc, are superior to that on the other versions.

Each of these performances, in its different but equally valid ways, has much to offer, but the DG must take preference on account of Stratas's mesmerising interpretation of the title role and Böhm's superb reading of the score.

Elektra

1. Leonie Rysanek (Elektra), Catarina Ligendza (Chrysothemis), Astrid Varnay (Klytemnestra), Hans Beirer (Aeghist), Dietrich Fischer-Dieskau (Orest). Vienna Philharmonic Chor and Orch/Karl Böhm. A film by Götz Friedrich. Decca VHS 071 400–3; LD:−1.
2. Eva Marton (Elektra), Cheryl Studer (Chrysothemis), Brigitte Fassbaender (Klytemnestra), James King (Aeghist), Franz Grundheber (Orest). Chor and Orch of Vienna State Opera/Claudio Abbado. Dir: Harry Kupfer; video dir: Brian Large. Pioneer LD PLMCB 00221.

The ghost of Agamemnon, the mythological Greek king, head of the House of Atreus, slain by his wife Clytemnestra and her paramour Aeghistus, pervades this, the most tragically grand of Strauss's operas. Here, in 1909, he is among the avant-garde, relentlessly moving forward the boundaries of harmony, scoring, textural concentration and psychological insight expressed in music. The intensity of mood is maintained throughout the 100-minute-plus, one-act drama, Strauss's first collaboration with librettist Hugo von Hofmannsthal, depicting the possessed and single-minded Elektra intent on revenging her father's murder through the aegis of her brother Orestes.

The Friedrich film is a fit successor to his version of *Salome* (see page 196). Set in some dark, dank, doom-laden courtyard (actually an old factory), with the House of Atreus a grim-looking range of sinister grey shutters, it leaves little to the imagination. Friedrich opts for a kind of silent-film style of acting as seen in the work of Fritz Lang, highly stylised and enhanced, as with his *Salome*, by a deal of close camerawork, characters confronting each other face to face most notably in the Elektra/Klytemnestra dialogue. The appearance of Agamemnon's ghost, the pawing of Chrysothemis by Elektra, the horribly vivid murder of Aeghist and much else makes manifest what Hofmannsthal intended us to envisage in our mind's eye, but this is the work of a really imaginative man of the theatre with his own vital vision of the piece, complete with an extravagantly fantastic retinue for Klytemnestra.

The singers are authoritative and experienced enough to carry out Friedrich's intentions with complete conviction and they effortlessly manage lip-synch. Rysanek's unforgettable Elektra crowns her career as a Strauss soprano (she had previously sung Chrysothemis and has since undertaken the mezzo part of Klytemnestra). A documentary made at the time this set was made showed her dedication to the task in hand, her final cooperation with Böhm. She was determined to give every ounce of energy and voice to a part new to her, learning the notes and phraseology under Böhm's still-sharp ear and eye in a stint of hard, concentrated work. The results are all-consuming, surpassing other recent interpreters, certainly Marton on the rival version, in depth of feeling and refinement of utterance.

Throughout, Rysanek conveys the distraught, deranged and finally maniacal aspects of Elektra's character both in her singing and her acting. The recognition scene with Fischer-Dieskau's solemn, still Orest is a heart-stopping experience. Friedrich allows us to see the fallen beauty of Rysanek's Elektra's face only at the moment of recognition when her expression evinces her elevation and relief. This is a great and historic assumption.

Ligendza, as Chrysothemis, makes a suitable contrast in white to Rysanek's black, and her keen-edged, clear soprano is set off against Rysanek's warmer, more occluded tones. Encouraged by the staging, Varnay as Klytemnestra exults in the character's superstition, fear and decadence, mighty convincing if slightly over the top. As Orest, Fischer-Dieskau sings nobly, acts movingly with his eyes. Beirer is a fittingly eupeptic, feeble Aeghist. In the small role of the Tutor, veteran bass Josef Greindl makes a farewell appearance.

Böhm's conducting is elemental, taut, emotionally overwhelming, a fit adieu to a composer he knew so well and loved so much, and the Vienna Philharmonic's playing, in its last cooperation with its revered conductor, is refulgent but both players and conductor also emphasise the score's refined attributes. They once more play superbly for Abbado on the rival version taken from a live performance at the Vienna State Opera in 1992, but Abbado's reading is often relentless and loud, wanting his senior's variety and subtlety. Ferocity is all: the sensuousness is missing and the recording has none of the space or atmosphere of its counterpart.

Similarly Marton throws her appreciable resources unstintingly at the taxing part of Elektra, but evinces little of the care for detail or ability for vocal colouring shown by Rysanek. Studer sings an opulent Chrysothemis and obediently acts out the fantasies proposed by director Kupfer. Fassbaender faithfully presents, in voice and mien, a woman racked by guilt and inner disintegration, but one more physically attractive than is customary. Grundheber is the avenging Orest to the life with savagely piercing eyes. King is a suitably futile paramour.

Little of the detail of Kupfer's staging can be gleaned in the Stygian gloom, defeating even as experienced a hand as Large. The treatment of the principals is all that is left and they emerge more as characters in a weird pantomime detracting from their humanity. For some reason in a gaggle of mad people, Elektra is the only sane creature – and that's surely not how the creators intended it to be. This is very much second best to the magnificent alternative.

Der Rosenkavalier

1. Lucia Popp (Sophie), Gwyneth Jones (Marschallin), Brigitte Fassbaender (Octavian), Benno Kusche (Faninal), Manfred Jungwirth (Baron Ochs). Chor and Orch of the Bavarian State Opera/Carlos Kleiber. Dir: Otto Schenk; video dir: Karlheinz Hundorf. DG VHS 072 405-3; LD:−1.

2. Barbara Bonney (Sophie), Felicity Lott (Marschallin), Anne Sofie von Otter (Octavian), Gottfried Hornik (Faninal), Kurt Moll (Baron Ochs). Chor and Orch of Vienna State Opera/Carlos Kleiber. Dir: Otto Schenk; video dir: Horant H. Hohlfeld. DG VHS 072 443–3; LD:−1. Subtitles (LD only).

3. Janet Perry (Sophie), Anna Tomowa-Sintow (Marschallin), Agnes Baltsa (Octavian), Gottfried Hornik (Faninal), Kurt Moll (Baron Ochs). Vienna State Opera Concert Chor, Vienna Philharmonic Orch/Herbert von Karajan. Dir: von Karajan; video dir: Hugo Käch. Sony VHS S2HV 48313; LD S2LV 48313.

4. Barbara Bonney (Sophie), Kiri Te Kanawa (Marschallin), Anne Howells (Octavian), Jonathan Summers (Faninal), Aage Haugland (Baron Ochs). Chor and Orch of Royal Opera House, Covent Garden/Georg Solti. Dir: John Schlesinger; video dir: Brian Large. Castle VHS CVI 2017.

Strauss followed the revolutionary ideas, inspired by mythology and the Bible, of *Salome* and *Elektra* with a deliberate attempt at a return to the era and style of Mozart. If he and Hofmannsthal didn't achieve quite that, they succeeded in writing one of the few works of the twentieth century to remain a regular staple of the repertory, one attempted by any and every opera company, but it has always flourished most potently in Munich, Vienna and Salzburg, the cities with which Strauss was most closely associated and where his music has always played a central part. Three of the four videos listed above stem from live productions in those centres.

The first of the two versions conducted by Carlos Kleiber derives from the famous Schenk staging at the Bavarian State Opera that achieved classic status, performed repeatedly with the cast seen here. It remains a benchmark by which others have to be judged. Schenk's orthodox yet highly detailed and perceptive staging within Jürgen Rose's handsome, traditional sets eschewed fashionable modernities and has therefore stood the test of time.

Kleiber's reading, unsurpassed since his father Eric conducted the work, has all that combination of warmth and élan the score calls for, also lightness of touch allied to controlled but never effusive sentiment. The Bavarian orchestra plays for him with a confidence gained from long acquaintance with Kleiber's impulsive ways. The shots of him in the pit during the preludes to Acts 1 and 3 show both how incisive his beat can be and how much he actually enjoys conducting this piece.

The instinctive reaction of the principals to each other is another indication of the rapport achieved in this staging. The intimacy of the dialogues between Marschallin and Octavian in Act 1, between Sophie and Octavian in Act 2, and the interplay among the three in the closing scenes is at once rewarding and deeply moving. In the name part Fassbaender acts the ardent, impetuous youth to perfection, sensual with Marschallin in Act 1, lovestruck with Sophie in Act 2, and highly amusing in the Mariandl disguises. Nothing is exaggerated, everything rings true in this ideal assumption, sung with richness and warmth.

Although by 1979, when this video was made, Popp was looking a shade old for Sophie, she conveys all the charm, indignation at Ochs's boorish behaviour, and in Act 3 confusion at her awkward predicament, and she sings with the right mix of sensuousness and purity. Gwyneth Jones's Marschallin looks appealing and girlish in Act 1 and then switches to dignified authority in Act 3. She is right inside her role and suggests all the heartbreak at the close, as Marschallin resigns her lover to Sophie. Jungwirth is a ripe, experienced Ochs, occasionally too boorish in behaviour and a shade approximate with his note values. Kusche is a too elderly but rightly tetchy Faninal, Araiza a mellifluous Italian Singer. Smaller roles are filled with long-serving artists of the house. The sound is excellent, especially on laserdisc.

In 1994 DG went to Vienna to video another Kleiber rendering with a new generation of Straussians, whom Kleiber declared his 'dream cast'. Well, while he himself remains a nonpareil in this score and persuades the VPO possibly to even greater finesse than their Munich counterparts, none of the ladies seem quite a match for their predecessors. For all her vocal suavity and innate sense of phrasing, Lott is a shade too contained for Marschallin, both as lover and as respected Princess, although at the very end she does catch the sadness of the character's situation. Von Otter's gawky, wilful Octavian is an endearing assumption but for those who have encountered Fassbaender in the part, von Otter's portrayal can seem contrived and her singing, clear and fresh enough in itself, lacking in warmth. Bonney, poorly bewigged, never catches the inner sentiment of Sophie's part, though she sings it exquisitely. The gain here is Moll's well-observed, jovial and rotundly sung Ochs, more precise in action and diction than Jungwirth's. Hornik is a nicely fussy Faninal. Small parts are well taken.

Schenk's staging is not so very different from his Munich effort, though he sensibly adapts certain ideas to suit his new singers. Rudolf Heinrich's decor is more intimate than that of Rose, equally apt for the piece. Curiously the sound is often inferior to that on the earlier set and the video direction less alert.

Ten years earlier, in 1984, Sony recorded Karajan's final attempt at the work, both as conductor and director, at the Salzburg Festival. Unfortunately he retained Teo Otto's sets from the 1960 Salzburg production, dully traditional in this case, but perhaps an apt backcloth to Karajan's lethargic direction. His conducting, as one would expect, is luminous and saturated in texture, but it misses the *Schwung* of Kleiber and is, at times, desperately slow.

Moll's Ochs, ten years the junior of his Vienna assumption, is even more persuasive, voice, accent, acting, expression wholly convincing. Tomowa-Sintow offers a blend of creamy, vibrant tone and finely shaped phrasing, but her singing is a shade under-characterised as regards the text. The sadness of Act 3 suits her better than the flirtatiousness of the opening scenes. Baltsa's Octavian, tangy in tone, is hangdog and static, no match for Fassbaender or von Otter. Perry is an anonymous Sophie. The absence of subtitles here and in the other versions (the Vienna DG on laserdisc apart) is particularly regrettable in this work depending so much on understanding of the subtle libretto.

Solti's ebullient conducting, in the 1985 Covent Garden

performance, is a relief after Karajan's somnolence. Schlesinger's earthy direction in William Dudley's pleasing scenery has its moments but doesn't precisely march with the feeling of the score. Te Kanawa is a gracious, ingratiating but slightly bland Marschallin. Howells offers a fresh, lightish Octavian. Haugland's boorish, falsely genial, darkly sung Ochs is not idiomatic in accent or facially responsive enough to make an ideal Ochs. There's nothing here to match Kleiber/Schenk in terms of authenticity.

Ariadne auf Naxos

1. Edita Gruberová (Zerbinetta), Gundula Janowitz (Prima Donna/Ariadne), Trudeliese Schmidt (Composer), René Kollo (Tenor/Bacchus), Heinz Zednik (Dancing Master/Brighella), Walter Berry (Music Master), Erich Kunz (Major-Domo). Vienna Philharmonic Orch/Karl Böhm. Dir: Filippo Sanjust; video dir: John Vernon. DG VHS 072 442–3.
2. Kathleen Battle (Zerbinetta), Jessye Norman (Prima Donna/Ariadne), Tatiana Troyanos (Composer), James King (Tenor/Bacchus), Joseph Frank (Dancing Master), Anthony Laciura (Brighella), Franz Ferdinand Nentwig (Music Master), Nico Castel (Major-Domo), Metropolitan Opera Orch/James Levine. Dir: Bodo Igesz; video dir: Brian Large. DG VHS 072 411–3; LD:−1.

This work began life in 1912 as a one-act opera to be played after Hofmannsthal's abridged version of Molière's *Le Bourgeois Gentilhomme* for which Strauss wrote the incidental music. In the revised, more practical version of 1916 the opera is preceded by a musical Prologue depicting events before it is to be staged. For that Prologue, Strauss created one of his most endearing characters, the Composer, a soprano role now usually taken by a mezzo. In the opera proper the soulful, romantic musings of Ariadne, deserted on the island of Naxos before being rescued by Bacchus, are contrasted with the ebullient music for the *commedia dell'arte* troupe headed by Zerbinetta, sung by a coloratura soprano who has a long and taxing aria declaring her views on men.

The piece was always a great favourite of Karl Böhm who

conducted it at various stages of his career. Here, in 1978, he shows all his old love of the piece in his deft, well-paced interpretation. He is conducting a video version of a production made for the Vienna State Opera by Sanjust whose view of the work is traditional but highly inventive when set beside its only competition, attractive in its setting, full of pertinently observed detail and, where the *commedia dell'arte* participants are concerned, a deal of balletic movement. Vernon, the video director, persuades all his principals to act with conviction so that the many close-ups reveal few specifically operatic gestures and plenty of genuine feeling.

Gruberová, the most compelling Zerbinetta of her day, and vocally stronger than Battle on the Levine version, performs naturally in front of the cameras, presenting her appealingly seductive portrait by means of facial and bodily expression. She sings the taxing part with complete aplomb and plenty of the required insouciance. Towards the end of the Prologue she moves into serious vein as the flighty girl finds herself falling in love with Schmidt's personable Composer, looking suitably boyish, but vocally showing some strain at the top of her range and explaining just why Strauss intended the part for a soprano. Berry's classic Music Master and Kunz's unerringly accented, superior-sounding Haushofmeister – the Major-Domo, a speaking role – are both faultless.

Janowitz is in the royal line of Ariadnes, singing with beauty and poise, and finding ecstatic form when Bacchus arrives for the long, impassioned duet that ends the opera. Although her acting can be awkward, she makes a conscious and partially successful effort to convey Ariadne's infatuation with her god-like, idealised partner. He appears in the handsome form of Kollo, but his singing, not always free of strain, isn't quite a match for his figure. The *commedia dell'arte* figures are fleetly led by Zednik, doubling as the Dancing Master of the Prologue, and by Barry McDaniel as the amorous, suavely singing Harlekin.

The picture and sound are quite the equal of those on the disappointing Metropolitan performance of 1988, taken off a live relay. Levine's account of the score with his heavy-sounding band is earthbound beside the luminous, taut reading of Böhm and the Vienna Philharmonic, and none of the principals is a match for their Vienna counterparts. Battle's Zerbinetta is delightful as far as it goes, but tends to be self-regarding rather than outgoing in the Gruberová manner.

Norman, whose singing is sensitive and always responsive to the score's minutiae, has an unsuitably mezzo-ish, thick timbre, which never soars easily in the Janowitz manner. Her acting is conventionally adequate. King's Bacchus has frankly seen better days but remains a remarkable effort for a tenor of sixty-two. Similarly Troyanos at fifty cannot suggest the youthful tomboy of a Composer she used to present so convincingly. None of the supporting singers is in the class of their Vienna colleagues, but Castel is a nicely cynical Haus-hofmeister.

The staging is uneventful to the extent of becoming a bore, an unusual complaint in a piece that tends to be over-directed, but such a static staging really calls for a more characterful cast to sustain it than what we have here. Even the experienced Large seems unable in his video direction to breathe life into the event. So this version is strictly for Norman and/or Battle enthusiasts, who may also be delighted with the fourteen-minute rehearsal sequence after the Prologue, showing Levine as a subtle psychologist when dealing with his two temperamental prima donnas. This programme must have been recorded before a different performance as Hermann Prey, rather than Nentwig, is briefly glimpsed as the Music Master. How sad that the wonderful Glynde-bourne version of twenty-five years ago, televised then, has never appeared on video. In its absence, the DG film will suffice to fill the gap.

Die Frau ohne Schatten

Cheryl Studer (Empress), Eva Marton (Dyer's wife), Marjana Lipovšek (Nurse), Thomas Moser (Emperor), Robert Hale (Barak). Chor of Vienna State Opera, Vienna Philharmonic Orch/Georg Solti. Dir: Götz Friedrich; video dir: Brian Large. Decca VHS 071 425–3; LD:—1.

This vast fairy-tale-cum-allegory was the most ambitious,

anti-Straussians would say most pretentious, project Hofmannsthal ever undertook. It attempts an overview of the human condition in terms of an Eastern-inspired fantasy concerning the contact of mortals with supernatural beings and forces. The score, the most complex ever attempted even by Strauss, stretches over three long acts, usually foreshortened (as here) for theatre performance.

This video is taken from a production by Götz Friedrich at the Salzburg Festival of 1992. Some day a designer and director will find an inspiring solution to the almost insoluble problems set by the opera's creators. Here the basically plain, uninviting decor fails to match the metaphysical challenges of the libretto and not all its most outrageous elements are properly confronted. Transformations are clumsily handled. Where are the bridge and waterfall in the finale? What are the Baraks doing at the Emperor's trial? Nor does Friedrich himself seem to give much detailed guidance to his singers as regards interpretation. Yet the reading has its moments of wonder, particularly where the immortals are concerned.

Studer's Empress is the most cogent reason for acquiring this video: she gives the forbidding part a vocal interpretation that is accomplished both technically and expressively, and she is committed dramatically to exploring the dilemmas presented by her role. Her tone cuts strongly and vibrantly through the heavy orchestration. Marton achieves the same effect but in her case the tone is worn and becomes ugly under pressure. Nor can it be said that her acting, when submitted to close scrutiny, really passes muster. Hale makes a suitably sympathetic Barak but his resonant singing sometimes fights a losing battle with the pit. Moser has the heroic tone for the Emperor and looks imperious, but he also shows signs of strain in his voice. While Lipovšek has the measure of the Nurse's music, the butch interpretation imposed on her, suggesting a lesbian attachment to the Empress, is uncomfortable. Bryn Terfel, in his Salzburg debut, makes a strong showing as the Spirit Messenger.

There's visceral excitement in Solti's conducting, but he misses the natural flow of the piece. Solti lives more for the moment than for the whole, as has always been the case with his Strauss. The Vienna Philharmonic plays magnificently in a score they know well. Sound and picture are excellent in both mediums.

Intermezzo

Felicity Lott (Christine), Elizabeth Gale (Anna), Ian Caley (Baron Lummer), John Pringle (Robert Storch). Glyndebourne Festival Chor, London Philharmonic Orch/Gustav Kuhn. Dir: John Cox; video dir: David Buckton. Castle VHS CVI 2024. In English.

Strauss's blatantly autobiographical work is a domestic drama involving the composer Robert Storch and his turbulent but loving wife Christine who at once begins an *amitié amoureuse* with the weak but scheming Baron Lummer while being outraged by her husband's supposed affair with the courtesan Mitzi Meier. When the misunderstanding is eventually resolved the pair fall into each other's arms. Once scorned by superior persons as a homespun, feeble piece, the opera came into its own when staged by the Bavarian State Opera in the early 1960s.

When Glyndebourne first produced the work, for Elisabeth Söderström, in 1974, its reputation was further enhanced. It returned to the house in 1983, when it was given in Andrew Porter's fluently idiomatic translation with Felicity Lott taking over the title role. As such it was a runaway success, now happily preserved on video. The piece fitted ideally into the intimate surroundings of Glyndebourne's old house, where the text could be easily projected even over quite a large orchestra.

Then Cox's staging in Martin Battersby's finely detailed, *Jugenstil* decor exactly catches the milieu of the piece and takes full advantage of the genre scenes: the toboggan-run, the dance, the card-game are delightfully delineated – but so are the home scenes. Battersby's front-drops during the orchestral interludes, showing the Strauss family and various photos of the period, and the wonderful costumes all add to the visual pleasure of this perfect staging.

In Lott we have an almost ideal Christine. She enacts the termagant, paradoxically irritating and adorable, with unremitting zeal and charming absurdity, every facial *moues* deliciously timed to make the greatest effect. She sings all through with silvery tone, a refined feeling for phrase and clear diction. If she is at times more English than specifically German that's a price that has to be paid for performing in the vernacular.

Pringle nicely balances urbanity and earnestness in his genial portrait of the composer Storch. Ian Caley acts and sings the weak scoundrel Lummer as best he can. Elizabeth Gale offers a witty cameo as Christine's maid Anna, and the smaller roles are all intelligently done. Kuhn conducts with a Straussian zest tempered by the need for the words to be heard. It is all a delight. Both sound and picture are excellent.

Arabella

1. Gundula Janowitz (Arabella), Sona Ghazarian (Zdenka), Edita Gruberová (Fiakermilli), Margarita Lilowa (Adelaide), René Kollo (Matteo), Bernd Weikl (Mandryka), Hans Kraemmer (Count Waldner). Vienna Philharmonic Orch/Georg Solti. A film by Otto Schenk. Decca VHS 071 405–3; LD:−1.

2. Ashley Putnam (Arabella), Gianna Rolandi (Zdenka), Gwendolyn Bradley (Fiakermilli), Regina Sarfaty (Adelaide), Keith Lewis (Matteo), John Bröcheler (Mandryka), Artur Korn (Count Waldner). Glyndebourne Festival Chor, London Philharmonic Orch/Bernard Haitink. Dir: John Cox; video dir: John Vernon. Castle VHS CVI 2036. Subtitles.

Arabella marked the final collaboration between Strauss and Hofmannsthal before the latter's untimely death. They were hoping to compile an operetta-like piece, but ended up with a fairly serious love story although the waltz is the predominant rhythm. The mettlesome heroine of the title is searching for the 'right' man and finds him in Mandryka, an outspoken, bluff landowner, nephew of an old friend of her father, Count Waldner. The situation is complicated by Zdenka, Arabella's younger sister, being brought up as a boy to save family funds. By a ruse the frustrated girl manages to spend an illicit night with her secret passion Matteo, who imagines her to be Arabella. The following complications and accusations are only cleared up after disaster threatens.

Working in Vienna as a Viennese, Schenk obviously catches the Viennese milieu to perfection in his well-made film that sensibly doesn't try to take the piece far from its given settings, hotel suite and foyer (Acts 1 and 3) and ballroom (Act 2), looking like proper locations rather than stage sets. Within them Schenk directs his principals with his customary feeling for relationships but he is somewhat hampered by post-synchronisation which some singers find more amenable than others. Janowitz seems most bothered in fitting her expression to her disembodied singing, and often acts stiffly. Not flirtatious or wilful by nature she finds the opening scenes uncongenial, but rises to the serious hurt and final forgiveness of Act 3. Her singing hasn't the ideal plush tone the best Arabellas command, but she phrases with her usual sense of Straussian style.

Weikl is to the life the rough, impulsive and ardent Mandryka, a role that ideally suits his high baritone. Ghazarian is just right as the androgynous Zdenka, plausible as both putative boy and adoring girl, and she sings her high-lying phrases a treat. Kollo does what he can with the somewhat ludicrous part of Matteo. Kraemmer's Waldner is _echt_ Viennese and old Mödl launches the opera in uproarious manner as the Fortune-Teller. The Vienna Philharmonic capture the _Schwung_ of Strauss's writing under Solti, who has always shown a penchant for this score. The Decca recording is vivid. Subtitles are sadly lacking in a work where every word counts.

Julia Trevelyan Oman's sets for the Glyndebourne staging of 1984 are minutely based on 1860s Vienna with Hotel Munsch in the Neumarkt as the model for Acts 1 and 3 while Act 2 is a replica of the anteroom at the Sperl ballroom. Within these she has paid attention in details (e.g. crinolines and smoking caps) to the feeling of rococo-cum-Biedermeier that the work needs. Cox, whose sixth Strauss production this was in the house, exerts his skills at catching the true flavour of the joint authors' work, adding just a touch of acceptable caricature where Waldner and Matteo are concerned to his straight treatment of the rest.

Putnam is a lovely looking, agreeably singing Arabella who manages practically all of the part's emotional overtones, and is essentially moving in Act 3. Apart from one ugly break in a rising phrase during the Act 1 finale and a few moments of strain, she does the part vocal justice, although a shade more attention to consonants would have helped to make her phrases more pointed. Rolandi is a literally incredible Zdenka. No one could possibly mistake this girl sticking out in all the right (or wrong) places for a boy and her singing has none of Ghazarian's ease above the stave.

As Mandryka, Bröcheler is no Weikl, rather stiff of mien and facially inexpressive, but there's an honest warmth to his singing and portrayal that eventually wins through. Korn makes almost too much of wily old Waldner. Lewis is a suitably fatuous Matteo. Bradley, a black soprano, is an acceptably vivacious Fiakermilli once you forget that 1860s Vienna was probably an all-white community. The smaller parts are no more than adequately taken (the heroic-sounding Glenn Winslade as Count Elemer apart), some less than that, yet the general excellence of the Glyndebourne ensemble and loving care over detail count for much, particularly in such carefully observed decor.

Haitink hasn't Solti's benefit of the Vienna Philharmonic strings in the pit but their London counterparts do him proud in conveying the vitality of his reading. The orchestra is however rather 'squashed' by the dim recording. The video direction and picture are, by contrast, of a high standard. Excellent subtitles are provided.

Neither of these performances is ideal all-round, but the Glyndebourne is truer to the work overall.

Capriccio

Kiri Te Kanawa (Countess), Tatiana Troyanos (Clairon), David Kuebler (Flamand), Michel Sénéchal (Taupe), Simon Keenlyside (Olivier), Håkan Hagegård (Count), Victor Braun (La Roche). San Francisco Opera Orch/ Donald Runnicles. Dir: Stephen Lawless; video dir: Peter Maniura. Decca VHS 071 426-3; LD:−1.

Strauss's last work for the stage is entitled a 'Conversation

Piece'. The libretto, by Clemens Krauss, who conducted the 1942 premiere in wartime Munich, discusses the conflicting demands of words and music in opera. The two sides of the argument are personified by the poet Olivier (baritone) and the composer Flamand (tenor). In a neat symmetry both are in love with the lovely Countess Madeleine who cannot choose between them. At the end, after a long, impassioned solo, we are left not knowing who has won her heart. The action takes place in the context of the rehearsal of a play (controlled by the worldly-wise director La Roche) at the Countess's château near Paris in which the Parisian actress Clairon is partaking. An old flame of Olivier's, she is now loved by the Countess's brother, the Count. Strauss and Krauss keep the closely woven plot in the air with the lightest of touches. By its very nature the piece is never likely to be a popular success, but the beauty of the music and the variety of characterisation have given it a dedicated following among those willing to master its verbal intricacies.

Its cause is hardly enhanced by Decca excluding subtitles from its video of the admired 1993 San Francisco staging. This production eschews the modern trend of updating the work to the 1920s, keeping faith with its eighteenth-century milieu in Mauro Pagano's attractive decor and Thierry Bosquet's lavish costumes. Lawless's direction also avoids modernistic tricks, playing the piece relatively straight, tracing the gentle progress of the argument with grace and some visual wit. Runnicles's sympathetic conducting catches the valedictory nature of Strauss's writing with evident affection in a carefully paced reading.

Te Kanawa glides through the role of the Countess with a nice balance between dignity, humour and passion. She inflects the music with shimmering, silvery tone, but she fails to make as much of the text's subtleties as her distinguished German-speaking predecessors. Kuebler is an ardent, bright-eyed Flamand, Keenlyside a quizzical, lyrical Olivier. Hagegård catches the right touch of puppy-like ardour in the Count's role. Braun is a dramatically experienced, vocally subfusc La Roche. Troyanos tends to be blowzy rather than seductive as Clairon. Sénéchal revels in the cameo role of the prompter M. Taupe.

Maniura's video direction is faultless, the sound – on VHS at least – is a shade muted, but as a whole fair justice is done to the lovable work.

Francesco Cilea (1866–1950)

Adriana Lecouvreur

Mirella Freni (Adriana), Fiorenza Cossotto (Princesse de Bouillon), Petr Dvorsky (Maurizio), Alessandro Cassis (Michonnet). Chor and Orch of La Scala, Milan/Gianandrea Gavazzeni. Dir: Lamberto Puggello; video dir: Brian Large. Castle VHS CVI 2073. Subtitles.

In his day Cilea was one of the most admired of the so-called *verismo* school of composers. His *Adriana* keeps its place in the repertory largely because it gives a prima donna of a certain age a sympathetic, not too demanding role, that of a Comédie Française actress, in love with Maurizio, Count of Saxony who has been courting her under a false identity. He is in turn loved by the jealous Princesse de Bouillon, who eventually kills her rival Adriana by sending her a poisoned bouquet. The score is pleasing enough in a mild, undemanding way with well-characterised solos for the three principals and for Michonnet, the theatre director, who secretly pines for Adriana, a gift of a part for a veteran baritone.

This performance from La Scala in 1991 is of only middling value. The production, in Paolo Bregni's beautifully designed and coloured sets, and the conducting of the veteran Gavazzeni, in great form, are authentic and worthy of the work. So is the Adriana of Freni. It has been one of her favourite parts in the latter part of her career. Although she fails to extract all the feeling from it of some famous interpreters of the past, she sings it with her innate sense of style and her customary warmth of tone, only bothered now and again by unsteady tone. Unfortunately Cossotto is afflicted thoughout by an intrusive wobble in a voice that is a travesty of its former self. Dvorsky sings an impassioned Maurizio but acts stiffly, no match for Domingo who has often partnered Freni in this opera on stage. The most rounded performance comes from the little-known Cassis, who makes an alert and deeply eloquent Michonnet. Smaller parts are well taken by Italian comprimarios.

The video direction is in the safe hands of Large. Unfortunately the sound, at least on my copy, is congested and sometimes distorted.

Umberto Giordano (1867–1948)

Andrea Chénier
1. Anna Tomowa-Sintow (Maddalena), Placido Domingo (Chénier), Giorgio Zancanaro (Gérard). Chor and Orch of the Royal Opera House, Covent Garden/Julius Rudel. Dir: Michael Hampe; video dir: Humphrey Burton. Castle VHS CVI 2058. Subtitles.
2. Eva Marton (Maddalena), José Carreras (Chénier), Piero Cappuccilli (Gérard). Chor and Orch of La Scala, Milan/Riccardo Chailly. Dir: Lamberto Puggelli; video dir: Brian Large. Castle CVI VHS 2002.

Although long-lived, Giordano never repeated the success of this work (1896), set at the time of the French Revolution and showing the love of the revolutionary poet Chénier for the aristocratic Madeleine de Coigny (Maddalena in the Italian libretto). Gérard, servant in Maddalena's family who then turns revolutionary leader, tries to use his new-found power to force himself on Maddalena, but when he realises her dedication to Chénier, he attempts to save Chénier from death. The piece is notable for its passionate solos and duets for the principals: what happens in between is often of middling quality, but in a convincing performance soprano, tenor and baritone can carry all before them – as happens in the Covent Garden production of 1985.

That video comes into competition with another, from the same company, taken from La Scala the same season. Maddeningly their attributes are complementary: were the Royal Opera singers performing under La Scala's conductor in La Scala's production, more ambitious and exciting visually than Covent Garden's, we would have an ideal interpretation.

Rudel's direction at the Royal Opera is at times lukewarm set beside Chailly's exhilarating reading at La Scala, and Hampe's conventional staging in London, borrowed from his own Cologne Opera, lacks the visual aplomb of Puggelli's in Paolo Bregni's attractively original sets and costumes at Milan.

The role of Chénier calls for a lyric-dramatic tenor of considerable force. That Carreras simply cannot provide: for much of the time one is saddened by the undue pressure he is placing on his once so plangent, smooth tenor. It is a case of a sweet, lyric voice extending itself into an unsuitably heroic part. By contrast Domingo gives a superb performance, pouring out his rich, perfectly placed voice unstintingly in solo after solo and making each a part of a vocally impeccable portrayal of an anguished lover. One cannot imagine his arias or his duets with Maddalena being better sung. Carreras may look more like the romantic poet than the somewhat eupeptic Domingo, but it is the older tenor who fulfils all the role's strenuous demands. Neither Maddalena is quite ideal, both looking too mature, but Tomowa-Sintow, at Covent Garden, overcomes a comfy-looking presence by the sincerity and beauty of her acting and singing. By the time she reaches 'La mamma morta', the aria in which she persuades Gérard to try to save Chénier, she is at her considerable best, phrasing with a long line and refulgent tone. By contrast, Marton's vocalisation at La Scala is squally and vibrato-ridden, and she looks and acts unconvincingly.

Zancanaro makes an ideal Gérard, combining fierce determination with eventual compassion, and singing his solo, 'Nemico della patria', with vibrant, exciting tone. Cappuccilli's burnished baritone was on the wane by 1985, but he remains a powerful presence and singer. Surprisingly most of the smaller roles (apart from the blind mother Madélon) are more pertinently enacted in London than in Milan.

There is nothing to choose between the visual direction of Large and Burton: both are sensitive. The sound is more than adequate in both cases. There is a deal of applause after numbers in both house with, it would seem, a claque at work in Milan. Castle's supporting material is cavalierly presented.

Bela Bartók (1881–1945)

Bluebeard's Castle

1. Sylvia Sass (Judith), Kolos Kováts (Bluebeard). London Philharmonic Orch/Georg Solti. A film by Miklós Szinetár. Decca VHS 071 147–3; LD:−1.
2. Elizabeth Laurence (Judith), Robert Lloyd (Bluebeard). London Philharmonic Orch/Adam Fischer. A film by Leslie Megahey. Teldec VHS 9031–73830–3; LD:−6.

Bartók's single-act opera has a libretto by the Symbolist poet Béla Balázs telling how Bluebeard introduces his new wife Judith to his palace, where she discovers and unlocks doors that reveal one by one Bluebeard's former wives incarcerated by, and in thrall to, him. This story is usually viewed as a psychological struggle between Bluebeard and Judith, man and wife, but it also has elements of mysterious myth and exerts in the theatre an eerie sense of unease. Bartók clothed the tale, first given in 1918, in vivid orchestration and broad-ranging harmony over which two voices of appreciable strength need to carry. Although the action is bound to be static, there is plenty of opportunity for an imaginative director to reflect the work's inner conflicts and to adumbrate the music illustrating what goes on behind those doors.

Balázs was a distinguished man of the cinema so it is hardly surprising that the opera works so well in cinematic terms as these two video versions confirm. A decision between them must partly rest on how successfully each director meets the exigent demands of the authors. There can be no doubt that the Hungarian Szinetár, steeped in the Hungarian tradition, wins hands down in his 1981 film, his treatment having a subtle fluency to it. Megahey's award-winning effort of 1988 seems, for all its touches of brilliance, less inspired, more contrived, not least because, beside its rival, it betrays signs of being studio-bound.

The Hungarian's concept catches to perfection the dreamy, *Pelléas* world of the work (after all, its inspiration is also a play by Maeterlinck). It acknowledges no spatial restrictions in creating the taut, tense world intended within a dark claustrophobic vault of a castle. Where the British film is literal in such matters as depicting the pervasive bloody images, the Hungarian portrays these things more subtly, symbolically nowhere more so than in the all-important episode of the tears in the middle of the piece. Altogether the watcher's mind is liberated as much as that of the creators'. The Teldec version is set more prosaically in a gloomy mansion, its walls dripping damp.

In musical terms, Decca also holds all the trump cards. It has in Sass and Kováts a pair who unerringly catch the erotic charge of scenario and score, and convey it, inevitably, in more idiomatic accenting of the text and more full-blooded singing than their English-speaking counterparts. Sass, with a more expressive body and face than Laurence, is ideally suited to Judith. Although Sass's approach to her music is sometimes a shade too calculated, she articulates it as to the manner born. Kováts is stiffer in his acting than his partner, but his singing is deeply expressive and has a timbre more applicable to Bluebeard than that of Lloyd, who is shown as a frock-coated Victorian gent, and offers more generalised singing.

Both conductors, Hungarian by birth, are at home in the score, but it is Solti who draws a more fiery, romantic reading from the London Philharmonic than does Fischer, whose reading is more subdued, though never less than involving. Neither quite has the piece in his bones as did Janos Ferencsik in his audio-only recordings. The earlier vintage of LPO players seems more at one with the music than their later counterparts.

Both films are naturally post-synchronised, Teldec's with marginally greater verisimilitude. Picture and sound are in each case superior on laserdisc. Teldec includes the spoken Prologue, Decca excludes it (though it's present in the audio counterpart of Solti's performance – strange). Decca also omits a libretto, Teldec prints it and a translation. Even with these marginal disadvantages, the Decca set is the one to have.

Sergey Prokofiev (1891–1953)

Les amours des très oranges (The Love for Three Oranges)

1. Catherine Dubosc (Ninetta), Michèle Lagrange (Fata Morgana), Hélène Perraguin (Princess Clarissa), Béatrice Uria Monzon (Smeraldina), Jean-Luc Viala (Prince), Georges Gautier (Truffaldino), Didier Henry (Pantaloon/Farfarello), Gabriel Bacquier (King of Clubs), Vincent Le Texier (Leandro), Jules Bastin (Cook), Gregory Reinhart (Tchélio). Chor and Orch of Lyon Opera/Kent Nagano. Dir: Louis Erlo; video dir: Jung. Virgin VHS VVD 805; Pioneer LD PLMCB 00211.

2. Colette Alliot-Lugaz (Ninetta), Nelly Morpurgo (Fata Morgana), Nucci Condò (Princess Clarissa), Fiona Kimm (Smeraldina), Ryland Davies (Prince), Ugo Benelli (Truffaldino), Peter-Christoph Runge (Pantaloon), Derek Hammond-Stroud (Farfarello), Willard White (King of Clubs), John Pringle (Leandro), Roger Bryson (Cook/Herald), Richard Van Allan (Tchélio). Glyndebourne Festival Chor, London Philharmonic Orch/Bernard Haitink. Dir: Frank Corsaro; video dir: Rodney Greenberg. Castle VHS CVI 2050. Subtitles.

In the composer's second opera, the Venetian *commedia dell' arte* tradition is set on its head in a topsy-turvy kaleidoscope of farce and fantasy based on a play by Gozzi. Prokofiev laced his bitter-sweet comedy with a deal of satire at the expense of convention and authority. The composer's score, to his own libretto, has an apt 1920s edge to it, but it is also full of well-contrived, genuine comedy and boasts one memorable tune, the frequently heard March. The Prince's hypochondriac melancholy is lifted at the sight of Fata Morgana tumbling over, in revenge for which she casts a love-spell over him for the three oranges of the title. His search for the oranges lands him in a never-never land where he encounters, among others, an outsize Cook (sung by a bass) and all kinds of vicissitudes perpetrated by those who wish him ill (eventually routed). Two 'oranges' die of the heat; the third reveals the beautiful Ninetta, with whom the Prince falls in love and whom he eventually marries, but not until she has been turned briefly into a rat by the evil ones.

The contrast between the two videos, one a 1982 staging at Glyndebourne, the other a 1989 production at the Lyon Opera, could not be greater. Corsaro's romp, set in Maurice Sendak's ingenious, literally fantastic decor, is a supershow intent on entertainment, and that alone; Erlo's is a witty, sophisticated recreation, set in Jacques Rapp's minimal but apt decor. Musically the differences are also marked: the Glyndebourne team do well in attempting a French style (why wasn't Tom Stoppard's English translation made for Glyndebourne Touring used?). The Lyon reading is sharper in accent, wholly authentic in accent and delivery.

Corsaro sets the piece in the French Revolution so that the argumentative factions, at once bystanders and active commentators, become aristos and sans-culottes. In general, director and designer obscure the meaning of the story with an excessive array of extra activity involving dancers, tumblers, jugglers, clowns, etc. The drop-curtains, quick-change screens, amazing costumes and inventive stage-machinery, including a Sphinx with articulated toes, leave little room, on the small stage, for the principals to act and interact. Not even the tender love scene for Prince and Princess is let off the high jinks, which hereabouts tend towards the camp. All great fun, but is it Prokofiev?

Haitink's conducting, though not as incisive or pointed as that of his Lyon counterpart, is attentive to the piece's complexities and never less than alert to Prokofiev's many changes of mood and feeling. The cast, apart from Alliot-Lugaz as an enchanting Ninetta and Davies as a winsome Prince, are unclear in their French diction, an almost fatal drawback, but Willard White provides a sonorous bass for the King, Pringle is a properly nasty Leandro, and Benelli's Truffaldino is a fleet assumption. The video direction isn't always as prompt as it should be. The sound is excellent.

At Lyon, by much more economic and well-directed means, Erlo and his designer create their own unreal world featuring white panels that slip easily into different shapes, through subtle, insinuating and sometimes threatening movement and choreography and through the precision and character of the singing actors who work incisively and with dedication to support Erlo's concept. Nothing is exaggerated, everything forms part of a unified idea, seconding the score by, for the most part, obeying the stage instructions in the libretto, yet interpreting them quite freely. The result is an amusing, lively, unpretentious show to delight children of all ages: besides being faithful to the author's intentions, definitely the version to have.

Nagano's conducting has a brio and brisk authority essential to the score and doesn't exclude exposition of its moments of menace. The Francophone singers are all equal to their roles and execute them to startling effect. Viala sings and acts the Prince to perfection, as adept at suggesting imagined malady as at playing the romantic hero. Le Texier's supercilious Leandro, Bacquier's dominant King, Gautier's exuberant Truffaldino, Bastin's plump, ridiculous Cook, Reinhart's dotty Tchélio, Perraguin's saturnine Clarissa are all ideal. Dubosc is a charmingly insubstantial, vulnerable Ninetta, and her love duet with Viala's Prince – so welcomed by the romantics among the onlookers – is one of many passages sensitively realised by Nagano. The video direction is as inspired as the rest of this enterprise, but English subtitles would have been welcome.

George Gershwin (1898–1937)

Porgy and Bess
Cynthia Haymon (Bess), Cynthia Clarey (Serena), Marietta Simpson (Maria), Damon Evans (Sportin' Life), Willard White (Porgy), Gregg Baker (Crown). Glyndebourne Chor, London Philharmonic Orch/Simon Rattle. A film directed by Trevor Nunn. EMI VHS MVB4 91131–3; LD:−1.

Once frowned on by superior persons as merely a glorified musical, Gershwin's multi-faceted score is now accepted as an opera in its own right, which deserves to be performed as such. Heard in its entirety as it is these days, rather than uncomfortably cut, its form, flow and dramatic tensions articulate the work's stature. The work may be a flawed masterpiece, a shade too ambitious for its own good, but a masterpiece it seems in the hands of Rattle, who was in charge of the revelatory 1986 Glyndebourne performances directed by Nunn, which were a runaway success. He revels in the buoyant rhythms, sensuous melodies and vivid orchestration in which Gershwin's score abounds.

This film was made in 1992, shortly after the Glyndebourne production was given at Covent Garden. Nunn opens out his stage production into a film studio, the principals miming to the EMI recording of 1989. His attempt to turn it into the equivalent of a 1940s MGM film musical risks losing some of the intense frisson of his own Glyndebourne original. John Gunter's clapboard decor for Catfish Row has been unobtrusively enlarged, but the outdoor scenes lack conviction with, for instance, a few palm-fronds making do for the picnic scene on Kittowah Island. Even with these drawbacks, the work's impact is for the most part conveyed.

Apart from some haphazard lip-synch, the cast performs impeccably. Haymon and White repeat their rounded, eloquent assumptions of the title roles. Evans is an insouciant, plausible Sportin' Life, Baker a massive presence as Crown with voice to match, Clarey a trenchant Serena. To no good purpose a few of the original cast have been replaced with other artists, and they are the ones who have difficulty miming to the singing of their recorded counterparts. The choral singing is stunning.

Camerawork is occasionally too restless, but by and large Nunn succeeds in achieving what he may have wanted, a reincarnation of the period of the work's conception. Most of the electrifying sound of the EMI recording has been preserved. Unaccountably the important Buzzard Song has been excised.

Michael Tippett (b. 1905)

King Priam

Janet Price (Hecuba), Anne Mason (Helen), Sarah Walker (Andromache), Enid Hartle (Nurse), Neil Jenkins (Achilles), Howard Haskin (Paris), Christopher

Gillett (Hermes), Omar Ebrahim (Hector), Rodney Macann (Priam), Richard Suart (Old Man), John Hancorn (Patroclus). Chor and Orch of Kent Opera/Roger Norrington. Dir: Nicholas Hytner; video dir: Robin Lough. Virgin VHS VVD 664.

Arresting resonances of the human condition inform the second and some (myself among them) would say greatest of his five operas. Its depiction of events in the Trojan War is used to discuss the 'mysterious nature of human choice' (Tippett). At the same time it is a pacifist's plea against the horrors, stupidity and inconsequence of war, a message as relevant of course today as at the time of the work's premiere in 1962. The spare, stark quality of the score is curiously moving in its restrained eloquence. In spite of the tragedy shown to us and its unremitting harshness, one comes away from it, as from a great play, uplifted and aware of the human predicament.

Throughout the vocal line is pure, even noble, and the climaxes have a lofty intensity of a peculiarly Tippettian kind. The work's import is tangibly conveyed in Nicholas Hytner's 1985 staging for Kent Opera, here caught on video, one of the productions that proclaimed Hytner's originality as a director. David Fielding's sets do not attempt to recreate an authentic picture of ancient Troy, but are confined as it were within a single mansion. The stage is framed by raw concrete beams from which rusty steel reinforcement protrudes in a careless way. Costumes are a timeless mixture of today or any day. The terror of war is suggested by bloody figures, not by cumbersome war machines. Within them Hytner presents the drama directly, unfussily but with plenty of telling bodily contact. Each scene seems to develop easily and naturally out of the preceding one in an effortless flow. The result is wholly credible, enhanced by the fact that everyone acts so convincingly and whole-heartedly.

Macann's Priam is a gnarled warrior-king, but one who is all too conscious of the force of destiny and the stupidity of war. His futile death at the close is only the final tragedy of many. His Greek counterpart, the warlike, epicene Achilles, is given an acute, brilliantly sung profile by Neil Jenkins.

Achilles's war-cry, ending Act 2, one of the most arresting effects in all modern opera, is vividly delivered and staged: his features are superimposed on the Trojan elite as they celebrate the killing of Patroclus, Achilles's dear young friend.

The three Trojan women are well contrasted. Janet Price is an agonised, authoritative Hecuba, Sarah Walker a fierce, fearsome Andromache (though she looks too old for the part), Anne Mason, a properly complacent Helen. Their long scene at the start of Act 3, difficult to make cohere, comes off wonderfully well in this staging. As Helen's wilful Paris, Haskin sings with appropriate ardour. Omar Ebrahim is a forceful Hector. As Hermes, a character somewhat akin to Loge in *Das Rheingold* in the sense that he is an outside, objective observer of events, Gillett sings with sensuous guile. All the smaller parts are carefully cast and acutely executed. Norrington conducts a technically assured and confident reading of the complex score. The production is keenly directed for video by Robin Lough, cleverly catching the special character of Hytner's vision. The sound is good average.

Benjamin Britten (1913–76)

Peter Grimes

1. Heather Harper (Ellen Orford), Patricia Payne (Mrs Sedley), Elizabeth Bainbridge (Auntie), Jon Vickers (Peter Grimes), John Dobson (Bob Boles), John Lanigan (Rector), Philip Gelling (Ned Keene), Norman Bailey (Balstrode), Forbes Robinson (Swallow), John Tomlinson (Hobson). Chor and Orch of Royal Opera House, Covent Garden/Colin Davis. Dir: Elijah Moshinsky; video dir: John Vernon. Castle VHS CVI 2015.

2. Janice Cairns (Ellen Orford), Susan Gorton (Mrs Sedley), Ann Howard (Auntie), Philip Langridge (Peter Grimes), Alan Woodrow (Bob Boles), Edward Byles (Rector), Robert Poulton (Ned Keene), Alan Opie (Balstrode), Andrew Greenan (Swallow), Mark Richardson (Hobson). Chor and Orch of English National Opera/

David Atherton. Dir: Tim Albery; video dir: Barrie Gavin. Decca VHS 071 428–3.

Peter Grimes was inspired by an article written by E.M. Forster, read by Britten in 1941 when he was in the USA, on the subject of the Suffolk poet George Crabbe. The libretto was fashioned by Montague Slater from Crabbe's long poem, *The Borough*, the scene being Aldeburgh where Crabbe was born and bred, and where Britten and his partner Peter Pears were to make their home shortly after Britten wrote this work. Its famous premiere at Sadler's Wells in 1945 made Britten's name and began a welcome renaissance of British opera. Its anti-hero is the rough, independent, self-willed but (in Britten's version) poetic fisherman Grimes. He is seen in conflict with the small-minded, prejudiced inhabitants of the Borough. The composer portrayed them and the protagonist unerringly within the context of a sea-drenched score which shows unflagging energy and inspiration. Britten's gift for dramatic timing and for subtlety of characterisation came of age at once.

The first version on video is taken from a Covent Garden performance in 1981, the second from an ENO staging in 1994. The singers at the Royal Opera comprise the second generation of Britten interpreters led by Vickers, who presents a tougher, even more tormented Grimes than Pears, the first interpreter, and Colin Davis, who closely identifies both with the music and, it seems, with Grimes's predicament. Vickers's reading may not have worn that well, now seeming a shade melodramatic, and his singing, strangely visionary as it may be, sometimes contorts note and word, but it remains a towering achievement rightly preserved for posterity.

As Ellen Orford, the widowed schoolmistress who tries and fails to save Peter from himself, Harper gives a wholly convincing interpretation, at once sturdy, felt, articulate and gloriously sung. Bailey, as the upright, burly Balstrode, offers another model performance, truly sung with the words always clear. The remainder of the cast, mostly Royal Opera regulars of their day, are all admirable, with particular praise for Robinson's fruity, well-upholstered Swallow, Tomlinson's surly Hobson, and Dobson's ranting Boles.

Davis's acute and vivid conducting misses nothing in projecting the sense of the sea and of a community dominated by it, and his Covent Garden forces respond in kind. Moshinsky's thoughtful staging is filled with emblems of the sea as designed by Timothy O'Brien and Tazeena Firth. Although it doesn't attempt a 'new' interpretation, it does move away from the traditional Suffolk village milieu of the libretto and throws a sharp focus on characters' motives, forming an appropriate setting for Vickers's Grimes. Its sense of a claustrophobic community at odds with its awkward outsider is finely caught in Vernon's video direction. The sound is reasonable but the range could have been greater.

In the ENO production we move even farther from the Suffolk coast than at Covent Garden, indeed from any sense of the sea. A basically dour, abstract set and timeless costumes lend Albery's staging in Hildegard Bechtler's scenery, dominated by concrete sea-walls and swathes of sailcloth, an Expressionist, almost Brechtian atmosphere with the Nieces' bright boots and blouses the only touch of colour on stage. All the fishy props are highly stylised. Within this forbidding, arresting decor, the characters are no longer recognisable as English eccentrics, however prejudiced, but louring figures of a universal bigotry out to destroy Grimes as an outsider, an outcast. That makes the message of the work even more frightening in its implications and, like Albery's *Budd* (see page 231) at times almost too terrible to watch.

But human feelings are there aplenty in the central roles. As directed by Albery, Langridge presents at once a pitiful and paradoxically heroic figure, searing in anger as in madness and in between catching the poetry of his two great monologues. He admirably conveys, from the start, a violent man on the edge of madness, a fanatical visionary and fisherman, eyes gleaming with an inner fire. It is an utterly riveting portrayal, and Langridge sings the role as well as any interpreter past or present. On screen it is more credible, more achingly eloquent than that of Vickers, and more accurately, more keenly articulated.

Cairns makes a profoundly sympathetic Ellen, a younger woman than Harper's, more obviously in love with Peter and desperately eager to comfort and abet him, thus making his rebuttal of her affection that much more moving. She sings with a sincere dignity and a refined attention to verbal detail. For the rest Covent Garden tends to have the stronger cast. Opie sounds too strenuous as Balstrode, missing Bailey's worldly-wise warmth, but as usual he is very much 'in' the given production, loyal to an ensemble performance. Mrs Sedley, a particularly vicious busybody in this reading, is given a forceful performance by Gorton and Howard is a formidable Auntie. The rest haven't either the voice or the character evinced by their Royal Opera counterparts, but the sum here is definitely greater than the parts.

Atherton's interpretation matches Albery's in elemental force and in uncovering the raw bone of the music. While allowing full play to the more reflective passages, especially the later interludes, he also can unleash a fury of biting sound in the set-pieces, gaining an answering charge from chorus and orchestra. The sound is first-rate. Gavin's video direction is always prompt, always in the right place at the right time. In the interludes he superimposes characters miming or in repose as appropriate to the moment and indulges in effective, impressionist glosses, something that can be attempted in a filmed version of a production without an audience in attendance.

Both versions are profound experiences, well worth seeing and hearing. Langridge's overwhelming performance and the more amenable sound would incline me by a hair's-breadth to the ENO, but anyone wanting something a shade more conventional will opt for Covent Garden.

The Rape of Lucretia
Kathryn Harries (Female Chorus), Cathryn Pope (Lucia), Jean Rigby (Lucretia), Anne Marie Owens (Bianca), Anthony Rolfe Johnson (Male Chorus), Russell Smythe (Tarquinius), Alan Opie (Junius), Richard Van Allan (Collatinus). Orch of English National Opera/ Lionel Friend. Dir: Graham Vick; video dir: Michael Simpson. Virgin VHS VVD 617.

Britten's first chamber opera (premiere at Glyndebourne, 1946), using the small forces of what was shortly to become the English Opera Group, is one of the most taut, compelling and eloquent scores he ever penned. With an unjustly vilified libretto by poet Ronald Duncan, the two acts each divided into two scenes, depict the ravishing of the chaste Lucretia, wife of the Roman general Collatinus, by the Etruscan Prince Tarquinius in or near Rome in 500 BC, a well-known legend and subject of earlier plays and operas. This one is based on André Obey's French drama, *Le Viol de Lucrèce*. It is set within a musical and dramatic frame provided by the dispassionate but not uninvolved Female and Male Chorus. The marriage of Lucretia and Collatinus torn apart by the rape, she commits suicide, unable to bear the shame.

Vick's 1987 staging for ENO was universally and rightly lauded. This video represents an intelligent studio reconstruction of that production, enabling the director Simpson to enhance the effects of Vick's arresting original. Vick mirrors the tensions and compassion of the writing in his extraordinarily economic yet pertinent direction, focusing with a luminous intensity, including startling use of silhouettes, on the direct unfolding of the drama and its inescapable conclusion. This ascetic staging is wholly appropriate to the austerity and restraint of Britten's inspired score.

Rigby's vulnerable, sensual Lucretia stands at the centre of the performance, exploding into fiery declamation in her apparent revulsion at Tarquinius's attack, which she is unwilling or unable to resist. There's a suggestion in this staging that the Prince holds a strange fascination for Lucretia, unlocking her deepest desires. Rigby sings the role with restraint, dignity, then passion.

Smythe makes a bold, priapic Tarquinius. Junius is just one of Opie's many character studies that goes to the heart of the matter: this time he depicts a man envious of Collatinus's faithful wife when his own has been promiscuous, and so prompted to dare Tarquinius to attempt the fatal rape. Van Allan is a moving, upright Collatinus, full of tragic feeling when he discovers from her the details of the rape.

The Female and Male Chorus, soprano and tenor onlookers, are here portrayed as anonymous figures in mufti (the soldiers are in uniform of fairly modern vintage). Harries and Rolfe Johnson strike just the right balance between objective concern and involvement. The tenor's description of Tarquin-ius's Ride to Rome, a famous passage, and – in _sotto voce_ tones – his approach to Lucretia's bedroom, are arrestingly managed. As Lucretia's two attendants, Lucia and Bianca, Pope and Owens provide a nice contrast, as Britten intended, between youthful high spirits and expectation, and wise resignation. Both sing, as do all the cast, with a fair degree of clear articulation although some earlier interpreters have provided a greater degree of clarity, and so more meaningful enunciation, in this respect.

Friend exercises complete control over the drama's progress and the solo players of the ENO Orchestra are all expert interpreters of their parts, but unfortunately the sound recording is no more than fair, with sibilants sometimes prominently caught and the range restricted. By contrast the visual direction is at all times clear and appropriate, in close-ups and distant shots, to the scene in hand.

Albert Herring

Patricia Johnson (Lady Billows), Elizabeth Gale (Miss Wordsworth), Jean Rigby (Nancy), Felicity Palmer (Florence Pike), Patricia Kern (Mrs Herring), John Graham-Hall (Albert Herring), Alexander Oliver (Mr Upfold), Alan Opie (Sid), Richard Van Allan (Mr Budd), Derek Hammond-Stroud (Mr Gedge). London Philharmonic Orch/Bernard Haitink. Dir and video dir: Peter Hall. Castle VHS CVI 2051.

This delightful comedy, another chamber work written for Glyndebourne, followed a year after _Lucretia_. Based on a French short story by Guy de Maupassant, Eric Crozier's libretto transfers the action from France to East Anglia. It tells how the local worthies in an imaginary village, unable to find a virginal May Queen, choose instead a virginal May King in the form of Albert. After getting drunk at the celebrations to enthrone him, he goes off on a binge that includes wine, women and song. Britten's gift for acute satire and sharp-edged characterisation are everywhere in evidence.

The work won new friends when the piece returned to Glyndebourne in 1985 in this delightfully authentic staging by Peter Hall. John Gunter's atmospheric decor and costumes aptly set the scene. The opening set, supposedly showing Lady Billows's breakfast room, here very much resembles the Glyndebourne Organ Room (it is a pity the video fails to show us the effect of rain, at one point, outside the window). This makes a splendid contrast to Mrs Herring's greengrocer shop placed in context on the village street. The vicarage fête, brilliantly observed by Hall and Gunter, is a tour de force of staging.

The adoption of Suffolk accents was frowned on by the powers-that-be at Aldeburgh, but they are so idiomatically done (under Peter Tuddenham's tutelage) that they seem justified in the event. Graham-Hall's tall, gawky Herring, hen-pecked by his mother and longing for release from her hold, is an original and welcome interpretation of a difficult role. As his mother, Kern is suitably domineering but earns sympathy in her grief when Albert is thought dead. Patricia Johnson's commanding yet faintly ridiculous Lady Billows is just right in her pronouncement of Mrs Whitehouse values. As her Puritan sidekick, Florence Pike, Palmer is equally in character. Among the other worthies Gale is a nicely fluttering, scatterbrained Miss Wordsworth, Oliver a pompous mayor, Hammond-Stroud a benign, vacuous vicar, Van Allan a staunch, slightly sly upholder of law. Opie's Sid and Rigby's Nancy are as amorous a pair of lovers as one could hope to see, and vocally perfect. All are unerringly directed by Hall, who also directs this video.

Haitink cleverly balances the lyrical, parodistic and humorous elements in the score and draws marvellous playing from thirteen LPO soloists.

Billy Budd

Philip Langridge (Captain Vere), Edward Byles (Red Whiskers), Barry Banks (Novice), Thomas Allen (Billy Budd), Neil Howlett (Mr Redburn), Phillip Guy-Bromley (Mr Flint), Clive Bayley (Mr Ratcliffe), Richard Van Allan (Claggart), John Connell (Dansker). Chor and Orch of English National Opera/David Atherton. Dir:

Tim Albery; video dir: Barrie Gavin. Virgin VHS VVD 545.

This, the second of Britten's large-scale operas (following *Grimes*), was first given at Covent Garden in 1951, conducted by the composer. The libretto, by E.M. Forster (who provided most of the words), and Eric Crozier (who provided the theatrical knowhow), is based on a story by Hermann Melville. The handsome Billy, perfect recruit to the navy in spite of being one of a press-ganged lot, has one flaw, a stammer which proves his downfall: when he is falsely accused of mutiny by the evil, homo-erotic Master-at-Arms Claggart, he cannot get his refutation out of his mouth, and – frustrated – strikes Claggart dead, suffering the fatal consequence.

Only the upright Captain Vere, worshipped by Billy, and witness to the events, can save Billy, but he remains silent at the court-martial – and suffers his own punishment, in the form of lifelong guilt at his sin of omission. These personal misfortunes are set unerringly by Britten against the background of the corrupt, harsh routine and discipline of the Navy in 1797, any sign of revolt on board Vere's the *Indomitable* made more heinous by the recent mutinies at Spithead and the Nore.

Albery's non-representational staging for ENO in 1988 emphasises the dark doings through the dour, harsh setting on a tilted stage with little sign of sea or ship, deriving its inspiration from modern stage practice in Germany. Sharp spotlights are used to concentrate the eye on key events and actions. Only in the scene when the crew prepares for battle are we allowed brilliant colour and movement, appropriately so as this is the one moment when the crew and its masters are united in a cause, hatred of the French. There's something a shade perverse about Albery's and his team's abjuration of the work's true setting (a mistake not made in Graham Vick's roughly contemporaneous yet equally up-to-date staging for Scottish Opera), but the ENO forces give the work such a convincing interpretation that the production's daring proves its own justification.

Albery directs with a strong eye for essentials, most of all in depicting the still, louring, baleful presence of Claggart as a man who uses his hold over his men to force them into betrayals and worse. When he finds the handsome beauty of Budd too much for his repressed emotions he sets out to destroy him with single-minded purpose. The character is frighteningly formidable as depicted in Van Allan's masterly acting and singing.

The old Vere of the Epilogue and Prologue, where he reflects on the long-ago events, is here shown as a shambling, Forster-like figure in modern overcoat and wearing spectacles. This cowed figure is marvellously depicted by Langridge. He is more conventionally represented in the opera proper in naval dress of the period. His doubts and indecisions after the fatal blow have been struck are expressed arrestingly in Langridge's features and voice. As much as Claggart, Vere is brought down by his own frustration and emotional hang-ups, and his very English refusal to show his real feelings. This is another of this versatile tenor's perceptive and involved portrayals, finely sung as always.

By 1988 Allen, who was here singing Budd for the last time in a distinguished career in the part, may look a shade mature for the role, but he conveys ideally the straightforward, forthright nature of the man, the very soul of fidelity and truth, his overwhelming shock at his moment of wilful anger, and his courage as he goes to his end, the final solos sung with deep pathos. There is no weakness in the support, but special praise is due to Connell's sympathetic Dansker, Howlett's authoritative, beautifully sung Redburn, and Barry Banks's cringing, distraught Novice. The chorus is superbly directed and sings magnificently.

There has been no better interpreter of the piece than Atherton, who paces it unerringly, finds just the weight and balance, and revels in the consistent excellence of the writing, not least in the important, reflective interludes, and his orchestra brings out every aspect of the score's inspiration. For the most part the video direction seconds Albery's efforts, but there are times when the darkness of the setting defeats Gavin, not really his fault. The sound is exemplary. The accompanying leaflet includes an essay by Crozier on the opera's genesis, telling us how Forster eventually fell out with Britten. That is history: in the event, the combination of their special talents produced a masterpiece done full justice here.

Gloriana
Sarah Walker (Queen Elizabeth I), Elizabeth Vaughan (Penelope Rich), Jean Rigby (Lady Essex), Anthony Rolfe Johnson (Earl of Essex), Neil Howlett (Lord Mountjoy), Alan Opie (Robert Cecil), Richard Van Allan (Walter Raleigh), Norman Bailey (Ballad Singer). Chor and Orch of English National Opera/Mark Elder. Dir: Colin Graham; video dir: Derek Bailey. Virgin VHS VVD 344.

This, Britten's work written for Covent Garden in 1953 to celebrate the coronation of Elizabeth II, caused a furore at its premiere. Rather than writing an innocuous pageant the composer explored instead Elizabeth I's inner torment as her love for the impetuous Essex conflicts with her public duty. After more than twenty years the piece was properly recognised through this ENO staging of 1966, here seen in its 1984 revival. The work is not unflawed: the second-act masque is superfluous to the nub of the action and the Ballad Singer scene is stilted. Then the subsidiary characters remain no more than ciphers, but the central, doomed relationship is unerringly depicted in Britten's persuasive music, and the score as a whole is as skilfully and daringly composed as any of Britten's operas, richly scored and imaginative in harmony. Elder makes the very most of it in his sure-footed, taut and luminous reading.

Graham's production has stood the test of time in his own and Alix Stone's well-designed, evocative, galleried set and Stone's costumes are just right. The action moves forward smoothly and unobtrusively, allowing the singers to dominate the stage as directed, firmly, by Graham. The title role, though not lying very high (the original interpreter Joan Cross was nearing the end of her distinguished career and Britten acknowledged the fact), really demands a soprano rather than Walker's mezzo: the tessitura sometimes strains her resources. She also presents a more youthful, ebullient Elizabeth than some, but she carefully develops the character from the impulsive, commanding ruler of the early scenes to the desolate woman of the later ones, and manages the final, difficult scene of *mélodrame* with tragic feeling.

Rolfe Johnson is a model of an Essex, volatile yet romantic, sensitive yet forceful, in both his acting and singing: the lute songs in Act 1 are as beautifully judged as by Peter Pears, the part's creator. Opie's sly, smooth Cecil is another of that splendid baritone's subtle creations. Howlett is an upright Mountjoy who makes his words tell. Vaughan is a positive Penelope Rich, Rigby a warm Frances Essex. Van Allan makes the most of the shadowy figure of Raleigh. The Ballad Singer is almost justified when sung as clearly as by Bailey. Even the cameo part of the Lady-in-Waiting finds a delicate interpreter in Lynda Russell. The video direction, cameras always in the right place at the right time, and the sound are both exemplary – and for once in a way a libretto is provided.

The Turn of the Screw
Helen Donath (Governess, acted by Magdalena Vásáryová), Ava June (Mrs Grose, acted by Dana Medrická), Heather Harper (Mrs Jessel, acted by Emilia Vásáryová), Lillian Watson (Flora, acted by Beata Blazicková), Michael Ginn (Miles, acted by Michael Gulyás), Philip Langridge (Prologue), Robert Tear (Quint, acted by Juraj Kukura). Orch of Royal Opera House, Covent Garden/ Colin Davis. A film by Petr Weigl. Philips VHS 070 400–3.

This chamber opera to a corruscating libretto by Myfanwy Piper based closely on Henry James's short story of the same title was first presented at Venice in 1954. It is usually considered Britten's masterpiece in the genre, so taut and consistent is the writing, so gripping its effect in any decent performance. This 1982 film by Petr Weigl, although it makes explicit the sexual undertones of the work left vague by both James and Piper, is an arresting interpretation of the work, set in a suitably Gothic-like mansion in Czechoslavakia. Not only lovely to look at, it also precisely mirrors the uncertainties and sense of misdeeds inherent in text and music. As ever we are left wondering whether the ghosts are really there or figments of the highly strung Governess's imagination as she attempts to solve or at least explain the strange behaviour of the children. The ghosts materialise palpably not from a cool English night but from the bright mid-European midday sun, the evil Quint on a striking minaret-like tower in the gardens, Miss Jessel across a misty lake.

Given an older Miles than usual means setting up an incipient erotic relationship between him and the Governess. Earlier, in a miming episode before the opera's action begins, Weigl shows Quint and Miss Jessel, when still alive, carrying on kinky games in the grounds with the children and with each other. That may shock Britten purists, but it sets up the tensions of the action in the opera, and is justified alone by the hypnotic performance given on screen by Juraj Kukura as Quint. Emilia Vásáyová's riveting Miss Jessel is just as astonishing a portrayal. Magdalena Vásáryová is a blonde stunner of a Governess, whose singing counterpart, Donath, nicely matches the actress's looks. In the other cases the voices aren't always as suited to those of the actors, though Tear's tone is an apt sound for Kukura's reading of Quint. Most troublesome is the chaste tone of Ginn which doesn't match the appearance of the pubescent Gulyás. Contrariwise Watson's grown-up soprano is ill-suited to the sweet, curly-haired Flora on film.

As a whole the enterprise can be accounted one of the most successful attempts ever at a re-interpretation of an opera in visual terms. The lip-synch is carefully and successfully managed. Davis's Philips splendidly cast and idiomatically conducted recording inevitably fares better on laserdisc than on VHS.

A Midsummer Night's Dream

Ileana Cotrubas (Tytania), Felicity Lott (Helena), Cynthia Buchan (Hermia), Claire Powell (Hippolyta), James Bowman (Oberon), Ryland Davies (Lysander), Dale Duesing (Demetrius), Lieuwe Visser (Theseus), Curt Appelgren (Bottom), Roger Bryson (Quince), Damien Nash (Puck). Glyndebourne Festival Chor, London Philharmonic Orch/Bernard Haitink. Dir: Peter Hall; video dir: David Heather. Castle VHS CVI 2008.

Peter Pears deftly reduced Shakespeare's long play into a manageable libretto, losing very little that is essential, for his partner Britten to set. The score, first given at Aldeburgh in 1960, is a miracle of lightness and delicacy, ideally evoking the various dream-like aspects of the story, most successfully of all in the scenes for Tytania and Oberon. Also inspired are the beginning, which suggests the awakening of the wood in highly original, shimmering sounds, and the close, an address in speech from Puck.

Hall's 1981 production, happily preserved here, responded in like kind to the arresting magic and beauty of the score in a well-nigh perfect production, based on John Bury's moving forest with leaves and branches meticulously detailed and aquiver in the breeze, made possible because each is supported by an actor. When Hall wants the stage cleared off they go, sideways or upwards. Into the setting come Tytania and Oberon, dressed and coiffured with literally fantastic imagination, upswept hair and pointed ears prominent. So is Puck, a red-headed gnome superbly acted and spoken by the diminutive Damien Nash. By contrast the Mortals and mechanicals are dressed in traditional Elizabethan costumes.

Not only does Hall unerringly catch the otherworldly feeling of the fairy world, into which Bottom as ass is wonderfully introduced, he also makes the lovers into real young people with true feelings, and he never allows the fun of the Pyramus and Thisbe play-within-a-play to flag. Everything is executed with an unerring ear for the music and eye for theatrical fantasy. Who could ask for more?

Haitink matches the inspiration on stage with his own subtly inflected account of the luminous score. Bowman's imperious, cold Oberon is partnered by Cotrubas's refined, sensuous Tytania. The lovers, each a personality, sing their music with mastery of tone and line, and act out quarrel and reconciliation with total conviction. Appelgren's Bottom is at once genial, ambitious, ludicrous and he sings with firmness and warmth. Power's Flute is cloth-headed and brilliantly amusing. Nowhere is there a weakness in this well-groomed and committed cast. Video direction and sound recording capture most of the visual and aural delight remembered from old Glyndebourne at the time.

Death in Venice
Michael Chance (Voice of Apollo), Robert Tear (Aschenbach), Alan Opie (seven roles), Gerald Finley (English Clerk), Paul Zeplichal (Tadzio). Glyndebourne Festival Chor, London Sinfonietta/Graeme Jenkins. Dir: Stephen Lawless; video dir: Robin Lough. Virgin VHS VVD 847.

Britten wrote this, his last opera, when suffering from the heart complaint that eventually killed him. Though composed under stress, it shows little or nor diminution in his powers, as he determined to finish it as a final gift to his life-long partner, tenor Peter Pears, who created the role of Aschenbach in the 1973 premiere. It is a long and taxing part as conceived by Myfanwy Piper in her libretto based on Thomas Mann's novella about a renowned writer visiting Venice and coming into disconcerting contact with the erotic element in his nature when he encounters, on the Lido, Tadzio, a beautiful Polish youth, a silent, danced role.

Lawless's production, done for Glyndebourne Touring Opera in 1989, dispenses with the Venetian milieu in favour of paring the action down to essentials in Tobias Hoheisel's sets. Everything has been stylised to the bare bones within a restricted box-like set using the modish device of high walls with narrow, upright openings serving as doors or embrasures. These allow for multiple exits and entrances, but kill any impression of space and light on the Lido and exclude entirely the backcloth, intended at one place, of St Mark's. Yet it has its own validity in creating a sense of claustrophobia and in thus forcing attention on to the interior feelings of the protagonist, turning the work into a personalised pyschodrama.

As this role is superbly taken by Robert Tear, climax of a distinguished career in singing Britten's music, this emphasis is justified by the event. He presents an egghead in sunglasses wrapped up in his own intellectual reasoning yet observant of everything around him, a man at once polished and objective in thought yet capable of being passionate and subjective in feeling. Tear is a master of the extended, continuo-accompanied recitatives during which Aschenbach muses on, and becomes alarmed by, the change in his emotions caused by contact with seductive Venice and sensual boy. Video allows us to perceive every raised eyebrow, curled lip, twitching limb in this highly detailed creation. Tone, text and accent are perfectly coordinated throughout, and with so little to interest the eye in the decor, Lough rightly concentrates his cameras on Tear, and on Opie's equally mesmeric Traveller and related roles as messenger of desire and death, true alter egos to Aschenbach himself in Lawless's concept.

In the role of Apollo, who represents the calmer side of Aschenbach's nature, Chance, dressed in silver suit, doesn't look entirely happy but he sings with the right, otherworldly counter-tenor tone. It is a mistake to have made his alter ego, Dionysus, manifest rather than just an offstage voice in the dream sequence. Finley makes his mark in the short but telling role of the English Clerk who finally confirms that cholera is rife, the cholera that kills Aschenbach as he finally seems to make at least visual contact with the object of his desire.

In this reading, Tadzio and the other youths, in designer beachwear, are far too knowing and too mature, somewhat defeating the essence of Britten's idea that Tadzio, at least, should be equivocally innocent of all except his own arresting attraction to Aschenbach. The role of his mother, so memorably done at the premiere by Deanne Bergsma, is here severely reduced in importance. The mimed and danced beach games at the end of Act 1 remain an unnecessarily long distraction and their music is the least convincing in the score. Given the confinement of the scenery, Martha Clarke's choreography is effective enough.

Jenkins conducts the London Sinfonietta with a fine ear for the often delicate economy of the score and reminds us of its haunting, atmospheric quality. He also allows for most of the text to be clearly projected. The recording, faultless in balance, also permits words and instrumentation to be heard to maximum advantage. Although this may be considered a somewhat one-dimensional view of the work, partly because of the exigencies of touring for which it was originally intended, it is none the less a unified piece of work that holds the attention from start to finish. The librettist's synopsis in the booklet doesn't always march with what is seen in this staging.

John Corigliano (b. 1938)

The Ghosts of Versailles
Tracy Dahl (Florestine), Teresa Stratas (Marie Antoinette), Renée Fleming (Countess Almaviva), Stella Zambalis (Cherubino), Marilyn Horne (Samira), Peter Kazaras (Count Almaviva), Graham Clark (Bégarss), Neil Rosenhein (Léon), Håkan Hagegård (Beaumarchais), Gino Quilico (Figaro). Chor and Orch of Metropolitan Opera, New York James Levine. Dir: Colin Graham; video dir: Brian Large. DG VHS 072 430–3; LD:−1.

For its first commission in a quarter of a century, the Metropolitan accorded the premiere of Corigliano's large, two-act gloss on Mozart and *Figaro* a lavish staging. This parodistic, grand *opera-bouffe* had the public and critics united in its praise. Because it is cinematic in concept it works well on video with plenty of cross-fades and attention to detail that may have been overlooked in the theatre, although some of the panoramic effects are inevitably lost. The score refers to Bach, Mozart, Rossini, Verdi, Strauss, Mussorgsky and others, yet paradoxically has a reasonably strong voice of its own. The style reaches its apogee in a lengthy, complex sextet, which is a technical tour de force. Much of the action and score is multi-layered. There are roles for almost every type of voice, and a large cast is deployed deftly. The performance also manages the feat of making clear most of William M. Hoffmann's intelligent libretto.

The singers have to act in an often agile way. As Figaro, Quilico sings much of his solo in mid-air. As the villain Clark, who has a superb, Iago-like solo, stands on his head. Horne, as an Egyptian entertainer (a role blatantly written to give the singer a brief but important solo), has a comedy turn of some ingenuity. In the final moments the work turns serious and moving, the authors achieving the turnround with an expert touch. Hagegård and Stratas stand out among the cast, he for his urbane Beaumarchais, she for her touching Marie Antoinette, but every one surpasses him or her self in the cause of at once fascinating, amusing, intriguing and eventually moving an audience.

Levine revels in the virtuoso qualities of the music, Graham provides an answering touch of invention in his direction. It's all entrancing once through. Time will tell whether or not the piece or the production will bear much repetition.

Concerts and Recitals

Maria Callas: Débuts à Paris
Arias from Norma, Il trovatore, Il barbiere di Siviglia: Tosca – Act 2, with Albert Lance (Manrico, Cavaradossi), Tito Gobbi (Scarpia). Chor and Orch of the Paris Opéra/ Georges Sébastian. Dir: Roger Benamou. EMI VHS MVD9 91258–3; LD: LDB9 91258–1.

Maria Callas at Covent Garden
Arias from Don Carlos and Carmen; Tosca – Act 2. With Renato Cioni (Cavaradossi), Tito Gobbi (Scarpia). Chor and Orch of Royal Opera House, Covent Garden/ Georges Prêtre. Dir: Franco Zeffirelli. EMI VHS MVD4 91283–3; LD: LDB4 91283–1.

All too little remains in picture of Callas in action, so these precious films, now available officially for the first time, are to be treasured, particularly as – by and large – they show her at her best and therefore inform a generation who never saw or heard what she was about and why she so mesmerised her audiences. It may also help those who have her very wide repertory caught in sound alone to relate those discs to her stage personality.

Where her Paris debut (in 1958) is concerned, she is at first obviously nervous and far from at her best. As John Steane points out in his invaluable note, those in the distinguished audience that night, including the French President of the day, may have begun wondering if they had paid over the odds to hear a voice that in Norma's 'Casta Diva' sounds worn and unsupported. Already by the piece's cabaletta, glimpses of her magic, in terms of verbal enlightenment and vocal nuance, can be gleaned even though the chorus is hopelessly at sea and Sébastian, as throughout the issue, proves a lethargic conductor.

The excerpt from *Trovatore* evinces a marked improvement. Alone on stage as the Act 4 Leonora, Callas, even without props or costume, suggests the woman's grief and loneliness in the recitative; then in the aria, 'D'amor sull'ali rosee' Callas sings with care for detail (adumbrated by Steane in his note) and hushed tone that silences a cough-ridden house and reminds me of her Covent Garden performance, absolutely riveting, in the role in 1953. Then in the 'Miserere' duet, all Leonora's longing for her Manrico are projected by voice, eyes and gesture.

Those eyes turn to gleeful mischief as Callas becomes the minxish Rosina incarnate in 'Una voce poco fa'. Here the tone clears completely so that Callas can do what she likes with the virtuoso piece – and that is a more vivacious, more delicately embellished account than in either of her recordings on disc. This is a fine example of Callas's relaxed vein at its most captivating – and it certainly enthralls the Paris audience.

The version of the second act of *Tosca* at Paris provides a fascinating contrast with that six years later at Covent Garden on the second video. The younger diva is able more naturally to conjure up the purely sensual appeal of the protagonist, explaining her attraction to both Cavaradossi and Scarpia, and her expressive wig and costume add to the magnetism of the diva. Already this Tosca is wilful, nervous and vulnerable. By 1964 those characteristics, under Zeffirelli's watchful eye, are more to the fore, but the ability to sustain and expand tone has sadly diminished. What we gain is Zeffirelli's imaginative direction as compared with a virtually non-existent staging at Paris (black and white against the Royal Opera's vivid colour).

Gobbi, all suave satisfaction and venially loathsome, exudes confidence and a subtle identification with the role on both occasions. At Covent Garden the portrayal has become even more refined; at Paris it is more freely sung. In Cavaradossi's brief incursions Cioni is superior to Lance, who is also a wooden, stentorian Manrico.

The three extracts from a 1962 Gala at Covent Garden, for which Callas announced her readiness to participate at a late stage, confound received opinion that she was then in vocal decline. Elisabetta's long Act 5 aria from *Don Carlos* shows her equal to all its stringent demands, also her ability to play with phrases – and what phrasing she offers! – at will because she is confident her voice will respond to her demands on it. Within the context of a concert performance, she conjures up all the feelings of sorrow, regret and determination so un-erringly expressed in Verdi's elevating music for the sad Queen. Here in action is the total involvement in a part, the inner identification with its emotional core, that so few since have been able to emulate, however hard they may have tried.

Yet this same diva of the sorrows can turn herself mirac-ulously into the most alluring of Carmens, one to tease and command men at will while remaining a free spirit. Yet every-thing is achieved within the strict bounds of the score, avoiding exaggerated expression or over-deliberate tempi. Prêtre here and throughout is a willing ally in everything Cal-las attempts. The sound is good enough to make this an absolutely essential purchase.

Placido Domingo: 'Hommage a Sevilla'
Excerpts from *Don Giovanni, Il Barbiere di Siviglia, Carmen, La forza del destino, Fidelio, El gato Montes*. With Victoria Vergara and Virginia Alonso. Vienna Sym-phony Orch/James Levine. A film by Jean-Ponnelle. DG VHS 072 187–3; LD:–1.

This astonishing product was entirely conceived and executed, visually speaking, at Seville. It shows extracts of operas set in and around the city and filmed on location with Domingo as the various protagonists – and singing a duet with himself in the extract from *Barbiere*, taking the tenor role of Count Almaviva and the baritone one of Figaro, while also singing another baritone role, that of Don Giovanni in his so-called Champagne aria. Each extract is introduced by Dom-ingo on location, and as audience-friendly as he always is.

The camerawork of Ponnelle and his team is as imaginative as ever. Seville itself is the background for the Rossini and Mozart numbers. Don Alvaro's elegiac aria from Verdi's *La forza del destino* is placed in a misty, deserted landscape where Alvaro's melancholic thoughts seem entirely appropriate.

The finale from *Carmen* is set in the local bullring. Most arresting of all is the evocation of Florestan's anguish in his opening scene – Act 2 of *Fidelio* – using some of the most savage images from Goya's *Los Desastres de la Guerra* for the introduction, then putting Domingo in the vault of some Roman ruins (Italica) outside the city.

The film was made in 1982 (it has since been re-edited, in 1992, by Horant H. Hohlfeld) when Domingo was at the height of his powers with the tone vibrant shading to heroic. His German may be unidiomatic in the Beethoven, but he shows total conviction in an unfamiliar role. So, as ever, does he as Don José in the *Carmen* finale where Vérgara, as Carmen, is rather too blatant. Domingo's other partner, in the zarzuela excerpt, is more pleasing to eye and ear. Domingo the baritone is as plausible as Domingo the tenor, with the trick photography in the *Barbiere* duet a permissible piece of licence.

The main drawback is the post-synchronisation. Even with such an experienced exponent as Domingo, it isn't always convincing, least so when he is in the open air. The visual and aural picture is excellent, especially so on laserdisc.

Pavarotti: 30th Anniversary Gala Concert

Excerpts from *L'ellsir d'amore, Lucia di Lammermoor, Il trovatore, La forza del destino, L'Arlesiana, La Bohème, Tosca* and *La traviata*, with Joan Anderson, Raina Kabaiwanska, Patrizia Pace, Shirley Verrett, Giuseppe Sabbatini, Paolo Coni, Giovanni Furlanetto, Enzo Dara. Orch of the Teatro Communale, Bologna/Leona Magiera and Maurizio Bernini. Dir: Christopher Swann. Decca 071 140–3; LD:−1.

This recital graphically illustrates the fact that Pavarotti's typically Italianate tenor has lasted longer than that of almost any other of his kind, throughout recorded history and perhaps in all time. Together with colleagues and friends he boxes the compass of his repertory in this 1991 recital (another is due from Decca masterminded by the *divo* given at London's Albert Hall in 1995). Whether as the lovelorn Nemorino in Donizetti's *L'elisir d'amore*, the distraught

Edgardo of the same composer's *Lucia*, the doomed Don Alvaro of Verdi's *Forza*, the painter-lover Cavaradossi, the youthful poet Rodolfo in the Puccini works, and perhaps best of all Federico's Lament from Ciléa's *L'Arlesiana*, he once more generously pours forth consistent tone in sincere, finely moulded phrasing, nowhere unstylish or forced.

His partners include some of the most experienced artists in the business, supplemented by a couple of comparative newcomers, including the new tenor hope Sabbatini, who provide their best in support of the star and host of the occasion. They take part in duets and ensembles, on a couple of occasions without him, completing a well-filled and interesting selection of numbers. Picture and sound are exemplary: we share in an inspiriting occasion.

'La Stupenda': A Portrait of Dame Joan Sutherland
Written and directed by Derek Bailey. Decca VHS 071 135–3; LD:–1.

The Essential Sutherland
Various orchestras/Richard Bonynge. Dir: Derek Bailey. Decca VHS 079 149–3; LD:–1.

The first issue combines documentary material with archive performances of the diva in action covering her forty-two years on stage, originally seen as an *Omnibus* feature on BBC TV. Although there are some invaluable examples of Sutherland in her prime most of the sung material comes from complete performances in Australia when she was a shade past her prime. What comes across is the patent sincerity and sheer professionalism of the subject. Wholly disarming in her own comments on her career, she was none the less always the thorough professional on stage, her standard of performance through her long career a model to any aspiring soprano. Her sense of humour in comic roles is as winning as her pathos in tragic ones. Future generations are also likely to acknowledge the immense contribution to her career's success of husband Bonynge, who is here, as always, loyally in support.

The second disc consists wholly of Dame Joan in action on stage, again in Australia. The sole exception is the Violetta/Alfredo duet from Act 1 of *La traviata* with Pavarotti from Sutherland's Covent Garden farewell. Still we must be grateful that at least the soprano has been preserved for posterity in such a wide variety of her repertory. Whatever opinion there may be about the state of the voice as such, its employment, in technical terms, remains something to marvel at.

Metropolitan Gala, 1991

Mirella Freni, Cheryl Studer, Barbara Daniels, Brigitta Svendén, Anne Sofie von Otter, Placido Domingo, Luciano Pavarotti, Leo Nucci, Hermann Prey, Justino Diaz, Nicola Ghiaurov. Chor and Orch of the Metropolitan Opera New York/James Levine. Dir: Brian Large. DG VHS 072 428–3; LD:−1.

This isn't your usual staid and/or bitty gala in the presence of an ignorant, well-heeled audience but a substantial evening in the theatre with some of the leading singers of the day taking part. The final act of *Rigoletto* features Studer as a more feisty Gilda than most, Pavarotti at his most ardent as the Duke of Mantua, and Nucci as an indignant jester. Svendén is a suitably alluring Maddalena. Act 3 of *Otello* features Domingo's classic Moor, Freni as a sincere, moving, but a trifle mature Desdemona. Diaz is, however, an anonymous Iago.

Then we have the party scene of Johann Strauss's *Die Fledermaus* with seemingly innumerable guests offering their party pieces. The results are of variable quality, though Aprile Millo, June Anderson and Frederica von Stade excel themselves. Pavarotti (tenor), Domingo (baritone), sing the Rodolfo-Marcello duet from *La Bohème* as the *pièce de résistance*. In the operetta proper, Daniels is an effusive Rosalinde, Prey a bouncy Eisenstein, von Otter a lively boyish Orlofsky. Levine presides benignly over his starry charges and the whole affair.

Three Tenors (Pavarotti, Domingo, Carreras) in Concert I
Dir: Brian Large. Decca VHS 071 123–3; LD:−1.

Three Tenors in Concert II
Dir: William Cosel. Warner Music Vision, VHS 4509 962 013.

You'll either own one or other of these bizarre, circus-like events, or you'll at least know about it through all the hype. Comment is really superfluous except to say that the filming and audio production on both occasions faithfully reflects the generosity of spirit shown by all three singers and conductor (both times), Zubin Mehta. But should this really be the way forward for opera on video?